WINNERS TAKE ALL

WINNERS TAKE ALL

THE 9 FUNDAMENTAL RULES OF HIGH TECH STRATEGY

TONY SEBA

Release 1.1

COPYRIGHT © TONY SEBA – 2006

Printed in the United States of America
First Edition

ISBN: 978-1-84728-953-7

To contact the author Tony Seba
Email: tony@tonyseba.com
Website: www.tonyseba.com

Cover Photography © 2006 by Tony Seba

To order extra copies of this book go to www.tonyseba.com

This book is dedicated to my mother.
Your values, foresight, courage, and determination
are still a source of inspiration.

Contents

ACKNOWLEDGEMENTS

"Success has many fathers. Failure is an orphan."

- John F. Kennedy

The first and main source of inspiration for this book came from teaching the "Strategic Marketing of High Technology Products and Innovations" at Stanford University Continuing Studies Program. My students are professionals and executives; they hail from marketing, engineering, finance, operations, and sales; they come from a cross-section of high technology companies in Silicon Valley. This group of students takes time from work and their families to come and learn practical knowledge that they can apply immediately. The joy of teaching such a highly experienced, engaged, and educated professional group is indescribable. They all are making things happen in their companies. I feel they are entrepreneurs whether they work in startups or multi-billion dollar companies. The feedback I get from them is invaluable. Every time I come back home from Stanford I modify and update my course based on that feedback. This book is the distillation of the essence of what I teach in that course. I want to thank each and every one of my students for contributing to this book.

I also want to thank the entrepreneurs and executives who have taken the time to come share their experiences for this book and for my classes at Stanford. Here is a partial list: Jim Bidzos, Joe Gatto, Jim Buckmaster, Konstantin Guericke, Ketan Kothari, Manish Kothari, Dieter Giesbrecht, John Girard, Jim Ritchings, Astro Teller, Alain Rossman, Jeffrey Jacobsen, Don MacAskill, Chris MacAskill, Gregor Freund, George Mueller, Hoshi Printer, Farrokh Billimoria, and Ian Campbell. I also want to thank Hal Louchheim for giving me the opportunity to teach at Stanford -- and therefore to write this book. I have created and taught four different courses for the Stanford Continuing Studies Program and Hal has always been supportive of my efforts.

I want to thank my agent and editor Roger Jellinek. He took a real interest in educating me and helping me traverse the world of publishing. He went out of his way to help me clean up both the book and the book proposal. I appreciate his honest feedback as well as his experience, skills and integrity.

Finally, I wish to thank my family. My mother Joyce and four brothers, Jimmy, Freddie, Johnny, and Jerry have always been supportive of my life efforts, whether it's writing this book or fullfilling my entrepreneurial, academic or other personal aspirations.

INTRODUCTION

"Technology: No Place for Wimps!"

- Scott Adams

"This is hyper-competition, make no mistake"

- Bill Gates

Building a winner in the high-speed, high-greed, hyper-competitive Silicon Valley technology world is not easy. The first few years of the twenty-first century were particularly tough for many companies. While success had a bigger payoff, mistakes became far more costly. As the Nasdaq stock market retreated from its lofty heights, many venture investors sharply curtailed their equity investments. Customers became king and played ever-hungrier companies against one another. The view from Silicon Valley during those years was gloomy indeed.

Entrepreneurs had a hard time raising funds to fuel their new innovations, startup companies had a hard time finding new customers and possible partnership opportunities, and established companies had a hard time convincing the market that growth was forthcoming. In the meantime technological progress kept accelerating faster and faster, geographic boundaries blurred, and industry boundaries disappeared.

Amidst these seemingly disastrous market conditions, there were a few companies that did exceedingly well: Symantec, Google, Apple, Netflix, Craigslist, Skype, and StarMine, to name a few. Their customers multiplied; they increased their revenues, profits and stock valuations, and they came to define or redefine their industries.

Learning the sources of success of these 21st century Silicon Valley was imperative. What was it that enabled these companies to succeed in tough environments?

As a high-tech entrepreneur I was interested in learning from the successes and mistakes of others before I started my next company. At the time, I was also teaching a course to professionals and executives at Stanford University on "Strategic Marketing of High Technology Products and Innovations." Hundreds of professionals from a cross-section of companies in Silicon Valley came back to learn how to go from idea, technology, or product to profits, and how to build a winning company. I was further interested in finding if there was anything we could learn about these winners that I could share with my students-- many of whom actually worked for these companies.

I particularly wanted to find out if there were new rules for success in fast moving, high-growth markets. Has the Internet changed everything? How has the globalization of markets, talent, and capital changed the rules of the game? Are we really living in a brave new world? How did the success of Google and Symantec compare with that of Microsoft and Dell before them?

Google's success was then the front cover story not only in Silicon Valley, but around the world. They went from idea to revenues of more than $1 billion and a market capitalization of $100 billion in only a few years–at a time when many other search engine companies died or were flailing due to a sharp drop in advertising spending.

Did such new rules apply to both small and large companies? Did they apply to existing as well as new companies? Could existing companies use such rules to be turned around and succeed in this tough environment?

Symantec was another star during this period. After moving sideways seemingly forever, Symantec suddenly exploded. In the five years to 2004, Symantec revenues more than tripled, from $592 million in fiscal year 1998 to $1.9 billion in 2004. The SYMC stock sextupled from the spring of 2000, going from about $10 to just under $60 (after two stock splits) in late 2004.[1] By then it employed 6,000 people in 38 countries and was still growing so fast it had more than 500 open unfilled employment positions. The company's market capitalization was higher than $12.5 billion.

How about startups? What rules applied to them? I looked at companies like StarMine, BodyMedia, and Clickability. These were small startups that grew their business by 50%-100% annually, even as competition became fiercer and prospective customers' budgets were being slashed. Was this newfound success the result of different strategies from what older tech companies like Dell and Microsoft used to win success? Were the rules different then?

I discovered that in some respects the world of high tech had changed radically. The bad news is that the stakes in the market are higher, the competition is keener, mistakes are punished more swiftly, and the market is changing even faster than it has in the past. Tech-based markets move so fast that getting things right becomes infinitely more important than it used to be. As a high tech entrepreneur, I personally know that it often feels like you're building a plane while flying it.

The good news is that I found a few really simple rules (or habits) that companies can follow to help them be successful in tough times.

9 Rules, to be exact:

Rule 1 – Feel the Pain. Then Develop Your Product.

Rule 2 – Focus, Win, Grow, Repeat.

Rule 3 – Add Value Not Features.

Rule 4 – Have a Story. Communicate It Clearly.

Rule 5 – It's A Risky World. Sell Confidence!

Rule 6 – Convert Champions Not Deals.

Rule 7 – Choose the Right Partners. Manage Them With Clarity.

Rule 8 – Design Products and Services That Are Easy to Adopt.

Rule 9 – You're Doing Well. Congratulations. Now Change or Die.

These 9 Rules apply to small and large companies. They apply at the beginning, at the middle, and at the end of the adoption lifecycle. The 9 Rules apply to companies that are product-based, service-based, Internet-based, innovation-based--and any combination thereof.

The fact that there are nine practical Rules for success in this increasingly complex scenario is encouraging. Some of the Rules are so simple in fact that they should not surprise many professional managers. For example, the concept of designing a product that's easy for the customer to adopt sounds like common sense. And yet, dozens of companies came out with MP3 digital portable players and didn't build them the right way. These companies had seasoned managers with MBAs from top schools – and yet they didn't build products that were easy to adopt. It took Apple to do it right – years after the category had been created.

The imperative need for succinct, clear communications and telling good stories about your product is not a surprise to many company managers. Yet this is one of the most underused and misunderstood rules of success in technology markets. And one of the most important. Why? Because tech products can be so risky, and tech markets move so incredibly fast.

To test the underlying rationale of the book, I set up two portfolios of public company stocks (to be published online.) These portfolios could not consist of "good" vs. "bad" companies. They were all to be "good" companies. One included companies like Symantec, Apple, and Google that were emblematic of the nine Rules. A second portfolio included comparable companies like McAfee, Sony, and Yahoo. A third tracked the stock market with a weighted average of the Nasdaq, NYSE, and S&P 500 indices. I "bought" $10,000-worth of virtual stock in each of the companies on April 1st, 2005.

The performance of the different portfolios was startling. By April 1st 2006, exactly one year after the creation of the portfolios, the "Winners Take All" companies had grown by more than 50% compared to the single-digit growth for the comparison portfolio and the 10% or so of the weighted average market in general. (Granted, this was not a scientific test and, as they say in Wall Street, this does not prove or guarantee future performance.) A portfolio performance can be skewed by one or two stocks that do extremely well or badly. Both portfolios had such performers. For instance, as of April 1, 2006, Netflix, Salesforce.com and Google, all in the "9 Rules" portfolio had gone up more than 100%, while Hewlett-Packard and Sun Micro, both comparison stocks , had gone up 53% and 42% respectively. What I liked best was that 12 of the 15 stock in the '9 Rules' portfolio beat the market while most of the stocks in the comparison portfolio were down. This finding seemed to indicate (but not prove) that the 9 Rules could be used in a predictive manner at the individual company level as well as in portfolios. You can see the latest performance of these portfolios at http://www.tonyseba.com.

I have used different versions of this book in class, first at Stanford in the fall of 2004 and then in the fall of 2005 and then in the Spring of 2006 in a course titled "Fundamental Rules of High Tech Strategy". The course participants were high-tech professionals and executives with many years' experience in the industry. I invited some of the executives I interviewed for the book to be guest speakers. This environment provided a natural testing ground for the ideas provided by this book. One of my students, the CEO of a new technology company, said it only took him a few weeks to get the largest deal in the company's history using the rules in the book. I hope this book is as useful to you as it was to that CEO.

The long gestation period of this book meant that many people had a chance to read it, apply it, and give me feedback. I published a Beta version of the book with the name "Winners Take All - The 9 Fundamental Rules of High Tech Strategy." Soon I got feedback from professionals in many industries, from consulting to financial services to non-profits, saying that the rules helped their businesses. I think we can all learn from the Silicon Valley innovators who have quickly built the winners that created the new 21st century industries - and amassed unimaginable wealth along the way.

The 9 Rules are common-sense business strategies that when properly understood and applied together have the power to help organizations in many industries and improve their performance, sometimes dramatically. I hope this book enhancesthe performance of your career and your company the way it already has my Stanford class participants and early book readers.

Please email me at tony@tonyseba.com and let me know what you think.

Enjoy!

– Tony Seba

RULE 1
FEEL THE PAIN.
THEN DEVELOP YOUR PRODUCT

"We don't go searching for technology as if it were some new compound on the element chart that hasn't been discovered. Instead we listen to our customers."

- Michael Dell

"Your most unhappy customers are your greatest source of learning."

- Bill Gates

Craigslist was a small (18-person) company in San Francisco, California whose community website got 10 million unique visitors and 2.5 billion page views per month (in September 2005.) That month alone, Craigslist users posted more than five million new classified ads, 160,000 new job listings and one million new forum postings every month in 190 cities in 23 countries. Measured by pageviews, Craigslist was one of the ten top companies in the English-language web world.[3] All other companies on that list had thousands or even tens of thousands of employees: Microsoft, Yahoo!, Google, eBay, Interactive Corp. And Craigslist was still growing by about 100% per year!

The influence of Craigslist was huge for a company that size. Some analysts announced the death of the newspaper advertising industry as we have known it. One wrote that "Craigslist makes newspaper publishers such as Gannett, Tribune, Knight Ridder, and E.W. Scripps quiver in fear by siphoning off a traditional cash cow: classified ads."[4] Internet auction giant eBay was so concerned it bought out the shares from one of Craigslist's company founders in order to sit on Craigslist's board and "learn about it."

HOW CRAIGSLIST BUILT A WINNER

What made this website so wildly successful? What is it that made executives in the $16-$18 billion newspaper classified industry quiver? Strategic insight? Venture capital? MBA types? None of the above.

The answer is the dynamic duo of Craig Newmark (founder and Chairman) and Jim Buckmaster (CEO). "Craig Newmark is the most important person in the newspaper business who is not in the newspaper business," said Sreenath Sreenivasan, Dean of Students at the Columbia School of Journalism in New York.[5] Mr. Newmark's secret? A large brain for sure, a heart of gold for sure, but more specifically, the fact that Mr. Newmark, the founder and Chairman of Craigslist spends at least half his working days and nights answering user emails. "My primary duty at the company is customer service," says Mr. Newmark "While others talk about customer service, we obsess about it."[6] Can you imagine the Chairman or CEO of Gannett or Knight Ridder (or your company) answering customer emails?

In 1995 Mr. Newmark started an email group list to which he broadcast San Francisco local events. He received dozens of emails about local events and would turn around and email them to the growing list. Soon he had to automate and create a list server. Then he started a simple website called craiglist.com.

In 1997 the apartment shortages in San Francisco made looking for an apartment a daunting task. List users started sharing leads on apartments for rent and roommate situations. At the time, the fast growth in the technology sector in the San Francisco Bay Area was attracting thousands of people, which made looking for workers a tough task for startups and established companies alike. Job listings became a staple on Craigslist. Newmark refused to run advertising banners, but he started charging for job postings. In 1999 Newmark quit his day job to dedicate himself full-time to the company.[7]

The company quickly broke even. Soon, Craigslist expanded across the United States to cities like New York, Los Angeles, Boston, and Seattle. The steady expansion took them as far away as Perth, Jerusalem, and Lima. Ten years later Newmark was still communicating directly with end users. He developed a sense of their concerns, fears and pain. The Craigslist website grew its offerings as a direct result of user input. In a web world full of banner ads, pop-ups, pop-unders, inline, floating ads, and myriad forms of online advertising, Craigslist didn't run them. The only way they made money was by charging companies for job listings. They charged $75 to employers in San Francisco, $25 in New York and Los Angeles, and nothing anywhere else. These prices didn't come out of someone's head. They were set with fully open input from users.

When the company decided to start charging for job listings in 1998, they ran open discussion boards. Anyone who was about to post a job saw a link to the discussion boards. Hundreds participated, and thousands viewed the proceedings. These employers decided that the price should be around $25. I repeat, San Francisco Bay Area employers who were posting free ads on Craigslist.com told company management to charge $25 per listing. Next year the same open discussion board process resulted in a $45 price per job listing. This was followed by an increase to $75 the following year–where it remained for the following five years. Every time the employers were the ones openly guiding the company in the price-setting process.

Craigslist CEO Buckmaster runs these discussion boards directly. Doing this helps him learn what the users need, want, and what their pains are. In 2005, Los Angeles employers asked Mr. Buckmaster to start charging for job postings there. As a strategist I needed to understand why these employers would want to do such thing. Why would anyone ask for the price of a service to be raised? Why would anyone want to pay for something they were getting for free?? The answer was that there were thousands of job listings for small contracts in the film industry and menial jobs like mowing lawns. A company looking for a software engineer or marketing manager would see its ad get lost in the clutter of lawn-mowing ads. They preferred paying a small fee for a more effective ad. The small gig posters saw it differently. Examples of a small gig were: $5 for mowing the lawn, $25 for an ornate stencil, or a free photo shoot. For these posters, even paying $10 would be prohibitively expensive relative to the size of the contract opportunity. Since the discussion board process is totally open, Mr. Buckmaster had to weigh all these users.

Buckmaster felt everyone's pain. What to do? The decision was to charge $25 for jobs, as the employers requested. However, the small contract opportunities were not left behind. Craigslist decided to offer a brand new category called "gigs" that would remain free. After the decision to charge $25 was implemented, the total number of postings in the "jobs" category fell by 80%. This was precisely what the employers wanted: more exposure for their jobs. The new "gigs" category became a popular and free way for the rest of the Los Angeles users to post their opportunities. Soon, Craigslist rolled out the gigs category to all their other sites around the world. Thus Craigslist users everywhere benefited from Buckmaster staying close to company users.

How to price services? What new services to offer? What new cities to serve? Pretty much everything at the company is done as a result of customer input. Why didn't they run advertising? "Because our users haven't asked us to do it" said CEO Buckmaster. "We get approached all the time by third-party companies wanting us to run ads on the site. But our users aren't asking us to put those on, and that's basically what it will take. I don't remember ever receiving a request to run ads on the site from our users."

Craigslist, one of the most successful companies of the web era, has made Rule 1 its mantra. Alphasmart also used Rule 1 to become the leader in its hardware category.

Alphasmart was a small company in Los Gatos, California that sold "education computers" that were smaller, slower, and less versatile than standard personal computers. These computers also ran fewer programs than either Windows or Mac computers. Alphasmart, however, kept beating computer giants like Dell and Apple in competitive contract bids in school systems all across the United States. They were profitable from the time their first product went out the door in the early 1990s, and they increased revenues and earnings nearly every year after that. In fact, despite a global technology recession that hit most of their competitors, Alphasmart (Nasdaq: ALSM) had a successful Initial Public Offering (IPO) in early 2004.

Alphasmart had the highest margins in their industry, high repurchase rates, and happy customers who were willing to champion their products around the world. The company's management truly believed that it was all about the customer. In fact, listening to the pain of prospective customers is what prompted CEO Ketan Kothari to start the company in the first place. The company's commitment to making every level of the organization listen to the customer flowed from the CEO. Alphasmart had formal and informal processes to ensure that customer relationships were both happy and mutually beneficial. These processes included all levels from the CEO to marketing managers to engineers and customer service representatives.

The Alphasmart experience is an example of why feeling the customer pain is essential to the success of hi-tech products and innovations. It can be the most effective way to discover new markets, target the right market segments, to design products in the way customers want them, to price them right, to use the right distribution channels, and, generally, to build the right strategy.

Dell Computers has built the market leader in the personal computer business by listening to its customers. "We don't go searching for technology as if it were some new compound on the element chart that hasn't been discovered" says Dell founder and Chairman Michael Dell. "Instead we listen to our customers."[8] At Google, which has built one of the most powerful web companies in the world, the number one rule is that the user is in charge. "The cardinal rule at Google is, if you can do something that will improve the user's experience, do it."[9]

I have seen many companies that build a product and then turn it over to a sales team to push it to potential customers. Then they wonder why it doesn't sell. They hire a "marketing" team to write data sheets and work on promotions. Meanwhile, the management looks at the competition that is supposed to have an "inferior" technology but is successfully selling in the marketplace, and point they finger in the wrong direction. They wonder what's wrong with customers: *don't they know what product is best for them? Should they be educated about the "right" technology? Why aren't they buying the "superior" product?* Managers in these companies claim they listen to their customers, while all they are doing is listening to their own echoes.

Not Alphasmart. From the moment Alphasmart first talked to a prospective customer, its whole strategy revolved around them. And it showed.

HOW ALPHASMART BUILT A WINNER

The most fundamental principle in marketing is that the product or service is solving a customer need, want, or pain. The customer doesn't have to buy a given product, she wants to solve a problem, fill a void, cure a pain, or make a dream or aspiration come true.

How do you know what the prospect or customer wants to buy? As simple as it sounds, the first thing you do is: ask them!

This is simple and obvious, right? Yes, but this is something many, if not most, technology companies don't do.

Alphasmart founder and CEO Ketan Kothari asked customers about their needs for 12 years. In fact, that's what prompted him to start his company. Mr. Kothari learned of the trouble that school teachers were having with standard PCs. He talked to teachers in person and via chatrooms (before the web era), visited them in classrooms and "PC Labs," and felt their pain as they tried to teach writing or reading.

No one disputed that a standard Macintosh or IBM-compatible (aka Wintel) PC had a more powerful chip and ran more software programs than an Alphasmart Dana. No one disputed that PCs could use more applications than the Dana.

But now imagine that you're in a classroom with 30 children aged 11 or 12 years old. Think about this simple problem: how many classrooms have 30 electrical outlets for that many PCs? Not many. Even if there were such a classroom, can you imagine how dangerous it would be for children to be running around with hundreds of feet of wires all over the classroom? Children's safety is of course one of our society's top concerns.

What about using laptop PCs with batteries? Laptops have many problems. I am writing this book with a standard Wintel laptop PC. Its battery lasts a mere two hours. Then I need to recharge it. If children needed to recharge their computer batteries every two hours it would totally destroy the classroom learning experience. Furthermore, my PC battery costs up to $100. This alone would make them an expensive proposition for school systems with hundreds of students. Alphasmart computers run on three AA batteries. These batteries don't disappear and if they do, it costs $1 or $2 to replace them. But wait, there's more! Incredibly these three AA batteries last a whole semester. Yes, you read that right, they last 6 months!

Computer safety is another issue. What do children do with their toys after playing with them for a few minutes? They drop them on the floor! Have you ever dropped your laptop PC from a height of 5 feet? No? Needless to say, it would probably be shattered beyond recognition! Alphasmart computers are built to survive being dropped from heights up to 6 feet–how many 11-year old children are even that tall?

Alphasmart builds the kind of computers that teachers want them to build. Schoolteachers have in fact been engaged in the whole product development process. Alphasmart's founders have felt the teachers' pain and have built a product specifically for children to use and teachers to manage.

Feeling the Pain

"Our relationship with customers is the company's most valuable asset," says Manish Kothari, Alphasmart's president.

Most technology companies *say* that they care about customer relations. In fact, many of these companies make these customers feel like they're a liability, not an asset. They have television ads touting their customer-centricity and customer-friendliness. In fact, many of these organizations are impossible to reach and talk to. If you do reach them on the phone, they may ask you for a credit card before they will even answer your questions, and make you pay whether they solve your problem or not. Many tech buyers don't even think about calling these organizations because they don't want to go through the hassle. Other companies outsource the customer service function to the lowest-bidder. Your calls or emails to them seem to go into a black hole where your information will be irretrievably lost–forever. Management at these companies then wonders why customers jump ship as soon as a viable alternative is available.

Many "enlightened" executives talk as if listening to the customer were some philanthropic endeavor. It may make these managers feel good–but they still see it as an expense to be avoided.

Not Alphasmart. Alphasmart considered customer service to be a competitive advantage. When a user dialed the free 800 number on the back of every Alphasmart product, his or her voice would make it to the executive offices. Every week the executive staff at Alphasmart went over the top concerns, suggestions, and complaints from these users.

So what was Alphasmart's return on this valuable asset? Let's count the ways:

Revenues

A full 80% of new sales in 2004 came from existing customers. This meant that school districts that had bought Alphasmart products were expanding its usage to more students within a particular school and expanding to more schools within the system.

Product development

As the company grew, most product features and even whole new products were the direct result of customer suggestions. Teachers asked Alphasmart for an easier way to manage classrooms using Dana computers. Managing a classroom had several dimensions: setting it up, organizing and running the class itself, and cleaning up and putting things away after class is over. This whole process needed to be done quickly, efficiently, and securely. Customers suggested, for example, that a "file cabinet" cart where they could store all the computers and wheel them away would make their lives easier. The teacher could easily cart all the computers in and out of the classroom. When she started class, the students would pick up the machines on their way in and drop them off in the cabinet after the bell rang.

This cabinet would also make it easier to use the computers in multiple classrooms. After teaching the 3rd grade writing class, the teacher could just walk two doors down and teach the 8th grade class without missing a beat. Alphasmart designers went to work and the result was the SmartOption Bundle. This 'cabinet' could fit not just a whole classroom worth of computers (about 30) but also all the cables, adapters, and documentation needed to run a classroom.

Ingenious. The SmartOption Bundle in 2004 represented 50% of new company sales.

As usually happens with successful innovations, new products spawn new uses, which in turn spawn more products. In this case, that new innovation was the Alphasmart Hub and the corresponding Alphasmart Manager software. The Hub was a physical storage and communications center for the Dana computers. It provided a console that easily allowed the teacher to automatically download and upload files to each machine so that students could pick up where they left off the previous day. The teacher could also check up on student progress and grade homework. The Manager was the software that allowed the teacher to run the entire classroom during and after class. Since student computers have limited memory, they cannot run several programs at a time.

The Manager allowed the teacher to download the appropriate program ("applet") to student computers whenever they need it. This way they could teach, for instance, typing during the first half hour and creative writing the next half hour. The transition from one to the other took a click of a button. This functionality had the unintended additional benefit that students had to focus on doing one task (typing, creative writing, testing) at a time. No distracting Internet messaging or email could be done in the background.

Champions

Since Alphasmart's inception, one of its best vehicles for growth had been the rave public reviews that its customers happily gave the company and its products. Whether in learning conferences, in the media, or acting as references for new accounts, customers spread the gospel of Alphasmart to the farthest education corners in America. [See Rule 7: Convert Champions Not Deals.]

Margins

Alphasmart maintained growth while keeping its gross margins around a healthy 50%. Even leading PC vendors like HP and Dell were hard-pressed to get anywhere close to that. Dell, the most

profitable company in the personal computer arena, made about
$7.5 billion gross profit on revenues of $51.4 billion in 2003, or about
an 18% gross margin. HP had next to no margin on its PC business.

How did Alphasmart do it? How did it generate such high
repurchase rates, high margins, and happy customers who were
willing to be its champions? The company management truly
believed that it was all about the customer. They were committed to
making every level and every function of the organization listen to
the customer: the CEO, the vice presidents, the marketing managers,
the engineers and the customer service representatives.

ARE YOU LISTENING TO THE CUSTOMER OR YOUR ECHO?

If customer relationships are an asset to your company, you need
to commit to making those relationships work. Many companies,
and indeed many people, see relationships as a one-way mechanism.
They see communications as a monologue: I speak, you listen. They
say they listen to the customer, but they're just hearing their own
echo. To make a relationship work, you need to understand the other
party, you need to listen to them, make sure they feel you are paying
attention to their needs (not just being nice with empty words), and
that you are investing in that relationship.

There's really nothing like listening to real customers using
real products in real situations. As a vendor, you can learn more
from those experiences than from any pretty report that gives your
customers trendy names like "global nomads" or "urban moms."
Mind you, there's a place in the universe for these reports. They may
help us look at the world in new and interesting ways. Your customer,
however, will provide you with the best learning experience.

Customer service

Alphasmart invested in customer relationships at every
level of the organization. Every product shipped by Alphasmart
had an 800 number that dialed straight into its customer service
department. What differentiated Alphasmart's customer service
representatives (CSR) from most tech companies was that this was

not an outsourced function; their customer service reps and managers were employees of the company, located right in California near company headquarters. Customer service reps and managers got constant training on existing and new company products. And they didn't just read from a script that popped up on their computers–they listened and carefully wrote down all customer concerns and suggestions. Customer service managers had direct access to top company executives (CEO, CTO, and President). They met every week to go over the top 5-10 concerns and suggestions gathered by the reps.

"The top five suggestions are pretty consistent across users," Manish Kothari told me. They might be as mundane as "Increase font size," or "Include writing templates," both of which were top five features included in the Neo, then the company's latest "education computer" product.

Engineers

Research and Development groups tend to be isolated from end users. The marketing team prepares market requirements documents (MRD), or product requirement documents (PRD), which engineers read and translate into a working product. This can be a big mistake. Few things are as valuable for a company as having research and development people get direct input from watching real products being used by real customers in real situations. Alphasmart's engineers have direct contact with end users. They observe them when they use the products, freely ask questions and get straight, direct, unfiltered feedback from them.

"Their technicians fly out here and talk directly to the students" said William Reeder, Director of Technology for the Fairfax, Virginia, Public School System. "They talk to teachers and to the technology infrastructure people."

Customer visits can thus be a profitable experience for both the engineer and the user. The latter will feel that her voice is being heard and that she can talk to someone who is in a position to solve her problem. For the engineer it's good to see exactly how the product is being used. There are no filters from salespeople or marketing people.

Product managers and marketing managers

Needless to say, the company product managers are in constant touch with the customers and prospects. That's their job. Alphasmart marketing managers go to more than 85 trade shows per year in the United States alone.

CEO, President and CTO

At least once every five to six weeks Manish Kothari, President, Ketan Kothari, CEO and Joe Barrus, CTO set out on field trips to talk to customers. They visit classrooms, talk to students, teachers, school administrators and school district managers. They get direct feedback from every one involved in the use or purchase of Alphasmart products.

These visits are not necessarily love-fests. Mr. Kothari specifically requests to meet with administrators from accounts that the company may have recently lost. He wants to learn what the company has done wrong and what can be improved in the future. Fairfax's Reeder added: "I have Manish's phone number and I can access him any time. He always listens to us."

Board of Advisors

There are many "Boards of Advisors" that are there just for show. Company management proudly rattles off the titles and influential positions of these advisors during investors' conferences or prospective customer meetings. While these boards can lend an aura of authority, if managed properly advisors can really make a difference in a company's or a product's success.

Alphasmart manages its advisory board well. The company has a board of advisors that consists of nine education industry professionals. In addition to regular communication with these advisors, the board met twice a year for a two-day retreat. At these meetings, they tested prototypes for products under consideration, talked about trends in the education market, shared new ideas and brainstormed about company strategy.

Everyone

This board activity is of course in addition to the customer feedback that account managers and marketing. It is the job of everyone in the organization, from marketing managers and account managers, to product managers, to listen to, record, and respond to what the customers are saying. Not every feature desired was implemented, but they were all carefully recorded and considered. Everyone in the company saw the good, the bad, and the ugly about their interactions with their customers.

As Bill Gates once said: "Your most unhappy customers are your greatest source of learning." If you create the proper culture and organizational mechanisms, your next big product idea may just come from those who need it most: your customers!

DEVELOPING A RADICAL PRODUCT

Most products are the result of incremental innovations. That is, they are the result of adding features and making improvements within a well-known product category: improve the speed by 20%, improve the keyboard, increase the size of the screen. These categories generally have well established product descriptions, customer bases, supply chains, and so on.

Many new technology products don't belong to an established category. They may be orders of magnitude more powerful than anything that the market has ever seen before. Research and development labs round the world are churning out innovations in software , hardware, processes, and technology areas like nanotech, genomics, proteomics, DNA computing, and materials science that have improvements in price/performance of 10 times over anything in existence Such technologies are also called "radical," and sometimes "subversive."

They are so different or so powerful that there might be no use for them in the current market. Who knew that the early microprocessors would lead to word processing at home? How could the creators of the public key encryption find profitable commercial uses for this revolutionary technology in 1978? Yet, both innovations have found uses in hundreds of millions of personal computers, mobile phones, and personal digital assistants.

By and large, tech companies develop a technology and then go out looking for a problem they can solve. This can work if you have a technology or a product that is orders of magnitude more powerful than anything that the market has ever seen before. Rule 1 can be expressed as "It's all about the customer, not you!" But how do you listen to your customers if you don't have any? How do you listen to them if they don't even know that the technology exists, let alone that they need it or want it? Do you just "throw the product out there and hope it sticks" as many companies do?

Craigslist didn't do that. Alphasmart didn't do that. Alphasmart's founders went out to the field and felt the prospective customer's pain. They understood and felt the pain and then developed their product. To develop a new product, you should first *Feel the Pain*, then develop the product and your strategy.

This is certainly easier said than done. Where do you start? How do you discover new untapped markets you can serve? How do you best use you precious few resources in this exercise?

ENTREPRENEURSHIP STARTS WITH PAIN!

Whatever your technology, your first priority is to find a profitable commercial use. You have to develop a product that both serves a customer need and has potential to create healthy profits for your company and your investors. There should be no contradiction between these two goals. In order to do this you need to feel the pain!

You need to feel the pain that will drive customers to consider buying your product. Here's a step-by-step guide for you to feel the pain.

Discovering your target market

Let's assume you are called upon to find a market for a next-generation artificial-intelligence-based "Pattern Recognition" technology. This technology helps find "patterns" in large amounts of data that our senses or existing technology would miss.

You probably have a good idea of the top candidates for whom your technology will be beneficial. Let's go on a customer discovery exercise. Look at Fig 1.1 – Customer Segment Discovery/Value Proposition Matrix.

First write down the names of the prospective or target customers on top of each column. You should be more specific than "the financial services industry" or "Fortune 500 companies." Write down their actual business titles. Picture the actual customer, and give him or her a name. For instance, Alexandra is a Systems Administrator at a Global 2000 industrial organization, Jonathan is a Credit Card Risk Management Manager for a medium-sized commercial bank, Allyson is an investment manager at a large global bank, Kevin is a software salesperson at an enterprise software company, Allen is a Purchasing Manager at a large department store, and Jimmy is an Airport Security Manager. You can also further specify a geographic area. Be as specific as you can.

Now think of the range of specific applications of your product or technology. Write in these applications down the left column. Choosing possible uses or applications is especially important if you have a horizontal product--one that can be used for many things. For instance a PC is a horizontal product, as is a content management server.

Different people have different uses for these products. For instance, your product could be used to look at a wide range of data and analyze and predict what the data owner will do next: the application could be called "Human Behavior Analysis." The technology can also be used to analyze the text within documents like emails for determining whether or not it can be spam. You need to find one use that brings big benefits to a particular customer or class of customers.

Use/ Application	Customer (segment) -->					
| V	Alexandra (Systems Administrator)	Jonathan (Credit Card Risk Mgmt Mgr)	Allen (Department Store Purchasing Mgr)	Kevin (Software Salesperson)	Jimmy (Airport Security Manager)	Allyson (Investment Manager)
Human Behavior Analysis	Allocate servers -> lower costs	Decrease fraud -> save costs	Predict fashion trends -> increase revenues	Predict likelihood of sale	Find criminals -> Increase security	Predict stock buying patterns -> increase revenues
Visual Pattern Recognition	Predict bandwidth usage -> lower costs	Predict card usage -> lower costs	Predict fashion -> increase revenues	N/A	Find criminals -> Increase security	Predict stock movements -> increase revenues
Weather Prediction	Predict consumer usage -> Lower costs	Predict usage -> lower costs	Predict usage ->lower costs	N/A	Predict usage -> lower costs	Commodity Trading accuracy -> increase revenues
Text Analysis	Spam filter-> lower server costs	Decrease fraud -> lower costs	N/A	N/A	Find criminals -> increase security	Scan blogs for tips -> increase revenues

[FIG. 1.1 – CUSTOMER SEGMENT DISCOVERY - VALUE PROPOSITION MATRIX]

In the case of our Pattern Recognition technology, we can imagine that it can be used for human behavior analysis, visual pattern recognition, weather prediction, and text analysis. Let's insert those uses or applications in the left column. Now we have a matrix where we can visualize all the many things we can do for many people. Each cell shows one possible application that one prospective customer can benefit from using our technology. Now we need to find the value proposition of each of those cells.

Focus on customer pain

On each cell, write down what the product can do and more importantly, what the benefit or value is for that specific customer. For instance, we could write an application to predict stock movements. This application can increase revenues of most of the above customers. Let's assume we can increase revenues by 2%. To Kevin, a software salesperson, a 2% increase may be meaningless. However, to Allyson, an investment manager who trades millions or billions of dollars in stock every day, a 2% increase in revenues could result in millions in extra income. Clearly that application has

RULE 1: Feel the Pain. Then Develop Your Product.

huge potential benefits to investment managers but not to software salespeople.

Similarly, we could develop a Human Behavior Analysis application which could bring different types of benefits to the above potential users. Alexandra, a systems administrator, could use it to better allocate computer servers based on consumer demand; Kevin, who is a software salesman, could use it to predict who is likely to buy and even when to call them; while Jimmy, an airline security manager, could use it to increase the likelihood of catching a potential troublemaker.

Go through this type of analysis for all combinations of applications and customers. You'll notice that each cell has a different type of benefit for the customer.

How intense is the customer pain?

Not only is the pain different for each cell, but the intensity of this pain or need is also different. Let's go back to the Segment Discovery Matrix – Value Proposition (fig 1.1 above). Now we're going to change the value proposition or benefit to a number reflecting the intensity of that benefit. The resulting matrix is the "Customer Discovery – Value Creation Rating Matrix (Fig. 1.2).

For each combination of application and customer, let's assign a rating of the value we can create for this customer. This number is based on the level of pain or need that the customer is experiencing currently that this product would cure – what's the intensity of that pain (and by extension the benefit of our application)? Let's use a rating scale of 1 to 10. For instance, if that specific use or application is a "can't-live-without" for the customer, then it's a 10. If it's a "nice-to-have" product, then it's a 5, if it's a "total waste of value" situation, then it's a 1.

	Customer (segment)	-->				
Use / Application | V	Alexandra (Systems Administrator)	Jonathan (Credit Card Risk Mgmt Mgr)	Allen (Department Store Purchasing Mgr)	Kevin (Software Salesperson)	Jimmy (Airline Security Manager)	Allyson (Investment Manager)
Human Behavior Analysis	6	8	6	9	10	9
Visual Pattern Recognition	4	5	7	2	9	8
Weather Prediction	5	6	6	2	6	5
Text Analysis	8	8	5	2	6	3

[FIG. 1.2 – CUSTOMER DISCOVERY – VALUE CREATION MATRIX]

Let's look across the rows or up-and-down the columns for consistently high numbers. We should focus on areas where the need is really intense. Metaphorically speaking, you want to sell industrial-strength pain relief not vitamins. Think about it for a second. You're in your car just pulling out of the driveway to go to work in the morning. Suddenly you're hit with a painful headache and notice that you forgot your pain relief pills. Would you get out of the car and walk back into the house to pick them up? Probably. Had you forgotten your vitamin C pills, would you go back and get them? Probably not. For our exercise above, you want to look for the industrial-strength pain relief.

Think about other products that would make you turn back your car in the morning. Mobile phone, laptop computer, personal digital assistant, and prescription drugs come to mind. Now remember, you are not your target customer. These are assumptions that need to be confirmed. She might turn back for her Apple iPod even if you wouldn't.

At this point, we need to answer two questions:
1. Who is the customer we are going to focus on?
2. What is the application that we are going to develop for that customer?

Focus on clusters of really intense needs. They should have ratings close to 10 (preferably 8, 9 or 10). Notice that there is a small cluster of 8s on the lower left part of the matrix for the "Text Analysis" application. Better yet, there's an even better looking cluster that includes a 10, two 9s and three 8s at the top right corner. This analysis leads us to believe that the best opportunity seems to lie in developing the "Human Behavior Analysis" application (it has an 8, 9, and a 10) for the "Airport Security Manager" customer segment.

Get prospect feedback early and often!

Product development can be an expensive undertaking. Before investing money in developing the applition you would certainly need to go back to the prospective customer to validate that the above assumptions are correct. In fact, even after you have decided to develop a full-fledged application, you need to fully involve the customer in its development process. Don't go away to your R&D ivory tower for a year and come back with a "complete" product. The customer may tell you that's not quite what she needed. You will have spent a lot of time and resources chasing the wrong rabbit.

Instead you should develop inexpensive proof-of-concept vehicles to gain feedback for the customer. Spend a little money on different versions of your ideas that a prospect can see and even play with. That way you can get feedback for what exactly the prospect finds valuable and wants to see (and importantly, pay money for) in such a product.

Alphasmart's development process is a good guide. Creating Value Remember, you're developing the product for a set of customers not for yourself.

THE WHOLE iPod

One of the key reasons that Apple's iPod became such a huge success was that product managers understood that all the pieces of the music listening experience needed to be in place, and they needed to be tightly integrated. They understood that they were not just selling a music player–a box. In fact, there were already more than two dozen competing MP3 portable digital players in the market. There were also tools to download music from the Internet (albeit not always legally) or transfer them from a CD to the PC. There were also tools to download this music to the music players. What they lacked was Apple's "whole product" perspective. From the iTunes website to the cables and the software built into the iPod, Apple provided the buyer with an easy, legal, and seamless way to listen to music.

One of the most important tools available to the product strategist is the "Whole Product (or Service)." You need to deliver the customer's product, not yours. You need to feel the customer's pain.

The "whole product" is the combination of products and services that can achieve the customer's buying objective. The whole product needs to work as an ensemble. If something as simple as a cable is missing or faulty, nothing will work. Imagine going home and finding that you don't have the PC networking cable. This alone may render the computer printer, Internet access, and home networking useless. We expand on this concept in Rule 8 (Design Products and Services that are easy to Adopt).

Research In Motion's Category-defining product, the Blackberry, is an example of a product that broke through the crowd to achieve category leadership because of careful attention to delivering the whole product. Many companies attempted (and failed) to introduce wireless handheld products that combined mobile phone and e-mail functions. When RIM introduced the Blackberry, it included everything that the user needed to run email: the handheld hardware, operating system and applications; the wireless phone service to send and receive emails; and the backend email servers that connected to the user's company or personal email servers. Everything worked together seamlessly. Users became so fanatical about the Blackberry that they started calling it "Crackberry."

Rule 1 Summary: Feel the pain. Then Develop Your Product

The way to create winning products and avoid costly and rapid failure in the high tech market is to feel the pain of your prospective customers and users. That's how Craigslist was started and grew into one of the top web companies in the English-speaking world. That's how Alphasmart was started and grew to beat some of the largest companies on earth in contract bid after contract bid.

These winning companies did not develop a product and push it out the door. Their success was based on listening to the customer. To develop your product you want to involve your marketing team from the beginning in defining it. You should build a product or service the customer needs or wants. These products should be about fixing a customer pain, helping achieve a goal, an aspiration or dream. That is how you *create* winning products.

A "feel the pain" approach is especially important when you have a brand new (or "radical") type of product, technology, or service. It is essential even when potential customers may not initially know what the uses might be. Focus on the benefits that your product might bring to them. Think of the intensity of their pain or need that will move them to purchase your product. The intensity of this pain can provide a guideline to prioritizing your development resources.

RULE 2
FOCUS, WIN, GROW, REPEAT

"Without exquisite focus, the resources and energy of the organization will be spread a mile wide – and they will be an inch deep."

- Andy Grove

"Leadership means holding the No. 1 position in the categories that you go into,"

- John Chambers

Symantec spent most of the 1990s moving sideways engaging in a series of unrelated businesses. Known for its Norton™ series of personal computer tool products, Symantec had a hard time figuring out where to grow. So it went in many directions. "The company had dozens of products whose only commonality was the yellow boxes they were wrapped in," says Symantec Senior Vice President and General Manager Dieter Giesbrecht. Today, Symantec is the world's leading Internet security company. Few large technology companies have had the revenue and stock price growth that Symantec had in the first five years of the new millennium. Their revenue tripled and their stock sextupled. What did Symantec do to turn itself into the best company in its marketplace and one of the largest software companies on earth? It focused, built strength, became a leader, and grew large through focused acquisitions.

Why are technology giants like Cisco, Microsoft, Dell, and SAP who have many products and dominate several market categories so successful? Business pundits might say that these companies have superior execution, or superior strategic insights, or superior management teams, or top engineers, or they just got lucky. But the one thing these giants have had in common is strategic focus. They have focused on dominating the products and markets they entered, and then they used their dominant positions to expand into new adjacent markets.

Take Dell. They started selling PCs to home users. They then moved to selling PCs to small businesses (an adjacent market), and then to large businesses. After achieving remarkable growth rates and dominating the competition, Dell started selling PC storage (an adjacent category) to the same markets, followed by PC networking equipment and Dell-branded printers.

These companies change one thing at a time and take "small" steps in that direction. (Granted, a 'small' step for Microsoft or Dell is a huge leap for most companies around.) When they expand, they offer new products to markets they already know, or existing products (or variations) to new markets. Both new products and new markets are "next door" or adjacent to where they already are.

You can't compete successfully with several powerful enemies at the same time. You can't be good at everything and you can't successfully address every market opportunity. You need to focus your resources on products and markets where you have the best opportunity to gain market leadership.

The concept of leadership can be fudged by management, but in technology markets it's mostly clear: "Leadership means holding the No. 1 position in the categories that you go into," says John Chambers, CEO of Cisco Systems[10]. Your moves should leverage your existing strengths, whether that is in product development, supply chain, research or market domination.

Apple has taken small steps with its wildly successful iPod line. For the first few years the main application was playing music. In late 2004 Apple added photo display capability, followed a year later by the capability to play video. Only after the iPod thoroughly dominated the category did it make sense to add new applications. Now the iPod has "horizontal" capabilities that may help establish it as a platform in its own right: Podcasting, Internet radio, video, audio, photo, and many innovative and previously unplanned applications. Last year I bought a microphone and an adapter and used my iPod to record my classes. This and other applications may turn the iPod into the center of a technology "ecosystem" where hundreds of companies develop products to complement it – just like many developed software and hardware to complement the Wintel personal computer over the last few decades.

In high technology as in the Olympics the gold comes from being number one.

Microsoft's product strategy looks haphazard but its competitive strategy is brutally focused. Since their inception, they took on one competitor at a time: Digital Research in the PC operating system category, WordPerfect in the word processing market, Lotus in the spreadsheet market, Borland in the development tools market, Netscape in the Internet browser market, Sun Microsystems in the business server market, Novell in the local area networking market. Microsoft has historically targeted one competitor and ruthlessly focused on it until it either drove them out of their market or turned them into non-threatening players. Once Microsoft felt they dominated, they launched from that position of strength and attacked the next competitor. This is how they came to dominate so many categories in personal computer software markets.

Has Microsoft always won? Well, no. They have repeatedly targeted and lost to one company that is even more focused than Microsoft: Intuit. Microsoft has several times gone after Intuit in the personal finance software market and failed. At one point, they threw in the towel and offered to acquire Intuit. The Securities and Exchange Commission did not approve the deal and Intuit has since extended its leadership into adjacent vertical markets - one at a time.

What did Intuit do that many of the others didn't? Intuit is one of the technology companies that has most obsessively focused on their customers. They have combined Rule 1 (Feel the Pain. Then Develop Your Product) and Rule 2 (Focus, Win, Grow, Repeat). It has been hard, even for Microsoft, to beat a company that combines these two Rules.

As of late 2005, Microsoft again decided to focus its efforts on a single competitor. This time it was Silicon Valley wunderkind Google. Whether Google's fate becomes that of Netscape or Intuit remains to be seen.

HOW SYMANTEC BUILT A WINNER

In the 1990s Symantec had dozens of products whose only commonality was the yellow boxes they were wrapped in. "We didn't know who our customers were or why they acquired our products," Said Executive Vice President Giesbrecht. "We had no relationship with our customers." Symantec was an unfocused company. It went into many markets with many products without much regard to whether they leveraged company strength. Its main product line was the Norton ™ series of personal computer tool products. These tools offered the user tools to clean up the PC hard drive, recover files, and secure sensitive data. Symantec had a hard time figuring out where else to grow. So it went in many directions.

In 1989, Symantec released the ACT product line aimed to help sales people manage their contacts and sales pipeline. ACT became a profitable business but it leveraged neither the technology strengths nor customer base for the Norton products. Hoping to jump on the Java bandwagon, Symantec released Visual Café in 1998, a software development tool aimed at the software programming market. Programmers could use the Visual Café Interactive Development Environment (IDE) to develop Java code for PCs. By releasing this product, Symantec gained a new set of competitors, from Microsoft to Borland.

Just like its neighbor Borland (aka Inprise), Symantec had gotten into a series of unrelated businesses. Symantec competed with different companies in different markets including McAfee (later bought by Network Associates) in data security, Quarterdeck in PC utilities, and GoldMine in the sales management market. None of the businesses seemed to leverage Symantec's technical skills or market strengths. According to Dieter Giesbrecht, Symantec's Senior Vice President and General Manager "the common denominator was that products came in yellow boxes that were sold through a two-tier distribution system." Furthermore, selling through that channel prevented the company from establishing a direct relationship with its customers. Symantec didn't even know who its customers were. The company lacked a center of strength. It had no real vision to focus and energize the employees. It had no strategy to invest resources and be a leader in a valuable software market. The company didn't know its customers so it published dozens of unrelated products hoping some of them would stick. Innovating and taking chances on new technologies and products is a good idea but a hit-or-miss product development strategy is not the best road to industry leadership in the brutal world of high technology.

Revenue growth during the 1990s was tepid. The SYMC stock moved sideways within a narrow trading range during this decade, even as high technology was enjoying the highest revenue growth and stock market appreciation in recent memory. While the Nasdaq Composite appreciated by an order of magnitude, the SYMC stock was stuck.

Enter John W. Thompson.

Decision to focus

After taking over as Symantec's CEO in April 1999, John Thompson knew that the company needed a new strategic direction. He did what new CEOs are supposed to do: analyze the company's strengths and weaknesses; analyze its markets and competitors; talk to customers, analysts, and employees; and look at the trends and opportunities ahead. He got his management team together and went to work.

It was obvious to him what needed to be done. Thompson decided that the company needed to focus. Symantec's management team had to choose which products and markets made sense for the company. Their not-so-easy task was to look for a large addressable market that was going to grow in the foreseeable future, for which Symantec had the skills and resources to be the market leader.

The team decided to focus on Internet security. There were four main drivers in the marketplace that led the management team to decide on Internet Security:

1. Projected growth in broadband internet connectivity.
2. Projected growth in e-commerce.
3. Disappearing perimeters.
4. Lots of security companies, but no clear or emerging leader.

In 1999 it looked like *broadband access* was going to keep increasing for the foreseeable future. Both the number of users with access to broadband and the size of the pipeline itself were growing fast. While Internet traffic would probably soon slow down a bit, it was still growing anywhere from 90% to 400% per year–depending on who you asked[11]. Furthermore, business enterprises accounted for about 80% of Internet traffic. All this meant that interconnectivity, file-sharing, data sharing, and software sharing was going to not just increase but explode exponentially.

At the same time, *electronic commerce* was becoming a major driver for both the operations and the growth of enterprises around the world. As a result, they had to open up the information technology infrastructure to partners, customers, and suppliers. The days when companies could just lock up their IT infrastructures from outside access were over.   This clearly increased data security risks and posed a huge challenge to corporate data managers. The perimeters of individual PCs and company information technology infrastructures were going to keep blurring fast. Standalone PCs are isolated. The only way to read or copy data to them is by physically accessing them. Once these PCs are connected to a network many other users have access to them. Where does a *personal* computer stop being personal? This was a big question then. Think of tens, hundreds, and even thousands of computers interconnected in corporate networks. Threats to the security of these computers comes as much from inside as from outside the networks. One may initially think of a disgruntled employee doing damage but you can also imagine that any outsider that has been able to crack into any weak spot anywhere on the network now would have access to the entire corporate data infrastructure.

Finally, there seemed to be *no clear leader* in Internet Security software, especially in the enterprise market. Several companies were relatively large (revenues larger than $250 million or so) but they either were point players with leadership in one product line or small startups with interesting technologies but no market power. The large companies included RSA Security, the leader in encryption and in the secure token access markets; Checkpoint, the leader in firewalls for enterprises; and Network Associates which had recently acquired McAfee, a well-known security company in the US, and Dr. Solomon's, a strong player in Europe. The lack of a clear leader was a key driver in Symantec's decision.

Many technology companies underestimate what it will take to defeat incumbent leaders, especially focused ones. Even giants fail to unseat smaller category winners. Cisco has been the clear leader in the networking gear space, accounting for more than 80% of the market. In its effort to expand beyond that core market, it invested time, resources, and effort getting into markets such as storage switches and network security. It gained leadership status in neither, mainly because of tough focused competitors. In the storage switch market, for example, Cisco, whose yearly revenues were above $20 billion, was a distant third to much smaller companies like Brocade (2004 revenues around $525 million) and McData (2004 revenues around $400 million). It also had a tough time in the enterprise firewall security space against much smaller but ultra-focused firewall vendor Checkpoint Systems (2004 revenues around $720 million).

In 1999, Symantec saw that the market opportunity in the emerging data security space was clearly a large one. "This was especially true in the enterprise market which accounted for 80% of Internet traffic." Said Executive Vice President Giesbrecht. Trends in the market also indicated it would be a fast growing opportunity.

Looking within the company, Symantec's executive management team believed that it had technical, market and management strengths in security. The necessary elements to win were there – if only they would focus. Thompson and his management team decided that Symantec should focus in the Internet security space.

Divesting sources of weakness

Former Intel CEO Andy Grove said that "hedging is expensive and dilutes commitment. Without exquisite focus, the resources and energy of the organization will be spread a mile wide – and they will be an inch deep."[12] Strategy is about making choices. It's a set of coherent decisions about the firm's approach to the market. Some of these decisions include what customers you're going to serve, how you're going to serve them, what resources you're going to invest, and how you're going to create competitive advantage. Once you decide what products and markets you will focus on, you have decided what businesses you don't intend to play in. Once you know you don't want to be in a given business or you can't be a leader in that business, the sooner you divest it the better. This may sound obvious but it's usually easier said than done.

It is common for CEOs and board directors of tech companies to punt on this transition. If you make a decision to focus, revenues and the size of the business will likely go down. This is something they may feel they didn't sign up for. Egos and paychecks may be proportional to the size of the business. Management teams and company directors may want to have it both ways. They want to have the revenue of the old unfocused business while the "new business where we're going to focus takes off."

They may say things like "synergy between the different businesses" or "the parts are bigger than the whole"–anything to keep the old divisions within the company.

In all likelihood the business may not take off at all *unless* and *until* it focuses.   Furthermore, focusing may be a heart-wrenching exercise. You may disappoint some customers, partners, investors, and employees. It may get messy for a while. There may be uncertainty as to the process and even the outcome. How are decisions being made?   Who's in? Who's out? What's the business going to look like? What's plan B? So the board and the management team may wait and hedge for a while. Not making a decision is a decision. Waiting is a decision. Hedging is a decision.

Thompson would have none of that. Symantec divested itself of unrelated businesses including both ACT and Visual Café within a year.[13] These businesses brought in around $55 million in yearly revenues, almost 10% of the company's total. Visual Café was getting rave reviews but was losing money so the decision to sell was relatively straightforward. It was sold to WebGain for $75 million in cash.[14] ACT, however, was a profitable product. There is always the temptation to keep a profitable business going as a cash cow to finance the business. We will see later this chapter how Kodak did it with its dying film business. This, however, may not be a good idea for all the reasons stated above. ACT™ was licensed to Interact (previously SalesLogix) for stock then valued at $20 million and future royalties of up to $57 million. Once divested of these businesses Symantec would be all about Internet and enterprise security.

Getting smaller to get larger

Focusing didn't mean that Symantec wanted to be smaller. On the contrary, it meant it wanted to be larger. Much larger.

Growth needed to come in a focused way. Thompson understood that the best way to do this was to set clear goals for growth for the near future. In 1999, the company set out to achieve two clear (and overlapping) goals:

1. Become a $1 billion revenue company by fiscal year 2002.
2. Become the Internet and enterprise security leader by 2003.

They were both audacious goals. The company had revenues of $580 million. To get to $1 billion in two years they needed to grow 72% in two years. Looked at another way, they needed to grow revenues by more than 31% year over year. This is not an unheard of growth rate in the software business, but it was clearly a stretch for a company that had been mostly moving sideways for a decade and was not used to steady fast growth. They needed to change the company momentum upwards and they needed to do it immediately. In order to have everyone moving in a single direction, the management team also had to change the company culture to one that was focused and measurement-oriented. Furthermore, they didn't know it at the time, but the information technology market was about to head into a terrible recession–one that saw many smaller companies go under, and even crushed leading companies like Siebel Systems and Sun Microsystems whose revenues hit less than half their 2000 fiscal year totals.

The second goal, that of being the Internet and enterprise security leader, was even bolder. It meant coming out of the pack of large companies in the security space and becoming number one. This is never easy to do in technology markets, especially in such a porous place as Silicon Valley, where management and technical talent turnover can be very high. This area is so porous that some venture capitalists sit on boards of directors of competing companies, and corporate strategies are well known outside your organization even as they are being crafted within. Almost anyone in the market can copy your strategy and hire your best people as you announce your new strategy to the world.

Symantec aspired to be the security leader in enterprise security software. Yet, it did not even have a single salesperson focused on selling to that market. They did have high usage within enterprises, but that was mostly because end users bought Symantec's products at the retail store and used them in their workplaces.

The company had set lofty goals and needed to work smart, fast and hard to get there.

Getting larger one company at a time

Symantec looked at where they wanted to be in the near future and where they currently were. They knew that they had product, market, process, and skills gaps that they needed to fill quickly. Management knew they could and should train their employees to develop in these new directions. Given the aggressive timeline, they also knew that many of these gaps could only be filled with outside resources, mainly through acquisitions. As a software publisher, Symantec had developed skills in acquiring companies and technologies and integrating them into their fold. In fact, most of Symantec's business came from corporate acquisitions:

- Peter Norton Computing (acquired in 1990) brought its line of PC tools.
- Central Point Software (1994) brought backup PC tools.
- Delrina (1995) brought WinFax.
- Quarterdeck (1998) brought PC diagnostics software.
- Binary Research Ltd brought its imaging technology.

The company had also developed technology acquisition expertise. Its antivirus technology came from acquisitions from IBM and Intel in 1998.

Customers told Symantec management they didn't just want a bunch of unrelated products. Symantec already had that! Customers (and prospective customers) wanted to easily integrate and manage their software products. "Manageability" of all the technology they brought into the fold would be a key element of the strategy going forward.

To achieve its goals company management knew they would need to step it up. Symantec got ready to go on an acquisition spree. Symantec acquired Axent in July of 2000. This acquisition was a bold and risky gamble. Integrating high tech companies of substantial size is known to be notoriously difficult. Management can be distracted, there may be cultural fit problems, technology integration problems, logistical issues, and so on. Axent was a relatively large company with revenues of $112 million in 1999 (vs. Symantec's $704 million). They were across the country (in Maryland) which presented logistics and possibly cultural integration problems.

Axent, however, had well accepted products, a revenue stream, and an enterprise customer portfolio. It had a capable sales force that sold to the enterprise market (whereas Symantec only knew how to sell to consumers and small businesses). Axent could also bring a security and systems consulting arm and 24/7 customer service that the enterprise market required as well as several products that Symantec needed:

- Firewalls (technology that protects computers and networks against penetration by outsiders)
- Intrusion detection (technology that identifies suspicious patterns against the user's network)
- Policy compliance management (technology that performs regulatory compliance analysis), and
- Vulnerability assessment (technology that helps determine the adequacy of security measures.)

Axent could fill many of Symantec's gaps but it was not cheap: the final purchase price was $975 million,([15]) a premium of 75% above its then stock price. This represented a market valuation of nearly nine times yearly revenues. Thompson's management team decided that it was worth the price and risk.

All told, five years after taking over as CEO, Mr. Thompson and his team had managed to make 19 acquisitions in the Internet and enterprise security areas. These are some of the businesses Symantec has acquired and the product lines, services, or technologies that they have brought into the company:

- L3 - network security business of L3.
- Lindner and Pelc – managed security services.
- Mountain Wave – multi-vendor security analysis technology.
- Recourse Technologies --network intrusion detection technology.
- Brightmail – antispam product line.
- SecurityFocus – vulnerability assessment technology,
- @stake – security audits and risk management.

Measurements and goals

Successful execution requires careful measurement. If you don't have clear goals you can't know if you're successful at what you do. The company may have employees going in different directions and canceling each other's actions out. Previously, Symantec had no real vision, no real growth strategy and no goals. That was true at the corporate level and it was even truer of divisions, teams, and individual employees. Since the company lacked clear goals, it lacked metrics to measure success. Product development deadlines were often missed and product quality was often substandard. Employee performance was not measured. Lack of consistent metrics meant that management had no way of improving product quality, plan effectively, or discipline inferior performance. John Thompson changed all this.

One of the advantages of focusing the company is that management can set goals and metrics that are simple, clear, and consistent. Handing employees clear metrics is like giving them a compass that points in the direction the company wants to go. Management and employees could then know when they are off course and how to measure the discrepancy from the goal. Hopefully employees would also be given the training and the tools to head back in the right direction.

Symantec's goal was to be the leading internet and enterprise security company. This goal would guide every single employee in the company. Every division, every product group, and every employee was handed clear directions and metrics to measure their performance. Many employees were not used to being managed, let alone measured. Many of them packed up and left. After its decision to focus on internet security, Symantec turned over half the company's 2,300 employees and most of its executive staff.[16]

Winning the Gold

Remember the two audacious (and complementary) goals that the company had set out for itself? Symantec achieved both these goals. The company reached $1 billion dollar in revenues in fiscal year 2002 and they became the leader in the internet and enterprise security market in 2003. By early 2005, more than 120 million users worldwide ran Symantec products. 950 of the Global 1,000 companies were its customers.

Take the antivirus market. Symantec's achieved a market share of 64% in the consumer anti-virus segment[17], and a 36% share of the overall market, followed by Network Associates with 24% market share. Its dominance in this market was demonstrated by the fact that it has raised prices several times[18] including a 33% price hike in 2003, while still growing at rates higher than 60% per year-- consistently faster than the market. Competitors like Network Associate's McAfee couldn't manage to do either.

As a result of its market dominance, Symantec's financial results were stellar. Revenues in the first five Thompson years more than tripled, having gone from $592 million in fiscal year 1998 (before Thompson) to $1.9 billion in 2004. The SYMC stock sextupled since the spring of 2000 going from about $10, to just under $60 (after two stock splits) in late 2004.[19] Symantec achieved a market capitalization of $12.5 billion, which would provide valuable currency to acquire even more companies.

Symantec's focused strategy and clear execution path had clearly paid off.

Raising the bar

Symantec had achieved and surpassed the lofty goals that John Thompson and his management team had set out when they decided to focus, grow and win. Technology markets haven't been kind to leaders who rest on their laurels (see Rule 9).

How do you maintain your market leadership in a brutally competitive marketplace? You keep raising the bar. You hire the best talent. You get closer to your customers and keep adding value. You stay focused. When you focus and become the market leader, you can acquire skills, resources, and opportunities that you would otherwise not be able to acquire. This allows you to raise the bar in the industry and make it expensive or pre-empt others from attempting to enter the market.

As part of its effort to manage all aspects of the security of its customers, small and large, Symantec assembled a set of technologies, skills, and information that is *truly* unequaled anywhere in the world. For instance, because of its *direct* relationship with almost all the

Global 1,000 companies and more than 120 million users, Symantec assembled the largest security intelligence database containing threats and vulnerabilities in the world. The development of this massive threat database allowed Symantec to literally listen to its customers, maintain a close relationship with them, stay ahead of the competition, and develop valuable next-generation security products that its competitors would have a hard time conceiving or deploying. As an example, the U. S. Department of Defense relied on Symantec's threat database.

The ability to hire (and manage well) the most creative and talented technical and management staff can set in motion a virtuous cycle. Google, for instance, is said to continually hire 90% of the best search-engine people in the world.[20] Talent can develop and market the most innovative and valuable products and services which solidify and extend a company's leadership position. This brings in even more of the top talent and the virtuous cycle gets going again. Once it became the industry leader, Symantec, could attract and hire the industry's top engineering and management talent – and raise the bar even higher.

Symantec, a company that not long before had been an unfocused publisher of shrink-wrapped PC software, had joined the ranks of SAP, Oracle, and IBM. Focusing, becoming a leader, and growing from there in a focused way clearly paid off for Symantec.

Coda

After achieving its enterprise security software leadership position, Symantec management felt the company needed another goal. The company decided it wanted to be a $5 billion organization. How to get there? Customers told Executive Vice President Dieter Giesbrecht that "you can have a secure infrastructure only if you have a well managed infrastructure." Symantec management understood this mandate to mean that the company's next expansion phase was to step into the systems and storage management area. Symantec called it "Information Integrity." At the beginning of 2005 Symantec officially acquired storage backup software company Veritas for about $13.5 billion. By adding archive and backup technologies to its security arsenal, Symantec believed it recast the whole security space in a new light. By adding Veritas's almost $2 billion in revenues and thousands of the largest corporate buyers on earth to its customer base, Symantec became the fourth largest software company in the world.

Symantec had succeeded as an enterprise company and shared these customers with Veritas. However, from the product perspective, it would be hard to define storage backup as an adjacent move for a security software company. Furthermore, Veritas was a company about the same size as Symantec and it would be a large bite to swallow. Focus had made Symantec great but this move was not within the security domain. Why did Symantec do this? This was more of a game-changing acquisition. Management felt that the company needed to change while it was strong or face the consequences if it did not. (This is more in line with Rule 9).

BORLAND CONFUSION

The flip side of Symantec's focused strategy was shown by Borland Software. Based in Scotts Valley, California, Borland was an early leader in the software development tools category. A classic Silicon Valley success story, Borland was founded in 1982 by Philippe Kahn, a brilliant French entrepreneur who had overstayed his visa to start the company. The company sold products like Borland Turbo Pascal, Borland C, and Borland C++ that programmers used to develop software applications for personal computers. In the early 1980s, Borland was synonymous with PC languages and development tools.

Flush with cash from its success in its core tools business, Borland expanded into several products and markets in a seemingly incoherent way. It started writing a series of products that had no relation to or in any way leveraged its successful core business. Then in 1983, Borland took some of its best engineering talent away from its core product line development projects, and reassigned them to the development of "Sidekick," an early personal information manager (PIM) software product. While a technically accomplished piece of software, Sidekick leveraged neither Borland's core technology infrastructure nor its customer base.

Borland then produced Quattro, a spreadsheet that was to compete with the leading spreadsheet software company at the time: Lotus Development. Again, this new product leveraged neither Borland's customer base nor its technical product infrastructure. In 1987 it acquired a company called Ansa, and then published Paradox, a PC database software product that competed with dBase, the clear market leader

Borland's sales strategy suffered from a number of disconnects. The market was predictably confused about what the company stood for. Instead of assigning the best engineers to work on projects they were best at, they were shuffled from project to project according to the new product du jour. The company went out to fight in thoroughly competitive races and left its core business unprotected, while Microsoft's shadow loomed larger and larger.

In 1991, Borland acquired Ashton-Tate, the maker of dBase, the leading database software for PCs at the time. Ashton-Tate had been going through internal problems and increasing external market pressure that it had not been able to manage well. The company was bloated, hadn't kept up with product innovation, and was losing market share. Its CEO reportedly couldn't run dBase on his computer.[21] In one fell swoop, Borland doubled its quarterly revenues to about $138 million (equivalent to $550 million/year) and was sitting on 75% of the PC database market. To put these numbers in perspective, Microsoft revenues had grown 56% to $1.8 billion in 1991[22] while Lotus had $800 million in revenues.

Now Borland had not one, not two, not three, but four different database platforms to maintain (dBase/ DOS and Interbase from Ashton-Tate, and Paradox and Object dBase from Borland) going to different markets. Integrating all these platforms became a nightmare: "We haven't found much technology in Ashton-Tate that would really become Borland technology," said Philippe Kahn[23]. "We have the product that they should have—the next-generation product. We knew that their product development wasn't in very good shape. It seemed natural that our product would be the continuation of their product."

Lack of focus on both the technical and marketing fronts would soon cause Borland to suffer in the marketplace. Soon after the Ashton-Tate acquisition, Borland revenues peaked at $480 million[24]

and then steadily declined to $174 million in 1999. Its stock went from above $80 in early1992 to just over $3 in late 1999. This decline took place as the world of information technology experienced one of the greatest expansionary periods in its history. During this time the Nasdaq went up by just under 400% (and it would almost double again before it peaked in March of 2000.) Borland Engineers left in droves -- some to work for the competition. The marketing department was decimated. Bankruptcy loomed.

Insiders could console themselves that at least they had a well known brand name. So, what did management do? They changed it! The new name could not be more generic: Inprise. It meant nothing and stood for nothing. Now they had a few great engineers left, a confused market, and a generic name. Did the story end there? Fortunately for Borland, it didn't. A cash infusion from their erstwhile competitor Microsoft kept them afloat. Then the company got back to profitability and even grew revenues to more than $300 million in 2004. How did Borland (aka Inprise) get back to profitability? You guessed it: by focusing on its core business of software tools for programmers. They have exited all other businesses. And thankfully they also brought the old Borland name back.

How to Focus and Grow

The companies I have cited have used a common formula for focusing their products:
1. Focus on one product, market, or competitor at a time.
   - Build up strength. Commit. Divest sources of weakness.
2. Become the market leader.
   - Grow and dominate the market.
   - Protect your leadership at all costs.
3. Expand to complementary or adjacent products or markets.
4. Repeat.

In the early stages of your business you probably have limited resources. You should focus on one cell on the Strategic Market Expansion Matrix (Fig. 2.1, below). Which customer/application cell should you focus on? Here's the step-by-step guidance.

Expand to adjacent opportunities

We have seen how some of the great technology companies, like Symantec, Dell, and Intuit, have won by focusing, gathering strength and expanding mainly to adjacent opportunities. Your best chance of success in new markets lies in expanding to adjacent opportunities. These are several ways to expand to adjacent opportunities.

Expand to adjacent market segments.

Your product is the leader in a specific marketplace. At this point your company has invested time, money, and human resources to develop a platform, valuable knowledge, skills, intellectual property and processes to develop the product, service or application to win in that marketplace. You have understood the customer's pain, needs, and wants. You have made mistakes and learned from them. Your focus on the customer means that your product works well and is generally well regarded in the marketplace. You are an insider in this market. It's not just that you know the market. It's also that the market knows you. It would take a competitor considerable time and expenditures to attempt to replicate what you already have. To grow beyond this core market, you may want to look at adjacent markets that have needs that are variations of the ones that your product is addressing in existing markets.

Adjacent markets are customer segments that are similar, close to or somehow connected to your existing market. This would include their suppliers, buyers, and partners. For instance, if you supply software for small clinics, there are several possible adjacent markets you can look at. You can start with larger clinics and hospitals, military hospitals, or even veterinary hospitals. You can look at suppliers like pharmaceuticals and clinical equipment manufacturers. You can also look at complementary targets such as physical therapy clinics or nursing hospitals.

Expanding to adjacent markets helps you leverage your existing customer and industry knowledge. It may be possible to use the reputation you have created as a leader to create word of mouth (and word of mouse), publicity, and references, all essential elements when entering a new market. It also helps that you may not need to develop a brand-new product from scratch. You have a core product that you can probably develop into a whole product for a new market. At best your investment in product development is incremental in terms of time, financial and human resources. Time is not something to be underestimated. Even if you had the financial resources and could quickly acquire the human resources, time-to-market may be an essential competitive advantage in fast-moving markets.

If you were to create a brand new product from scratch, you may just be on a similar competitive ground as many competitors, existing and new. You would need to go up the learning curve in terms of industry knowledge, customer needs assessment, technology, promotion, and brand creation.

Expand to adjacent product categories.

Your product is the leader in its market. You have developed a customer base that trusts you and knows what you're capable of delivering for them. These customers have allowed you into their company, household, or organization. You have learned much about them too--about their businesses, their workflow, their pains, problems, challenges, needs and desires. You know them and they know you. The combination of intimate customer knowledge and the trust they have placed in you puts your company in a unique position to deliver new products and services to solve your customer needs.

Look at other sources of pain or wants your customers have. What other products and services can you develop for your them? Microsoft has leveraged the strength brought by the fact that its operating system runs on most personal computers to develop applications for users of those PCs. Today most of its revenues and earnings come from the Windows operating system and the Office application suite. After dominating its market Apple has leveraged its leadership and customer knowledge by expanding its iPod product line from music to photo to podcasting to video and other applications and services. Peoplesoft leveraged its initial human resources technology presence in large corporations to develop other applications like financials and enterprise resource planning. They all have developed new products leveraging their deep knowledge of their customers and their respective market positions.

Use / Applications	Customer (segment) -->					
| V	Veterinary Hospital	Large Hospital	Small Hospital	Pharma-ceutical	Medical Equipment	Military Hospital
Patient Record Management						
Clinical Trial Management						
Medical Office Management						
Enterprise Resource Management						

FIG. 2.1 – STRATEGIC MARKET EXPANSION MATRIX

Expand to adjacent geographies.

Geographic expansion should be treated similarly to segment expansion. Each market may have its own needs and the company may have to build a different product for each one of them. Many companies make the mistake of thinking that a simple translation of their product manuals will do. Nothing is further from the truth. Feel the pain of the local market segment before you expand there. SAP is an example of a company that carefully moved from building strength in its original core market in Germany to dominate Europe and then the United States and indeed the world. They built this expansion on the strength of its core ERP product line.

Sometimes company management forgets that their core markets are the source of their strength and ignore them in their rush to expand elsewhere. The following are tips that your company should heed as you seek to expand:

Defend your core market as you seek expansion opportunities

Your core market is what currently provides your company with its livelihood. It is your base of operations. While you may be in a position of strength, you're by no means secure. There are other companies eyeing your position in that market. If you abandon it while seeking other business opportunities you may come back to find someone else has moved in. Your customers will notice if you assign your top engineering and marketing talent away from them and into other opportunities. Your product will deteriorate, customer service will deteriorate, your brand (which means your relationship with the customer) will deteriorate. Once your customers feel abandoned and start looking seriously at alternatives in the market, your fate may be sealed. At best you will have to dramatically increase your investments just to hold on to your customers. At worst you may lose the leadership position. You may regain some of the market back, but it may be too late to save it.

Yahoo! was the first and early leader in the Internet search category. As the Internet grew exponentially in the mid-1990's, there was a clear need for an easy way to locate products, services, people, and information from the millions of websites that were springing up around the world every day. Millions of users flocked to sites such as Yahoo!, Excite, and Lycos. After a hard battle that cost hundreds of millions of dollars, Yahoo! beat them all and became the undisputed leader. Excite went bankrupt and Lycos became a shadow of itself and was later acquired by Terra, a subsidiary of Spanish telecom company Telefonica.

Feeling comfortable in its leadership position, Yahoo! went after a bigger market. They redefined themselves as a "branded media property" company[25] and went after companies like AOL. Yahoo! spent billions of dollars acquiring "media" property companies such as *Broadcast.com* with the goal of being the premier entertainment destination on the Web[26] They also hired a new CEO, Terry Semel, whose background included running such Hollywood mainstays as Warner Brothers and divisions of CBS and Disney. In the meantime, they neglected their core search business. They outsourced the search function to companies like AltaVista, Inktomi and later a small startup called Google. Yahoo! and Google shared a board member and venture capital investor. It was all in the family, right? Well, not quite. Not for Yahoo! anyway.

Google soon became the leader in the internet search category, outstripping Yahoo! of their leadership. While Yahoo!'s new core business suffered through the 2001-2003 recession, Google was more than doubling revenues each of those years. Yahoo! found itself playing catch-up in a category it once dominated and consciously walked away from.

Terry Semel, Yahoo's CEO said, "We woke up in time and we saw search ever present in the entire network. We saw an enormous opportunity to be the other major player in search."[27] He tried to acquire Google when the latter was still a private company -- but they had already become too expensive for Yahoo!'s taste. Semel then went on an acquisition spree to buy the search technology and market to fight again in the search world. Yahoo! paid about $2 billion for to buy Inktomi and Overture. The merged companies got Yahoo! back in the search game. Yahoo! was fortunate it had the financial resources (in terms of market capitalization and cash) to get back in the game. Most companies are not this lucky.

However, it is safe to say that Google is going to be a tough rival to Yahoo! in many areas. Google again struck at the heart of Yahoo!'s core business with their Gmail web-based email service, with up to ten times the free storage that Yahoo! offered. Then Google offered tools for users to create their own personalized home pages (with news, weather, email, groups, and so on), a Yahoo! staple since its early days. At the same time Google surpassed Yahoo in terms of advertising revenues, the latter's bread and butter. Google's 2004 fourth quarter net ad revenues (after paying other sites for their share) was $654 million against $618 million for Yahoo![28]   And Google never looked back!

Google's revenues have been growing at a higher rate than Yahoo! The quarter ending June 2005 saw Yahoo!'s revenue grow to $1.25 billion and its operating income to $261 million. There are great numbers any way you look at them. Google's revenues and operating income however went up to $1.38 billion and $475 million respectively in the same period. The following quarter Google announced quarterly revenues of $1.578 billion (almost doubling the equivalent quarter in 2004) and earnings of $381 million. Yahoo!'s revenues that quarter were $1.3 billion (a 47% increase over the equivalent quarter in 2004) and operating income of $270 million.[29] The fourth quarter of 2005 saw Google's revenues grow to $1.9 billion vs. $1.5 billion for Yahoo while their respective operating incomes were $569 million and $438 million.

More noteworthy was the fact that Google's CEO Eric Schmidt claimed that Google handled 45 percent of all search requests in the U.S., more than both Yahoo! (23%) and MSN (12%) combined.[30] In mid-October 2005, Google achieved a $94 billion market capitalization, almost twice Yahoo!'s impressive $49 billion valuation. Yahoo! let Google in the barn and they nearly took over the farm!

Don't overextend the company

While it is important to invest in new market opportunities, you should not overextend the company in such pursuit.

Palm Inc was the early leader in the handheld computer category. After they released the Palm Pilot in 1996 they went on to redefine and dominate this fast-growing market. In an interview in the fall of 1998, Palm co-founder Donna Dubinsky asserted they had more than 80% share of the market.[31] Life was good until established rivals started eyeing this market. In 1998, Microsoft released the first version of its PalmPC operating system (later named Pocket PC and later re-renamed Windows CE) and giants like Dell and HP created hardware around it. By the end of 1999 when Palm was ready to go public, it had about 45% of the market against 25% for Microsoft and 18% for Psion.[32]

At this point it became clear that Palm was overextending itself trying to compete against powerful giants in several categories at the same time. Palm was producing and marketing both the hardware and the operating system concurrently. Because of this fact, it was basically competing with its best customers! Companies like Sony, Samsung, and Kyocera found themselves licensing Palm OS and competing with Palm's hardware. This is not sustainable under normal circumstances.

Microsoft soon went after the handheld operating systems market. They aggressively licensed their new products to hardware manufacturers like Compaq, Dell, HP, and Gateway. Just these four companies had revenues in excess of $100 billion dollars at the time. Aggressive, well-capitalized startups like Handspring were also going after Palm from below. Palm soon found itself competing with giants like Microsoft in the OS market and Dell and Compaq (as well as its own customers) in the hardware business. By doing this, they overextended the company and lost their market leadership.

Eventually, they did the obvious and split the company into two pieces: PalmSource would produce and market the OS, and Palm Inc would produce hardware based on that software. Dave Nagel, CEO of the new PalmSource, said that they could now "focus 100 percent of our time on building the world's best operating system."[33] Their downward momentum was too steep and Microsoft's pressure too hard. The following year saw PalmSource's lead in the PDA OS market go down from 46.9 percent to 29.8 percent while Microsoft took the lead with 48.1 percent.[34] PalmSource's stock went on to decline by about 50% before selling itself to Japanese mobile software vendor Access for $324.3 million[35].

To get back in the hardware game, Palm Inc. (the second spinoff company) acquired one of its truly innovative licensees: Handspring. The latter was an expensive acquisition: at $378 million[36] that is more than a third of the outstanding stock of the joint company (renamed PalmOne). Palm, however, had very little choice. Handspring, founded by Donna Dubinsky and Jeff Hawkins (who had originally founded Palm itself before leaving the company) had produced award-winning products that were far ahead of anything Palm had been able to design and market. PalmOne had a tough time in the market but it subsequently managed to double its stock valuation. While both of Palm's spin-off companies face tough battles ahead, the split probably saved Palm from almost certain extinction, but it was probably too late to regain its leadership in either the hardware or software categories. Palm had overextended itself.

Stay close to home

Technology markets are synonymous with relentless change. You are constantly changing products, markets, supply chain, competitors, allies, competitors. Furthermore, tech market leadership implies going where no one has gone before. To succeed amidst this change you will need to experiment constantly. Many times you will be successful making these changes and other times you will not. If you are successful, you will want to know what worked and apply the lesson. If you are not successful, you also need to know what didn't work so you don't repeat that mistake.

The problem is: with so many changes seemingly happening concurrently, how do you know what worked or didn't? Whatever you do, stay close to home. Launch your attacks from positions of strength. Change one major variable at a time. Measure it. Then change another variable. Measure it. Then change yet another variable. You can do this quickly, but don't jump far from home—there might not be a home when you come back. Excite proves this point.

Excite was a successful web search company in the mid-to-late nineties. In 1998 it was still the number two search engine, trailing Yahoo! in terms of visitors and other then-prevailing measurements of success like page views. In its quest to expand at all costs, Excite paid the ultimate cost. It acquired cable Internet provider At-home. Again, these two companies shared a venture capitalist who sat on both boards. So it was all in the family. Well, again, not this time. At the time, At-home was burning through $350 million dollars a quarter in its quest to lay fiber to as many homes as possible.[37] Excite was fighting a good fight with Yahoo! and suddenly they took their eyes off the prize and went chasing another set of enemies to fight. Instead of investing in this fight, they took the cash to fight another more expensive one.

Some would say that good strategies are only known in hindsight. In many cases they are right. But not in this case. We know that AOL had been divesting itself from the access portion of its business to focus on the content and community. Early in its life, the access part of the business was a key to its growth and a differentiator. The access business, however, was becoming an increasingly competitive, high-investment, low-margin business with little hope of becoming a cash generator any time soon. The joint company was quite unfocused – and became even more so. In July 1999, Excite/Athome acquired iMall, a virtual shopping center, for about half a billion dollars, and BlueMountain.com, an online greetings card company, for just under 1 billion dollars, including $350 million in cash.

It ended badly. The once-proud Excite, which was valued at $10 billion at its peak, and which was still valued at $7.8 billion when it merged with At-home in 1999, was virtually liquidated for a mere $10 million in November 2001.[38]

How Texas Instruments Won Again

Ever since the 1950s Texas Instruments has been a paragon of technology innovation. It was first in inventing or commercializing the integrated circuit, the electronic hand-held calculator, the single-chip microcomputer, solid-state radar, the single-chip speech synthesizer, and the single-chip digital signal processor.[39]

The business side of TI hasn't always been the best in harnessing the company's innovative skills. In the 1980s the company's microprocessor products came under attack from competitors such as Intel and Motorola while its memory chips had become low-margin commodity products. In the 1990s it entered many unrelated businesses, from speech-recognition for toys, to radars and missile systems for the military, personal computers, systems for oil and gas exploration and automotive systems. Basically it used many of its technologies to go after many markets, none of which it dominated. TI's stock reflected this lack of focus by languishing in the single-digits for most of the 1980s and early 1990s.

The Texas Instruments story parallels Symantec's. An unfocused company moving sideways learns to focus, grows, wins leadership in a market and then grows in a focused way into adjacent opportunities. In 2003, TI dominated the $6.1 billion DSP chip market with about more than 47% market share, while Agere and Motorola fought it out for the number two position with less than 8% of the market each.[40] Furthermore, TI's $2.9 billion in DSP represented a growth of 39% over the previous year while Motorola's revenues actually declined by 7.7% to $631 million. Texas Instruments is consolidating its position as the leader in the DSP market.

So where does TI go from here? It is expanding laterally to Digital Light Processing applications. Much of the technology for DLP chips were also invented at TI's own research labs. They are mainly used in a new fast-growth market: digital television, although they could be used for applications like projectors, computer monitors, and other sophisticated types of displays.

How interesting is the DLP opportunity? Think about the shift from analog to digital movies and music. Most new movie content today is digitally encoded, whether it comes down from a satellite, a DVD, or downloaded from the Internet. Imagine that all those hundreds of millions of analog televisions will need to be replaced by or complemented with digital television sets over the next decade or so and you can start to grasp the size of the opportunity. This is why companies like Intel announced their intention to compete for this pot of gold at the end of the ever-shifting rainbow.

Focusing has given Texas Instruments strength and allows it to better address new market opportunities. Furthermore, because TI has announced that it will focus on the DLP business, it is signaling to the industry that whoever decides to enter the digital TV processor space will face tough competition. They are saying: "We have no plan B, so expect a battle to the death." Intel, for one, has cancelled its plans to develop Liquid Crystal on Silicon (LCoS) chips that would have placed it in direct competition with TI's DLP business.[41] This is a testament to both companies pursuing focused strategies. The response from the market would undoubtedly be different if an unfocused company announced they were getting into that market.

Intel would be a tough competitor itself should it decide to enter a market that's adjacent to its areas of technology or market strength. However, it has decided that it cannot chase every new market, even if it looks promising. Its new chief executive officer, Paul Ottelini, is the first CEO in company history without a technical degree. He grew though the company ranks in marketing, not engineering or R&D like the three previous company CEOs.

Mr. Ottelini has announced that Intel plans to focus not on technologies but on platforms – complete systems aimed at both computing and consumer electronics markets. "The strategy is a significant shift–a "right-hand turn," as Mr. Otellini likes to say– from Intel's long-term obsession with making ever-faster computer chips.[42]

Rule 2 Summary: focus, win, grow, repeat

Because many high tech markets tend to be winner-take-all battlegrounds your goal is to achieve the gold medal that goes with market leadership.

You can't be good at everything and you can't address every market opportunity. You have to focus your resources on areas where you can be the best in the market. Lack of focus is one of the surest ways to failure in fast-growth high-tech markets.

After Symantec decided to strategically focus the company in 1999 that strategic decision it invested resources in developing and acquiring skills, technologies and markets to help them achieve that single goal. It also shed unrelated businesses. The result was a tripling of revenues and sextupling of stock price in just five years.

Leading companies such as Dell Computers and SAP have succeeded by bringing out one new major product line at a time or by extending their existing product categories into adjacent markets. Microsoft focuses on one powerful competitor at a time and they only do so from positions of strength.

Only when they dominate a market or have conquered a competitor do these companies move on successfully to the next target.

Commitment goes hand in hand with focus. Sometimes good companies get overextended. They go into unrelated markets and dilute their resources, brand equity and strength. They compete with strong players in several markets before dominating any of them.

Having clear goals and a focused execution path allows the market to understand you better, ensures that employees make better decisions, and signals to possible competitors that they will face a tough and likely losing battle should they attempt to enter into markets you focus on.

Only by focusing their strengths have these companies become dominant, and have been able to beat their competition and successfully expand into new markets.

RULE 3
ADD VALUE NOT FEATURES

"We don't really worry about staying ahead of the pack. We just focus on what our users are asking us to do, and try to do better at that."

- Jim Buckmaster

"The biggest challenge is to avoid unnecessary complexity and gratuitous engineering"

- Andy Bechtolsheim

StarMine is a small San Francisco-based software company dedicated to measuring financial analyst performance. Its customers are in the business of managing other people's assets and guarding their money fiercely. Yet, they pay five or six figures to license the company's services. StarMine has achieved a 145% compound growth rate during 2001-2004, even though the financial services industry went through a sharp slowdown in information technology spending.

After going sideways for most of the 1980's and 90's, Texas Instruments became the undisputed market leader in the Digital Signal Processing marketplace. In 2003 TI's DSP chips powered about half the world's 460 million phones and earned TI $2.9 billion in revenues. How did TI, a company that seemed to be playing mostly in low-margin commodity markets, beat powerhouses such as Motorola and Intel to win the huge DSP prize?

Why do products from these successful companies become market leaders, command premium prices and repeat business even when faced with tough competition? One word: *value*.

Value is not about multitudes of features. In their own unique ways, both StarMine and Texas Instruments products are simply and cleanly designed to take the noise and clutter out of their customer's lives. Many companies claim they "add value" and talk about a "value proposition." What they're really thinking about is their product features, their technology, their process investment, and the value to their own company. Prospects may see it as just that: a pitch for their product.

Here's the key to understanding if you're providing value: *value resides in the customer and features reside in the product.* In other words, value is in the customer's heart and mind, not in those of the product developer.

Featuritis and power-hunger can be devastating to many companies. This is not just endemic to high tech-based companies. It happens to mature markets everywhere. But tech markets move so fast that feature hunger can be deadly.

In the mid-1990's Silicon Graphics was the undisputed market leader in the graphic design computer market. It had the most powerful workstations, the top graphics modeling language, the most prestigious clients. Walking into the company headquarters lobby in Mountain View, California, you couldn't help but be impressed by the life-size dinosaur replicas that had been rendered using SGI's technology for the movie *Jurassic Park*. SGI was so power-hungry that it in 1996 it acquired supercomputer vendor Cray to add its technologies and market to the company's portfolio. In the meantime, SGI was losing market share not to more powerful computers but to less technologically powerful products: personal computers.

A few short years after the *Jurassic Park* glory days, SGI was hanging by a thread for its life. Its revenue went from a high of $3.66 billion in 1997 to $842 million in 2004.[43] Four years after acquiring Cray for $734 million, SGI sold it for around $100 million.[44]

Detroit carmakers had an obsessive pursuit of horsepower of their own. For decades the Big Three automakers (GM, Ford, and Chrysler) engaged in a horsepower race: the more horsepower and the more features the better. In the early 1970's the environment changed due to the convergence of several factors, but primarily because of the rise in oil prices. The public consciousness had also changed. Consumer rights and environmental movements were inspired by the publication in the early 60's of works such as Ralph Nader's "*Unsafe at Any Speed*" and Rachel Carson's "*Silent Spring.*" In the 1970s there seemed to emerge a critical mass of American automobile customers who cared about (and demanded) quality, safety and fuel efficiency instead of just horsepower. Detroit didn't listen and stayed with its pursuit of power. The Big Three slipped from their collective leadership and market share position in the US. For instance, between 1973 and 1985 General Motors' market share in the US went from about 44% to 30%.

Detroit hadn't recovered yet in 2004. In fact, it kept sliding. The big three (GM, Ford, and Daimler-Chrysler) saw their combined share of the US market go from 73% in the mid 1990s to about 60% in 2003, and lower yet in 2004.[45] The trend still looked bleak in 2005 when the competitive environment got even worse. In the fall of 2005 a series of events disrupted oil markets again, sending gas prices to levels not seen since the 1970s. After three decades, Detroit still didn't have the right products. Many high tech companies are not much different from Detroit.

Value Resides In the Customer

A Silicon Valley marketing manager once said in my class: "We add features to the product in the hope that customers will find value in them." She was repeating a common way of thinking in the high tech business world. According to Gartner, an IT consultancy, only 7% of software functionality that is paid for is actually used. Many software development vendors waste resources developing functionality that will not be used. Companies pay dearly for developing useless technologies.

First of all, technology products are costly to develop: top engineers and marketing talent are expensive. Cash burn is a huge issue in hi tech economics, especially with startup companies. Secondly, the opportunity cost they incur can be huge. Instead of wasting resources developing functionality and features prospects don't value, they should invest their resources developing value for the customer, enabling them to price their more valuable products higher, and thus earn more revenues, profits, and, importantly, market share. Worse still, while vendors waste their resources pursuing unnecessary features, their competition may be developing competing products that their customers do value.

You should not just add features to the product in hopes that someone will find value. Focus your effort on understanding what customers do value and are willing to pay for, and invest your resources in delivering that value.

SWATCH: SUCCESS THROUGH DESIGN SIMPLICITY

When designing a high tech product you could do much worse than imitate Swatch. We may not give wristwatches a second thought these days. They are very simple: they show the time and the date. When digital watches first came out in the seventies, many people, including industry pundits, thought that old-style mechanical watches would disappear. They though they would soon join eight-track tapes and 78-rpm records in flea markets and nostalgia shops. Whoever thought that they would not just survive the onslaught from digital watches but fight back and triumph?

Digital watches offer you much more than just the time. They may turn into a calculator, show you the time in every city in the world, or turn into a stop-watch so you can figure out how much time you need to wait for the bus to take you to work. And yet, consumers keep buying and using old-style watches. They are elegant, light, and low-maintenance. That's what consumers value. To these users, everything else is a waste of the manufacturer's money and resources.

When Swatch in 1982 came out with even simpler, lighter-weight watches, pundits gave them little chance of success. More than two decades later, these simple Swatch watches were priced higher than "Dick Tracy"-type digital watches. It was digital watches that ended up in flea markets and nostalgia shops! In the meantime, Swatch had a market valuation in excess of $3 billion and had revenues of $ 2.5 billion in 2004. Not bad for a simple product brought into a crowded and supposedly dying market.But Swatch is not really a technology company, some would say. How about an Internet company?

CRAIGSLIST: VALUE IS SIMPLE

Take Craigslist, one of the top Internet companies in the world, with its ten million unique visitors and 2.5 billion page views per month (Sept 2005). "We try to keep things as simple as we can," says CEO Jim Buckmeister. "We don't want to overwhelm the users with categories, fancy technologies, or a site that can't be navigated."

Since the web exploded in 1995 there have been many new technologies that many companies and users have adopted, so many that it was hard to keep track of all the browser plug-ins we needed to keep up. In the midst of this barrage of technology, Craigslist vowed to keep it simple. "We try to be compatible with the simplest HTML (website building) technology that dates back to the beginnings of the Web in 1995," says CEO Buckmeister, who started out at the company as a programmer himself.

That's not to say you shouldn't innovate. Far from it. You can't survive without innovating in today's marketplace. However, many seem to equate innovation with spending in research and development–so they may not understand that companies like Swatch, Craigslist or Dell are innovative.

Technology markets especially are brutally competitive and relentless in their innovation. You have to innovate. If you're in a profitable market, you can be certain that someone else wants a piece of it, if not all of it. You never know where your competition is going to come from–whether a large multinational or a two-person startup, your enemies or your partners, within or outside your industry. You need to keep innovating in a way that makes your product increasingly valuable to your customers. Adding features and "neat" technology for their own sake rarely helps you–your technical innovations may be exceptional, but may not mean much to your customers. Again, value is in the customer's eye, not the vendor's.

Soon after starting to write this book, I bought a new laptop with a processor that was less than half as powerful as that in my old laptop. For that privilege I paid about twice the market price of the latest and greatest version of my old laptop. Half the power at twice the price? Some readers might be mumbling something about selling me a bridge in Brooklyn or the San Francisco Bay. They may not be asking the right questions.

MARKET IMPACT, SPEED AND NEEDS

"My role as a CEO is to prioritize the feedback that Craiglist gets from users." Said Jim Buckmaster. "We can't do everything that's suggested to us. We look at impact, speed and needs. What features will have the largest possible impact? Which ones can we get out the door quickly? Which ones solve multiple needs out there?" Intel forgot that for a while.

While writing this book in 2005, I posted an old laptop PC on Craigslist. It was a five-year-old souped-up IBM Thinkpad. The computer originally cost around $5,000 and I was selling it for $140. Almost everyone who emailed me wanted to know whether it had wireless connectivity. Nothing else seemed to matter. In other words, they valued wireless Internet connectivity more than anything else.

Intel built a $20-billion business built on the pursuit of raw computing power. Every chip they design is many times faster than the last. This was a strategy that worked until customers stopped paying for that additional power. PC users cared about other things, like lower energy consumption (so laptop batteries could last longer), and connectivity (so they could have Internet access anywhere). As the wireless connectivity boom raged on in the late 90s many in Silicon Valley thought Intel didn't get it. When an open market senses business opportunities that incumbents do not seem to be addressing, it will redeploy money and talent to tackle them. New companies like Transmeta were started to design and sell chips that were compatible with and many times more energy-efficient than Intel's "mobile" chips. During 2001 AMD started gaining market share at Intel's expense.

Does this tale sound familiar? Does it sound like Detroit's Big Three all over again? Many thought so and were worried about Intel. Intel, however, wouldn't have any of it.

Starting in 1999 the company spent billions of dollars acquiring dozens of companies to beef up its offerings in the areas of networking and communications. [46] It later added wireless technologies to that charter. In early 2003 Intel launched its Centrino ® product and spent hundreds of millions to reposition itself as a "Mobility Technology" company. The strategy worked. Intel recaptured its leadership in the PC semiconductor marketplace. Furthermore, this roadmap may have opened opportunities for them in fast-growing markets like cell phone and handheld processors.

The market was telling Intel that the new areas of value were in mobility. Like Detroit automakers in the past, Intel kept going with its (processor) speed technology race. Unlike Detroit, Intel eventually listened to the market and invested in creating value – for its customers. It invested in both developing and acquiring the necessary skills and technology. Before it was too late it brought out products with low energy consumption and built-in wireless connectivity. Intel regained its clear leadership status.

Which brings me back to the laptop computer I acquired last year. What I wanted was what I then defined as a "coffeehouse" computer. A lightweight computer (4 pounds or so) with wireless internet connectivity, a decent screen, and the ability to run email, browser and standard applications like word processor, spreadsheets, and business presentation. Just basic stuff. Note that processor power was the furthest thing from my mind. Using a word processor to write a book doesn't really require supercomputing power! If you're caught up in the power race then you would have missed me and millions of other customers who want something other than raw horsepower in a personal computer.

How Starmine Built a Winner

A technology is not a product. Whether you are developing the next generation of your product or service, the next minor release, or you have a new product or technology that's early in the adoption lifecycle, there are several tools you may need to use before getting it out to the marketplace. Your product development investment should involve prospective customers, and there are several ways by which you can make sure your product is valuable to them.

Prototyping

"Prototyping is a great excuse to get in front of the customer," says Joe Gatto, CEO of StarMine, Inc. He should know. StarMine prospects taught Mr. Gatto how he should turn his initial idea into a valuable product. He was careful not to *tell* his prospective customers what they needed; *they told him*! It is this attention to the prospective customer that has allowed his company to grow its business by at least 50% every year since its inception (including the tech bust after 2001). "Adding value" is often just rhetoric in the mission statements of many companies. Not StarMine's. StarMine's SmartEstimates started as an idea in Mr. Gatto's mind in 1995. He noticed that stock prices move up or down on the basis of earnings predictions by financial analysts. FirstCall, a division of Thomson Financial, aggregates thousands of earnings predictions and publishes them as the "FirstCall Earnings Consensus."

If you are trying to evaluate whether to buy or sell a stock, *future* earnings are critical to that evaluation. Of course the problem is that future earnings of a company are uncertain. One way the sell side earns its keep is to have analysts predict the future and share those predictions with their money manager clients. But what do you do if you are a money manager and 20 analysts on a stock all have vastly different opinions about the future earnings of a company? For example: back in 1994, 20 analysts from different sell-side firms each had different estimates of a stock, ranging from $1.98 to $4.14 per share. Most of the world punts on the uncertainty and uses the simple average of the 20 analysts--in this case $3.00/share. This was called the "consensus estimate."

Why are future earnings important? Because many stocks are priced by the market based on a multiple called "Price/Earnings" or "P/E ratio". That is, investors take the expected earnings, multiply it by expected growth to arrive at a price. For instance if Dell is expected to earn $2.50 this year and its earnings growth or P/E ratio is expected to be 20, then Dell's stock price would be $50 (20 times $2.50).

If you used the consensus estimate for earnings prediction then you would be weighing all analysts equally. However, some of them may have been following the company for ten years and some only ten months. Some analysts might know the products better than others, know the industry better, or have better insight into customer purchasing patterns. If the $3.00 consensus estimate turned out to be right, then the stock would jump to $60 (20 times $3.10) as soon as Dell's CFO announced the "real" earnings. However, if the announced earnings were closer to $1.40, then the stock would drop to $28. That represented a variability of more than 100% between the high and low expected stock prices. For many investors this was a lot of risk to bear.

Imagine that you knew who the most consistently accurate analysts were. You'd probably "know" what the "real" earnings were going to be. If you thought you knew the stock was going up, then you could make more than 20% on the stock run-up by buying (or keeping) stock, or avoid a 40% loss by selling early. The variability was large enough to warrant a closer look.

With all this in mind, and armed with a Stanford degree in Engineering-Economic Systems and heavy-duty consulting experience in statistical decision-making analysis, Joe Gatto decided to start StarMine. Gatto imagined that the SmartEstimate® product would be most valuable to customers who invested a lot of money (see Rule 1). He designed the first version of the product for money managers in large investment funds.

Validate the market

A customer is not a market. It's a customer.

Once you know that your product is valuable to a single customer, you will want to validate that there is a larger market out there. You want to engage a number of prospects in conversations to validate that the needs that you found in your original customer exist broadly.

There are many ways to do this. Go to trade shows and talk to them. Interview them. Use prototypes and ask for honest feedback. Joe Gatto actually rented a small inexpensive booth at an investment conference in New York and showed his prototype to anyone who would stop and listen. He asked for feedback. He asked many questions. How would you use this? Would you pay money for this? What's right? What's wrong? Mr Gatto never stopped asking questions. Flying back to San Fancisco he serendipitously sat next to an investment manager. Gatto promptly pulled his laptop computer, showed him the prototype and asked for advice. Four hours later, Mr. Gatto was still writing notes, getting invaluable and extensive feedback about his prototype and the market in general.

Segment the market

Segmentation involves breaking up the world into distinct groups of customers and/or prospects who are more similar to each other than to other groups. Segments should have similar needs (or wants) and buying patterns. Members of the segment usually look to or reference one another before adopting a product. Segmentation is about creating value for a customer. You ask users questions like:

- Do you have a huge pain that I can help with (can I create value for you)?
- Can I serve your market well? What else are you looking for in a vendor?
- Are there others already serving this market with a similar offering?
- What would prevent you from purchasing my product?

There are many ways to segment the market. If we look at the financial services investment world from the top down, we can start with two sides: buy side (those who buy stocks and other financial assets) and sell side (those who sell them). To give you an idea of the scale involved, the buy side managed $10 trillion dollars in assets in 2004. This was just about the size of the United States Gross Domestic Product (GDP)! We can further break this market down in many ways. The question is: who could StarMine create value for? Who could benefit from StarMine's products?

Joe Gatto found three distinct types of potential users: fundamental analysts, quantitative analysts (or "quants"), and technical analysts. They all have distinct needs and work with different tools to do their job. The quants usually have advanced degrees in math or science and build sophisticated computer-based programs to find patterns and analyze stocks. The fundamental analysts study balance sheets and profit and loss statements, but also look into quality of management, micro and macro economic factors. They take all these objective and subjective factors to arrive at estimates of future earnings and growth rates. The technical analysts look at price and volume trends to predict stock movement.

Focus on a Target Market

You can't go after every market, especially if you're a small company. (See Rule 2.) After you segment the market, you need to choose the one target segment that you can serve the best and focus on them. You have probably already established that there is a need for your product in a few segments. In other words, you can create value for customers in those segments. How do you choose which one to target? You ask yourself questions like:

- Do I have the resources or can I acquire the resources to create the customer's whole product?
- Is my product valuable enough (relative to the status quo) that these customers will take a chance on a small company like mine?
- Can I charge premium prices to justify my investments in developing the market?
- Can I use my investments in product and market development to expand to adjacent opportunities in the future?

Targeting is ultimately about capturing value. It's about finding a market your product can dominate. Creating value for the customer is the first step.

StarMine decided to target the quantitative analysts. This was, interestingly, the smallest market segment, with barely over 200 target companies. To put this number in perspective, there are more than 50,000 fundamental analysts. Many executives and investors would scoff at this choice: why not just go for the big market? Don't you want to be a large company? Whether you are a small or a large company, you should probably target a market small enough that you can dominate–and large enough that you can create a business around it or use it as a stepping stone to other adjacent opportunities. Other companies like Bulldog Research decided to go after broader markets and did not do well.

Develop their whole product

The whole product is specific to a target market. Technology that is valuable to one set of customers may be useless to others. After making the decision to target the quantitative analysts, StarMine learned that they needed to reinvent their product to make it valuable. While their underlying engine was valuable, StarMine's product had features that were useless to this market.

Quantitative analysts deal with large quantities of numbers that are constantly crunched by powerful computers. StarMine's first product had a great looking graphic visualization tool. It plotted the consensus earnings estimates vs. the StarMine smart estimate and the stock price. Most everyone who saw it mentioned how "nifty" or "neat" it was. However, they would not pay money to have it! It wasn't valuable to them! Because they deal with number-crunching, the quants would want just that: a number or a set of numbers for each stock. They could load these numbers onto their program together with many other numbers and figure out what to buy or sell. So, as nifty as StarMine's graphic was, it was useless to the quants. Joe Gatto went back to re-engineer the product to output 'the number' for each stock. The result was that StarMine developed the product that the target customers wanted. If Gatto had been out pushing his original product and telling the prospects how valuable it was, the company would have gone nowhere. Instead, StarMine became the leader in its segment and achieved growth rates in double and triple digits over the last few years.

Communicate it

Success begets success. Once you have successfully created a product that fills a market need, you need to communicate it broadly. Even for a small startup companies there are many ways to do this. You should make sure that you articulate the value clearly (see Rule 4) Go to other prospects and tell them how the product is being used. Tell them customer stories that they can identify with. Generate word of mouth. Generate publicity in media that your users read and trust. Have others communicate the value of your product. The prospects won't just come to you!

Do it again

Go back to the prospects. Prototype again. Ask for honest feedback. Can you target more finely? Are there other customer needs that you're not addressing? Are you communicating well? Are there new or different ways in which you should be deploying the product? Value generation is a never-ending process.

Starmine Finds Family Value

How do you find out what your existing customers value? Joe Gatto, StarMine's CEO, has a simple answer: "Ask them." But don't just go out and call your customers yet! There's a little more to it than that. If you have the right process, you may just find out that the customer values the time he spends with his wife and children. Your product is just a way for them to do that. Here's StarMine's process:

Get in front of the right customers

StarMine marketing teams starts this value creation process by looking for those customers who love their products: those for whom it has changed their life positively in one way or another. But who knows who the happy customers are? Account managers should know. They are the ones who get the angry calls if the product doesn't work as advertised. They are the ones who don't get the repeat orders if the product is just OK. They are the ones who also get the happy calls if the product works. They are the ones who know which customers are willing to be a reference for others. Product development and salespeople don't always communicate well – or at all. Even the marketing department may not communicate well with sales. That's too bad because salespeople have a wealth of information that you can use to develop a better product. So talk to account managers. Ask them who the right customers are.

Get in front of high-usage customers

A parallel step for StarMine marketing and engineering teams in the "value generation" process is to look for its highest-usage customers. They assume the customers who use the company's products the most are the ones who find them most valuable.

There are several ways to find out who the highest-use customers are:

- Web logs are one way to identify high usage customers. They show who is using the product and how much time they're

spending using it. You can complement that knowledge with other people who have contact with your customers.
- Customer Service Representatives also log phone calls and know who the high-usage customers are.
- Account managers who are in constant touch with their customers also know.

Ask questions

"You need to ask good questions. You need to ask questions in different ways until you're sure you understand," says Joe Gatto, adding that "asking good questions is the key to customer engagement and learning."

These are some of the questions that you should ask:
- Why do you like the product?
- How does it make your life better?
- What specific features do you like?
- How do you use it?

Drill down: why, why, why? Some of these questions may be obvious, but the mistake that many marketing managers make is to assume they know the answers. The answers will vary from customer to customer. The same customer's answers may vary over time. Like the StarMine managers you should ask plenty of "why" questions to understand precisely what customers value. Keep asking why until you get to the bottom of the "value chain."

Finally, there's a very important question you need to ask: "In your own words, how does this product make your life better?" After one of these "why" sessions, a customer told Joe Gatto: "It's folks like you who allow me to go home to my wife and kids early every day." That is true value! You couldn't define customer value better than that.

Have a process to feed the answers back into the product

Even if you ask good questions, you need to have a mechanism to report it back. This is the only way everyone within the company can understand and use the information. Using those answers, the marketing team should then generate "use cases" that detail how customers use the product and what benefits they get out of it.

So what did StarMine's customers find of value? Remember, these customers are asset managers. They usually invest in many public stocks, and they need to monitor all of them (maybe as many as 80-100 stocks). In late 2005 there were 5,000 new or revised earnings estimates each day globally--and that did not even include recommendations or other estimates like revenue or cash flow. In total, StarMine processed about ten million unique analyst predictions per year, generated by 6,000 analysts at 600 brokerage firms on 14,000 stocks around the world.[47] Additionally, there were press releases, news, new analyst reports, emails, and myriad other data for each stock. Clearly, an asset manager can't keep up with all the information. However, they can't ignore anything, in case they miss something important. Moreover, they have to constantly look out for new stocks to invest in. They can't miss out on a growth opportunity because they didn't have time to read an additional email or two, right?

Here are two major reasons StarMine's customers found its software valuable:

1. It helped them monitor what they had. Because StarMine alerts its users to surprises (up or down) they can focus their attention on those stocks first. Investors can read the analyst reports, press releases, customer emails, and other information specific to these "surprise" stocks. Then they can make decisions on whether they want to buy more, sell, or do nothing.

2. It helped them look for new investment opportunities. Idea-generation for new investment opportunities is an arduous and time-consuming process. There are too many investment choices. If they can see who's generating surprises, they can follow those who are trending up.

Both these reasons involve saving time. Customers wanted to get through the clutter and noise out there so they could focus their valuable time on stocks "deserving" of their attention. They didn't want to worry about certain stocks if they didn't have to.

Communicate it

Once you understand what your highest-use customers find most valuable in your product, you need to communicate it. StarMine generates "use cases" and "war stories" that tell in a simple way how these significant customers are generating value (see Rule 4: Have a Story). These "use cases" are fed back to other customers who may find additional benefits that they may not have perceived before. Prospects are usually eager to hear what leaders in their industry are doing (see Rule 6: Convert Champions). "Use cases" create structured stories that help the sales team communicate with prospects who may identify with how the leading users are getting value.

Do it again

This value-generation process is never-ending. High tech markets move too fast for you to rest on your laurels. You need to go back to your customers and keep asking questions until you understand what they find valuable. How's their job changing? How's their industry changing? How are their customers changing? You may find that your product mainly helps your customer spend time with what he or she values most: her family. And that's priceless!

TEXAS INSTRUMENTS CREATES VALUE

After a decade of declining fortunes, Texas Instruments was looking to enter new growth markets. Intel had all but pushed TI out of the microprocessor markets. However, TI's Digital Signal Processing (DSP) chips looked like great candidates for entering the new mobile device markets. Investments in DSP development requires committing massive resources in technical infrastructure and market development. Doing the usual process of developing technology and then going out to sell it would clearly not do.

But TI didn't just create a product and go out selling it. TI went asking. It talked to Nokia, a hungry upstart mobile phone company in Finland, about developing a DSP chip for its phones. TI developed prototypes specific to mobile phones, and Nokia, then a relatively small company, gained a partner who would develop semiconductor products specific to its needs. Digital Signal Processors (DSP) packed a hundred million transistors on a single chip and processed information ten times faster than general purpose chips while also using less than one-sixth the battery power of competitive chips.

This is no mean technological feat, but TI had the technical prowess to pull it off. What it didn't have was the market knowledge to understand where the customer value was. In Nokia, TI gained a partner who would help it develop new products that had clear customer value and commercial viability.

After many prototypes, and fits and starts, TI's DSP business grew in great part thanks to this attention to Nokia. As Nokia's fortunes grew in the mobile phone marketplace, so did TI's. Nokia alone represented 14% of TI's $11.5 billion in revenues in 2003[48]. Furthermore, about half the world's 460 million cell phones have TI's DSP chips.[49]

Value–The Way to Beat Microsoft

In high technology winners take it all. However, having it all doesn't guarantee that you can keep it all forever (see rule 9 for some examples). Microsoft is one of the nimblest large companies on the planet. When they feel threatened by a new technology, they can muster the will and the ability to move the company on a dime and confront the attacker head on. And they usually win.

Microsoft all but ignored the Internet in the early 1990s. In his 1994 book *The Road Ahead*, Bill Gates mentioned the Internet once--in an appendix. While Silicon Valley was buzzing with the sound of Netscape's IPO and those of countless other Internet companies that quickly followed, Microsoft kept underestimating the power of the Internet. Only after it became painfully clear that the web was a major threat to its operating system platform dominance did Microsoft embark on a major counter-attack. To their credit, once they understood the threat, it took them just weeks to turn the company around. They killed off project after project and moved hundreds of their best engineers to develop the technologies necessary to compete in that market.

Microsoft acquired browser and server technologies to accelerate their entry into the Internet market. Their attack on Netscape was ferocious. They left no stone unturned in their attempt to win the Internet gold. This victory drew costly and lengthy lawsuits from the regulatory authorities of both the United States and the European

Union. A U.S. District Judge ruled that Microsoft had violated the Sherman Act by using it monopoly powers to block Netscape from marketing its browsers. The U.S. government threatened to break up Microsoft into two or more parts (operating systems, applications, and others). The reports of Microsoft's tactics also did much to ruin goodwill amongst customers and the information technology industry in general. In the end a much-weakened Netscape was acquired by AOL. After a protracted fight, Microsoft paid a then-weakened AOL $750 million as a settlement.[50]

One of the lessons from Netscape is that Microsoft can be overcome with a valuable product that is easy to adopt. It need not do everything under the sun, but it must do what it does very well. Netscape achieved a user base of 40 million people within a few months, a feat previously impossible to achieve without the Internet itself.

Microsoft's operating system dominance is again under threat. Again, it is a simple, light, and inexpensive product. It is easily downloadable by anyone who wants it. It doesn't have all the features of Microsoft Windows. However, it does what it does really well. Its name is Linux. In 2004 Linux achieved market penetration approaching one-third of the server operating system market.

How did Microsoft commit the same error again? It didn't listen to its customers. Windows has become fatter and fatter without adding value to the users. Windows consumers have been crying for years about the need for a stable and secure operating system. Instead Windows keeps crashing (mine does all the time) and has so many security holes you could drive trucks full of viruses, Trojans, and spyware through them. If you use Microsoft Windows, you have probably seen the little paper clip character that pops up at the most unexpected moments. Instead of spending time and money adding useless features like this one, Microsoft should add value to Windows, that is, make it secure and crash-proof. Otherwise users will keep migrating to other operating systems like Linux that do add value.

The rise of Google must surely have woken up Microsoft to the fact that millions of computer users value efficient and effective search. Apple also brought out a search product called *Spotlight* that may change the way the computer world thinks about search altogether. David Pogue, of *The New York Times*, wrote: "This isn't just a fast Find command. It's an enhancement that's so deep, convenient and powerful, it threatens to reduce the 20-year-old Mac/Windows system of nested folders to irrelevance."[51] Spotlight, however only runs on Apple Macs, which haven't broken trough the 3%-5% marketshare in two decades. Google, however, has already invaded "Microsoft's territory" with a downloadable PC search program that runs on Windows. Is this worrisome for Microsoft executives? I recently did a search for a research document that Google found in much less time on the web than Microsoft did on my own hard drive. Think about that for a second. The web has billions of pages and my hard drive probably has a few thousand. In the past Microsoft has been able to recover after missing several paradigm shifts like graphical user interface and the Internet. How many times can Microsoft forget about what users find valuable and still recover?

RULE 3 SUMMARY–ADD VALUE NOT FEATURES

Customers purchase products and services that create value for them – not just for the vendor. The key to understanding value is that value resides in the customer, whereas features reside in the productMany companies have engaged in the pursuit of features and horse-power instead of the pursuit of value. They are looking for value in their own product, not the customer.

To create value you have to get your customers and prospects involved. Don't just push your products, build the whole product that prospects find valuable and will pay money for. If you have a new technology you need to test prototypes with your prospects. You should then validate the market by making sure that the need for your product lies beyond just one customer. You should segment the market according to the benefits that your technology provides, then choose one target market and focus all your resources on it. The target market should be small enough that you can dominate it but large enough to build a business on–or it should be a stepping stone to other opportunities. Once you start generating sales, communicate your product's value to other users. Do this again and again until you have a solid customer base.

If you already have a customer base you should get them involved as part of your value-creation process. Get in front of winning customers and high-usage customers. Ask them questions to help you understand precisely what they find valuable in your product. Don't assume you know the answers. Ask how it's making their lives better – in their own words. Establish a process to get these answers fed back into your product development and marketing process. Communicate success within your company and to the market. Value-creation is a never-ending process. Do it again and again.

RULE 4
HAVE A STORY.
COMMUNICATE CLEARLY.

"In general, the bigger the film, the simpler the character"
- Matt Damon

"Humans are social animals, and the lifeblood of society is conversation"
- Andrew C. Revkin

Netflix grew to be the top online provider of movie DVDs, beating many other providers of the same service and giants Blockbuster and Amazon. In November 2005, Netflix had achieved half a billion dollars in revenues and a market valuation twice that of incumbent Blockbuster ($1.5 billion vs. $770 million). Netflix was in the business of selling Hollywood stories in more ways than one.

Salesforce.com was a San Francisco-based company that quickly rose to $100 million in revenue on the strength of publicity and word-of-mouth. As their name indicates, they sold sales force automation (SFA later CRM) technology—with a twist. Instead of large, complex and expensive software installation and customization projects, they delivered their product over the web. This software delivery model is known as Saas, or Software as a Service. They were able to gain market share over several SaaS companies like Salesnet.com with similar products—and steal customers from giant Siebel Systems, then the leader in the traditional SFA software category. Salesforce.com did much of this market penetration on the strength of word-of-mouth and a tremendous publicity machine - and no advertising.

Google also grew to a $1-billion revenue company without spending anything on consumer advertising. How did they do it? If you're a Google user, think back to the first time you used it. The reason was likely to be that someone within your personal or professional network told you about this website. Word-of-mouth and especially word-of-mouse played a tremendous role in Google's rise to the top.

Technology markets move extremely quickly. Speed of adoption may be essential to the success of your product or service. This is especially true if there are network effects in your product category. Network effects essentially guarantee a winner-take-all market. How do you grow demand for you business quickly and effectively? How do you do it without spending millions in promotions that you may not have or that may be better used elsewhere in the organization? Let's look at how Netflix, Salesforce.com, Google and other category winners did it. These organizations effectively used their customers, the media, and influencers as a way to spread the word and accelerate adoption of their product offerings. Surely they created valuable products and services, but (as thousands of companies have found out) that is not enough to win in today's hypercompetitive technology markets. What did these winners do?

They created good stories and a simple communications strategy that helped them get ahead of the pack and win it all. They engaged the market and used one of the most effective market growth strategy in the strategy toolbox: have your customers recommend your product or service to others. Like these companies, you want analysts and influencers know about you and recommend your product. You want prospects and customers to talk about your products, top investors to take interest in investing in your company, top employees to come work for you, leading distributors to sell your products, and opinion leaders to talk about you. You want the media to spread the word. Having others talk about and recommend your product is particularly significant in the early stages of a product category's adoption lifecycle when gathering a critical mass of adopters is key to winning it all.

ENTREPRENEURIAL COMMUNICATION CHALLENGES

Entrepreneurs and technology executives have several challenges working against them when getting the word out about their new products and companies.

1. Busy Minds. People are busy. Prospective buyers and influencers are even busier.
2. Tech Talk. The technology underlying your product may be complex. How do you get through to prospective users whose life and workflow is already complex?
3. Competition. There are probably several other companies offering products similar to yours. Differentiating your product or company may be an uphill struggle.
4. Short Timeframes. The technology adoption lifecycle may be exceedingly short. By the time you get the word out it may be too late.

Let's go over these points and then come back to how companies like Netflix, Google, and Salesforce.com have used their communication strategy to come out of the pack, distinguish themselves and win their categories.

Busy minds

Our civilization has turned from information-starved to information-glutted in only a few decades. In August 2005 there were more than 353 million website hosts[52] with billions of web pages containing data in dozens of formats. This is up from 213 Internet hosts in 1981! That's a million-fold growth in 24 years. Not that the web is our only source of information. The average American watches 4 hours of television per day and by age 65 will have watched more than 2 million TV commercials.[53] Additionally we listen to three hours of radio per day.[54] This is not to mention all the other media available to us: newspapers, magazines, movies, email, internet messaging, phone messaging, weblogs, podcasts, and mobile phone media, as well as variations and hybrids thereof.

Peter Lyman and Hal Varian of the University of California looked at newly created information in four mediums: print, film, magnetic, and optical–and seen or heard in telephone, radio and TV, and the Internet. They calculated that in 2002 alone the world produced 5 exabytes of information. That is about the information content of 37,000 new complete Libraries of Congress every year, or about the equivalent of 30 feet of new books for each person in the world (there are an estimated 6.3 billion people on earth.)[55] Since the US produces 40% of the world's new information, this means

Americans would need to process the informational equivalent of 265 feet (equivalent to a 20-story-high building) of new books per year. Furthermore, Lyman and Varian estimate that new information grew 30% per year for the previous three years. Assuming this growth rate stays unabated, that means that the information that we need to process is more than doubling every three years. At this rate Americans will need to process the informational equivalent of a stack of books taller than the Empire State Building's 1,250 feet by 2008.

How hard is it to process all this information? Even Google with its powerful farms of tens of thousands of networked computers could only catalog less than 2% of the world's websites in 2004! How do you expect anyone to keep up?

Even if you can get in front of your prospects, they can probably not give you much time to explain yourself.

Human capacity to absorb information is inherently limited. A seminal 1956 paper posited that human bandwidth seems to be limited to about 7 concurrent pieces of information, plus or minus two.[56] Have you wondered why automobile license plates are six or seven letters and numbers, local phone numbers are seven or eight digits, or the (western) musical scale generally has seven notes? Why do many management theorists say we should only manage about seven people (plus or minus two)? Can you remember your credit card number? How about your driver's license number? How many digits do they have? (Here is an old trick: ask anyone to repeat a sequence of numbers until they make a mistake. Most will do it after seven numbers.) Several management consultants asked me why it wasn't "7 Fundamental Rules of High Tech" instead of 9!

If seven pieces of information sounds like too little, brace yourself. Research over the last half century seems to be pointing to an even *smaller* rather than larger human bandwidth.[57] The number being mentioned is as small as 3 pieces of information. New entrepreneurs and technology CEOs face a quandary: human bandwidth seems to be genetically limited to a small constant and information is exploding to the point that not even the most powerful and technologically advanced new search and cataloging technology can keep up with it.

Tech talk

Tech talk is important but may be complex and intricate. It may take time to understand and digest important new ideas and technology. This inherent complexity makes tech talk travel slowly and will probably make it anything but memorable.

Tech talk may also rely on a feature-by-feature comparison, which is both an intellectual and an open-ended proposition. Features change on an almost day-to-day basis. On any given day any company may be 'winning' the features race. Furthermore, features tend to become commodities. Leadership is seldom built on features.

Imagine yourself getting on an elevator. Your dream customer, business partner, trade journal editor, or investor is there. They ask you what your company does. You know you only have one floor, maybe two to go. You have 10 seconds or less. What do you tell them? You can't go on a long-winded explanation about the functionality or the merits of the technology. You can't give complicated examples. You can say it in 10 words or less. If you grab their attention and they show interest they'll ask you for more details. In Silicon Valley they call it the "elevator pitch." If you can't say what you do and who you are in a few seconds, how do you expect others to do it?

Many entrepreneurs and tech executives are justifiably proud of their products. They will talk about them to anyone who will listen. In fact, many of them may talk a bit much about the underlying technology. This may be sometimes unavoidable because the technology may be in the early stages and there is no established category to define it. When you have a technology in an established product category, it's fairly simple to talk about it: "we make a Customer Relationship Management (CRM) software product," "reproductive health technology," or "anti-virus software." When they're talking about a brand-new technology that doesn't quite fit into any existing category entrepreneurs and executives often stumble. That's exactly when it's most important for a company to have a story and a clear, simple message that travels fast.

How do you talk about a technology that's new and complex? How do you explain quickly and succinctly about your new chip that has an architecture that radically changes the cost/performance of computing? How in 1993 do you explain something as radical as the Internet? How do you talk about a software infrastructure that allows you to develop software programs by drawing business processes, not by coding using standard programming languages? Or runs ten times faster than the current leader, or saves ten times the energy, or shortens hospital stays by 90 percent?

"How much time have you got?" It's not unusual for new technology startup executives to ask this when I ask them what their company does. Without waiting for an answer, they may go into long-winded explanations about the underlying bits, algorithms, or silicon and how it's going to revolutionize the world. If they were on that elevator, their soliloquy would lose everyone. Their audience would likely go back to thinking about the other 83 issues that they have in their minds. The entrepreneur may have lost the opportunity to get a new customer, investor, or partner.

Buzzwords are also a problem in management monologues. Many executives try to stuff as many buzzwords as possible into a single long-winded sentence. They think this makes them look respectable. This phenomenon is so negatively ingrained into public "communications" that a few journalists started a website in the late 1990s called "BuzzKiller" (www.buzzkiller.net) to debunk many of these buzzwords. They decried the use of words like "contextualized," "impactful," and "incent" (or its cousin "incentivize"), especially when they're all used in the same sentence!

Here's an example a Buzzkiller weblog contributor quoted from an email sent to him in which a company described itself as "a global leader in pressure-sensitive technology and innovative self-adhesive solutions for consumer products and label materials"([58]). By the time this executive is done saying this no one will know what he is talking about. If that had been your company, you could have lost the Wal-Mart CIO who could have adopted your technology and helped champion you to their dozens of major suppliers, the *New York Times* technology editor, and the investors who stepped off the elevator scratching their heads. What a mouthful! Wouldn't it be easier to say they make *stickers*?

Competition

One of the many mistakes that entrepreneurs and executives make is to say (and think) that "we have no competitors" or, when pressed, that "no one does it **exactly** like we do." I emphasize the word exactly because that might be a way to deny their competitors. If there is an attractive new market opportunity there will probably be a score of companies chasing it. Their products or services have roughly the same feature set and deliver similar benefits to prospects and customers (if they do it right – see Rule 1 "Build Value, Not Features"). More likely than not, points of differentiation are technical features and exist mostly in the mind of the entrepreneurs and executives. The prospect or customer may not know or care much about this feature.Furthermore, as a general rule, your new product is not just competing with products in the same category. It is competing with the established way of doing things – the status quo. It is also competing with a set of products in other categories.

Given that there are many products and services, both new and established, that perform similar benefits to yours, how can you make the market take an interest in your product? Why would they talk about a product that is basically similar to others in the marketplace? How are you going to get the word out about yours? Tech talk is usually not the way to do it and differentiating on features is not going to do it either. Furthermore, you don't have much time to communicate with the marketplace.

No time to waste

To say that the technology adoption lifecycle can be short is to overstate the obvious. Some categories have gone from market launch to full market penetration in less than 2 years. We talk about some of these technologies elsewhere in this book: weblogging, internet telephony and podcasting are but a few recent examples. Facebook.com went from launch to almost total market penetration of several thousand American colleges and universities in less than two years. This was as basically a word-of-mouse phenomenon. Adoption just spread like wildfire and when all was said and done it was over. There are network effects in social networks so facebook's market will not allow for a viable number two player. If you compete in a fast-growing category like this one you don't have time to waste. You have no time to talk about intricacies of technologies.

GETTING THROUGH THE CLUTTER - THE BASICS

Winning companies mentioned in this book use their communications strategy as a means of gaining and maintaining market leadership. They have surmounted the challenges of clutter and competition by using the following tools. These are tools that we believe are fundamental for the entrepreneur to know.

1. Stories. Leaders craft and tell stories.
2. Messages. Companies need to be adept at crafting simple and effective messages.
3. Positioning. A company's positioning is paramount to their success in the cluttered marketplace.
4. Branding. A brand is a durable element of leadership – but it may not be what you think.
5. Word-of-mouth. It is hard to overstate the importance of creating word-of-mouth and its Internet equivalent word-of-mouse.
6. Name. Your name is your badge. Naming a company or a product the right way can help you get through the clutter and deliver your messages.

It is important to say that no amount of communications will help a company without a valuable product. The companies mentioned in this chapter, and indeed this book created clear value for their customers. Buzz can be no substitute for value.

TELLING STORIES

Stories and images have always had the power to shape everyday human existence[59]. Marketing departments of products in mature industries know about storytelling and they have made it part of their promotion arsenal for at least a century. Take diamond commercials: they're sold with stories and images of love and lifetime commitment. Without stories diamonds are just commodities, sold in the world's financial exchanges along with copper, sugar, and pork belly futures. Cars are promoted with stories of freedom. Soda drinks are sold as embodiments of "youth" and "cool." Few of these associations have much to do with the functionality of the products.

Leadership is about telling stories. Leaders are great storytellers. That's what Harvard University cognitive psychologist Howard Gardner found out when he studied several 20th-century world leaders (such as Mahatma Ghandi, Martin Luther King and George C. Marshall.) "Leaders achieve their effectiveness chiefly through the stories they relate."[60] Are we to surmise that leaders can just be fake? Can they just be actors reciting stories they read in the morning? Not necessarily. A key finding of Dr. Gardner was that leaders embody the stories they tell. That is, they are and they do what they say. Importantly, leaders need to be perceived by their intended audience to embody them. That is, just because they say so doesn't make it so. Simply asserting their story is not sufficient; their audience has to buy into their story. U.S. Secretary of State George C. Marshall did not simply call for a massive aid effort to help Europe recover after World War II (the 'European Recovery Plan' later known as the Marshall Plan). His stories called for America to go beyond its immediate narrow self-interests and postwar victorious gloating to suspend rivalries and see themselves as citizens of the world. He had to battle many other rival and competing stories that asked for punishing those who did not support American causes. Only a man who was known for his integrity, strength, and selfless pursuit of public service could pull off the approval and implementation of the largest aid and reconstruction package in history. When the Nobel Committee awarded Marshall the Nobel Peace Prize in 1953 they said it was "the most constructive peaceful work...in this century."[61]

Similarly, many high tech company executives use stories to engage users on an emotional level. These stories enable the user and the prospect to identify with the company, to see their products as more than just bits, algorithms, and silicon. These stories build on many other stories we have within us; stories of smarts, hard work, struggle, temporary failure, and ultimate success.

The messages and stories these companies craft are short, succinct, and memorable. The simpler the story and the messages, the easier they can travel. The more customers identify with your stories, the more they will want to have a relationship with your company. The more they want to tell your stories to others, the more these stories will stick with them. Technology leaders don't just create valuable products, they also tell good stories.

Technology products may be complicated and impersonal. How can customers identify with complex encryption algorithms, impersonal computers or fast-changing web portals? Yet, we "love" RSA, Apple, Yahoo! and Google. When was the last time Apple users made a feature-by-feature comparison of their Macs vs. Wintel machines? How do these companies ask their users to tell others about what they do? How different are online DVD rental companies or SFA providers anyway?

THE NETFLIX STORY

Netflix is a Los Gatos, California-based company that rents DVD movies over the Internet. For a monthly subscription fee of about $10 to $18 the user can rent one to three DVD movies at a time. The user can create a long list of movies that they want to see. The company mails them in order and the user can keep them and watch them as many times as they want. When they are done with the DVD, they mail them back to Netflix in a company-provided envelope. As soon as Netflix receives the DVD, they send the next movie on the user's list.

This is a convenient process. Users don't have to get to the store to rent the DVD. Online providers have a much wider selection than the local store can possibly provide. Better yet, they don't have to pay late fees. Surely, the combination of Internet ordering, wide selection, top inventory operations, and mail delivery added up to lower costs and more convenience for the users. Netflix had all of that–but that was not the only story they originally sold. Read an article featuring Netflix and you will hear CEO Reed Hastings tell why he started the company. He rented the movie *Apollo 13* at Blockbuster in 1997 and had to pay $40 in late fees. The nerve of the movie rental company to charge him $40 for being late! He thought there had to be a better way, and started the company.

Who cannot identify with this story? Who hasn't been miffed at the movie rental company for slapping on a late rental fee? I stopped doing business with Blockbuster years ago for that same reason. The worst part was that Blockbuster and movie rental companies stiffed their very best customers: frequent renters. Americans paid about $1.3 billion in movie rental late fees in 2004.[62] When you hear Hastings's story you can identify with him. It is dramatic, immediate and engaging. You can feel his anger. Probably because a movie rental company did the same to you. So when you hear his story you start developing a relationship with the founder and the company even before you sign up. You care not only about what they do but also about who they are. You identify with him and his struggle.

Netflix eventually became the leader in the category, but it wasn't easy getting there! First the founder had to go through painful struggles. You didn't think Blockbuster would go without a fight, did you? Some type of David vs. Goliath story is ingrained in most cultures and Hastings told his to anyone who would listen. These stories are also engaging and ask us to take sides. Suddenly we're doing business with David who's battling the Goliath evil empire. We become emotionally involved in a simple DVD rental transaction.

Furthermore, what these stories do is help us simplify the world and narrow down the choices. They make us ignore other competitors. The DVD rental world becomes a fist-fight just between Blockbuster and Netflix. None of the other upstarts in the online movie rental business (Intelliflix, QwikFliks, Peerflix, DVDOvernight and many other general and niche-oriented sites) matter anymore. The media loves Hastings and his company's struggles. We identify with Hasting's struggles. Netflix is the one we root for!

Netflix eventually became the leader in the category: more than 2.5 million people had signed up as of late 2004 (more than 50% of the market) which was a growth of 60% over the previous year.[63] By late 2005, Netflix had reached annual revenues above $600 million and achieved a market capitalization of $1.5 billion, which was about twice that of Blockbuster. Netflix had also beaten back giant Wal-Mart's attempt to enter the market and turned them into a partner.

Aristotle and Netflix

Stories like Netflix's become a way to give meaning to otherwise complex, cold and meaningless technologies and establish them as part of the users' identities and world view. They are a way to differentiate their product or company in the heart as well as the mind of the user. They provide an easy way for everyone to talk about their product and their company: the media, users, allies, investors, suppliers, even competitors.

What is the secret to crafting and telling stories the way winning companies do? Can new entrepreneurs learn from them? Naturally! Here's the secret: most new stories are just retelling of old successful stories. New characters are used as variations of old characters and new story themes are variations of themes that have delighted and captivated human beings for millennia.

Notice that the Netflix story described above takes place in three acts: creation story, struggles to achieve the goal, and final success. Along the way there are events that incite the hero to action. Now think of the story of Google, Apple, Hewlett-Packard, Cisco, or Yahoo! In all these companies two friends or partners (the founders) met somewhere in Silicon Valley. There was an inciting event that led them to believe that they could do something better than the establishment. Then they started a company. They struggled against the prevailing wisdom. They ate nothing but pizza and soda for months while they were being turned down by investors. Regardless, they persevered. There were one or more turning points and scary moments along the way. Then the world turned around. In the end they prevailed.

Again, their stories take place in three acts, with provocative events along the way. They build on the stories we have ingrained in our personal and collective consciousness. Think of your favorite movie. Think of *Lord of The Rings*, *Star Wars*, or *Titanic*. They have a similar structure as the stories of Google, Netflix or Apple. This is not coincidental. Blame it on Aristotle. More than 2300 years ago the brilliant Greek philosopher penned the Three Act Structure[64] that Hollywood still uses to write screenplays. This structure is so important that "many studio executives now refuse even to consider a screenplay that does not perfectly match the three act structure."[65]

That Aristotle's storytelling secrets still work says something about this brilliant philosopher but also about the way the human brain and the human spirit work.

Simple Messages

Stories also have the power to carry your messages. They provide a context for your messages. The most important message you can transmit is your value proposition. Your value proposition messages can communicate to your listener (or viewer or reader) what the company or product does, who you are and what the value or benefit the product brings to the user - all in an effective, simple, brief way. For instance, during Skype's early days, their message was simply "Skype is free Internet telephony that just works." This is an effective as well as brief message.

Crafting simple messages is not always easy in the ever-more complex world of high tech products and services. Thomas Jefferson said that "the most valuable of talents is never to use two words when one would do." This maxim applies more than ever to today's high technology communications. The entrepreneur should invest time and effort to create messages that can be communicated effectively, simply and briefly.

I emphasize simplicity and brevity because they are sorely lacking from many companies. However, brevity is no substitute for effectiveness. For instance, the latest corporate incarnation of AT&T (SBC acquired the former AT&T and renamed itself) has probably spent hundreds of million of dollars repeating "Your World Delivered." This is a short message – but not effective. I'm not sure what this means. I see it when I go to AT&T Park to see the San Francisco Giants baseball team, I see it when I drive the 101 Highway to Palo Alto, and when I read the newspaper. I still don't know what it means. Any company in any business could say this - and it would still be meaningless. Contrast this message with Skype's (above).

Hollywood treatment

The movie industry is in the business of telling stories. Their stories tend to be clear and simple. They also craft simple and effective messages. Without a doubt, Hollywood has been quite successful at doing this, and offers a useful model. A long-time complaint about Hollywood is that their stories are too simple, but look at the most profitable or critically-acclaimed movies (they don't always fall on the same lists) and you will see simple stories and simple themes.

The *Star Wars* series probably grossed in excess of $20 billion dollars in box office, DVD, games, toys and other revenues[66]. *The Lord Of The Rings* trilogy is headed in the same direction. According to Time Warner, the worldwide box office take has been $2.9 billion and the consumer spending on home entertainment and merchandise was $3 billion.[67] What do these films have in common? Despite the heavy special-effects, they're all based on simple, enduring, and universal mythologies that Joseph Campbell wrote about decades ago in books like *Hero with a Thousand Faces*. They tell basic, archetypal stories. Matt Damon, actor, producer, and writer said once that "the bigger the story, the simpler the characters." Mr. Damon co-wrote the screenplay for *Good Will Hunting* and acted as Private Ryan in Academy-Award Winner *Saving Private Ryan* as well as many other successful films such as *The Bourne Identity* and *Ocean's Eleven*. Hollywood uses story-making skills not just to make movies but also to sell them. They know how to craft simple messages, create relationships between stars and customers, create word of mouth, and position their products.

But Hollywood does something else that is essential for high tech strategy. Silicon Valley did not create the concept of venture capital or fundraising for a new venture. Hollywood has been doing it for far longer. Entrepreneurs (writers, directors or producers) first develop a new idea for a movie. They then write a treatment and/or a screenplay, and a "business plan" that they use to attract studios, investors, producers, actors, and directors. Sound familiar? This is what a technology entrepreneur does. Only instead of studio investors they seek venture capital investors. Instead of directors, they look for an executive staff. Instead of actors, they look for engineers. Like studios they look for outstanding marketing managers.

Here's an exercise–explain the following movies in ten words (or ten seconds) or less:

- *Crouching Tiger, Hidden Dragon* (starring Michelle Yeow and Yun-Fat Chow)
- *The Last Samurai* (starring Tom Cruise)

Hint: don't explain the plot of the movie (and don't turn the page just yet!) You may only use ten words (or ten seconds) or less to explain it. Put the book down and think about it.

Here's how Ang Lee, director of *Crouching Tiger, Hidden Dragon* explained the concept when he was recruiting star actor Michelle Yeow. He said it was *Sense and Sensibility* with martial arts." *Sense and Sensibility* is a movie that Ang Lee had previously directed based on Jane Austen's book of the same title. This book portrays two sisters with polar opposite characters: one is diplomatic and restrained, while the younger sister utterly lacks emotional control. Ang Lee needed just six words to explain the new movie. Instead of going on with a long-winded explanation of the plot, he started with something Michelle Yeow knew (the movie *Sense and Sensibility*), and then explained how they were different (martial arts). Certainly, those six words can't tell the whole story, can they? They can. At a minimum, they pique investor or actor interest and start a conversation. That's precisely what you need!

How would you explain Tom Cruise's *Last Samurai*? A few minutes into the movie I thought: *Dances with Wolves* with Samurai. If I were on that elevator pitching a new concept to an investor and had no time to explain it, that's what I would say. If she had seen Kevin Costner in *Dances with Wolves*, she would imagine a former military man who has an existential crisis, escapes his world, and comes into contact with a different culture that was supposed to be "backward" and now faces extinction at the hands of a militarily, technologically, and numerically overwhelming group. The hero is transformed, finds redemption, his true self and the woman he loves in that strange culture. The main difference is that instead of Native American cultures, the culture is that of the Japanese Samurai. You don't need to explain the whole plot. Just start with something the viewer knows (Dances with Wolves) and say how the new product is different (with Samurai). The multi-billion dollar success of movies like *Lord of The Rings*, *Star Wars*, and *Titanic* and the seeming ease with which Hollywood keeps pumping new successful movies in a cluttered marketplace are testaments to Hollywod's deep storytelling and promotional skills.

POSITIONING

Ok, so Hollywood has brilliant promoters who can spout effective messages. How does this apply to complex, knowledge-intensive technology products? Let's look at an example from the field of genetics. There are very few fields that get more complicated than genetics. While doing research for this book, I came across a company called Applied BioScience. They sold technology products that were used to discover and experiment with genes–genotyping, resequencing and gene expression. On their home page (www.appliedbioscience.com) there was a banner ad that said in large fonts "See More Genes. Use Less Sample." At the lower left, in smaller font, it said, "Expression Array System."

The underlying technology for an "Expression Array System" is probably extremely complex and it would take an expert a skyscraper-high elevator ride, or more likely a cross-country flight to explain its innards. Notice, however, that even a biotech lay person (like myself) can understand what this product does and what the value is. "See more genes. Use less sample." Six simple but brilliantly effective words. Now the prospect has an idea of what it does and how it's different. If this is an area of interest to them, they'll click on the banner to go get more detailed information. It's also easy to talk to others about it. Now think about it. Is your technology more complex than an "Expression Array System"? Let's see how positioning can help distill a product to its market essence.

Positioning has emerged as one of the most important elements in marketing strategy since Al Ries and Jack Trout introduced it to the business world in the early 1980s. They defined positioning as "how you differentiate your brand in the minds of your customers and prospects."[68]

Before you differentiate your product, you have to get into the mind of the customers and prospects. The problem is that yours is one of tens of thousands of new technologies, products or services that are conceived every year. We have already seen how cluttered the tech world can be. In 2004 the United States Patent Office issued about 300,000 new patents. That's more than a thousand each working day! Even if only a small percentage of those patents turned into products, you would be going up against near impossible odds to get in front of your intended audience. New products are just the beginning of what you're competing with for attention. Even if your product does make it to a store shelf at a store somewhere, you're still competing with tens of thousands of products for the customer's attention. It's even worse online. In 2004, Ingram Micro, the largest distributor of electronics products in the United States, had a distribution catalog of more than 280,000 unique products[69].

New technologies are usually much harder to describe than mature products. This is especially true in so-called "horizontal" technologies. A horizontal technology is one that has many uses or applications. The personal computer, for instance, can be used in innumerable ways: writing, watching videos, emailing, calendaring, etc. The Internet, electricity, the car, are examples of horizontal technologies. They have many applications and can be used for many reasons by many users under a plethora of different circumstances.

So how do we explain a new complex technology? Make it simple! You need to do it with 10 words or 10 seconds or less. Remember the case of the "Expression Array System": you don't need to explain the technology itself.

To start the positioning exercise, you need to have the following elements:

1. What is the target market? Who's the user, customer, or prospect?
2. What is the product? This may sound redundant but you may bring a different "whole product" (See Rule 8) to different markets. Furthermore you probably want to focus on a specific use or application of the product, not the product itself.
3. What are the benefits your product brings to the specific customer in your target market?
4. Who are you competing against?

Understanding and clearly explaining technology benefits then becomes a key element in your positioning exercise. Many times it's not obvious what the benefits are. What is the pain you're trying to solve?

As you see, positioning helps your simplify not just your message but also your whole product strategy. Once you clarify to yourself who your target market is what the key benefits you will deliver are as well as who you're competing against then you can craft your strategy around those facts. It makes it easier to define who you should partner with, where to invest your research and development dollars, and your marketing dollars.

Here's a simple formula to create your positioning: (My technology) *is like* (something the prospect already - an existing product or process) except (how it's different – additional value/ benefits)

For instance Salesforce.com's positioning when they emerged would have been as follows: (Salesforce.com) is like (Siebel's CRM), except (there's no software to install).

Let's look at several ways to position a product.

Positioning relative to an existing process or something your target market already knows

This type of positioning should generally be used when a technology product is in an emerging category. In the beginning of the technology adoption lifecycle, when a technology is brand new and maybe hard to explain you want to compare your product with existing processes, products, or ways of doing things. You start by comparing your product with something your prospect already knows. This makes it easy for the market to understand what the product does or what the benefits are without necessarily understanding the underlying technology. It also helps the vendor compare its product line and explain the advantages relative to the existing way of doing things.

For example, when Apple Computers developed its desktop publishing product strategy in the early 1980s, they positioned themselves against existing publishing technologies like Linotype. If you published a newsletter in the early 1980s you understood very well the time, cost, and effort to do write, edit, and print it. By positioning Apple this way it was relatively straightforward to show the difference their products made.

Apple did a great job promoting the WYSIWIG (what you see is what you get) capability of their computers in the 1980s. To the user the benefits were clear: make all the changes and see what your newsletter is going to look like–before printing anything at all. No proofs to send back to the client, no round trips with minor (or major) changes, no wasted printing runs. For the vendor the benefit of this clear positioning was also clear: no need to explain RAM size, hard-disk access rate or CPU speed in a market that may not have understood or cared about any of this technology.

Notice that Apple didn't mention Microsoft. Wasn't the Wintel computer Apple's nemesis and main competitor? Not in this market. Microsoft and Intel were just too busy going after global domination in a horizontal way, a battle that Apple had already lost.

Thus, early in the life of the category, you need to compare yourself to the existing way of doing things, not the competition.

Positioning relative to the competition

Once a product category has emerged, the competitive landscape is better defined. The companies who make up the category, the product benefits, the rules of the game, and the general trajectory of the market are usually defined by this point. When the rules of the game are known, the battle is probably over. The winner is crowned and the rivals aspiring to leadership positions are lining up to battle for their piece of the action.

At this point, most companies need to define themselves or their products relative to the competition, usually the leader. For example, the relational database (RDB) category was a brutal fight that saw Oracle emerge as the clear leader. How did companies in this category position themselves? Relative to Oracle. Informix would say their products are faster than Oracle's. They would show tables with the results of countless tests that "proved" their superior speed. The positioning statement would be as follows:

Informix RDB is like Oracle, only faster.

These seven words would underlie the company's product strategy. Now the company knows that it needs to invest its R&D dollars in making the product faster and its market dollars in targeting organizations who need the extra speed.

Positioning as a new opportunity/niche/hole player

You can also position your product by findin new opportunities that haven't been exploited by or may still be too small for the bigger players. For instance, in the RDB case, Sybase has positioned itself as the mobility database company. Oracle won the battle for large corporate depositories of information where it is battling it out with IBM's DB2 offering for the big corporate dollars,

Taking advantage of its inroads into the medium-sized business marketplace, Microsoft SQLServer has positioned itself as the one to beat there, while Informix went for speed and online transaction processing. The open source movement brought free databases and MySQL has successfully positioned itself as the company to beat in that space.

How do you position your RDB company in this maelstrom? Let's look at how Sybase came back from the brink to successfully position itself as the one to beat in a database space. First of all, it would be useless for Sybase to say that they are 'better' than Oracle. That battle was fought in 1980s and 1990s. The market has already spoken there. How many people are going to rip out their Oracle infrastructure because another database is slightly better? Faster? Informix is there. Cheaper? Microsoft is there.

You go back to the customer and find out what their database-related pain is. What Sybase figured is that many enterprise information technology executives have a pain managing their mobile infrastructure. As new form factors, sizes, and shapes of computing devices have emerged, they are having problems managing it all. Corporate users walking around with cell phones, personal digital assistants, RFID devices, nano-laptops, and the like, need to be managed centrally. Whose database should inhabit those devices? Whose database can bring it all home seamlessly?

Sybase has found a large and growing pain within the enterprise and has uniquely positioned itself as the company to solve that pain. They are not attempting to compete with all the other companies in all fronts, even if their relational databases has many features that are fairly similar.

Sybase CEO now talks about the "Unwired Enterprise"[70]

Positioning as a leader

If you can credibly claim a position of leadership, you should. In that case, you have no need to compare your product to the competition or to existing processes. The king is the king, right? If you're the leader you become the standard bearer for the category, the one to beat, the one others aim their guns at. In fact when they come up with a new product upgrade, leaders usually compare them to their *existing* one, not the competition. When Microsoft came up with Windows XP who did they position it against? Win98!. Similarly, Intel would position its Centrino relative to its own Pentium (it's like Pentium with built-in communications). Transmeta had already had a similar product out there for a few years, but Intel did not bother giving them any credibility in the marketplace. AMD? Let them pay for their own promotions!

Positioning then is about getting into the minds of your prospects and customers. It's ultimately how they think about your product. It's also a way to focus your product/market strategy and simplify your messages.

BRANDING

Branding is one of the most important and misunderstood elements of strategy. Much has been said about brands to confuse us even more: it's a color, it's a symbol, it's a message, it's a name, it's about packaging, designing, and so on. Because of the speed of market development and the complexity of high technology products and services, creating a brand is probably more important in high tech markets than in more traditional ones. Why? To the same reasons stated above (busy people, complex technology, fast-moving markets, tech talk, and competition) we add another one. Technology features are usually hard to defend and can become commoditized quickly. A brand is durable and defensible.

Think of a brand as how the customer feels about your product, service or company. If successful, a brand becomes part of the user's identity. How can anyone identify with a technology product? Aren't we talking about feelings here? How can you have a "relationship" with a technology product? Before answering that, think about how you feel about Microsoft products. What do you feel when MS Windows crashes on you in the middle of a moment of inspired writing (as has happened to me countless times while writing this book)? Be honest, nobody is watching!

Now how do you feel about Google? Craigslist? Apple? Yahoo? eBay? We talked earlier in this chapter how some of these companies have developed stories that engage the customer. When you rent a DVD from Netflix, buy a Mac from Apple, or use Google search or Gmail it's not a cold and meaningless experience. There are feelings involved. You identify with the people and stories surrounding them. It's important that their products deliver value but at some point the interaction is less rational. For instance, when was the last time you compared Google with competitive search engines? How many Apple users compare Megs of memory or processor speed with their Wintel counterparts? Brands shelter users from having to make such decisions on an ongoing basis. It also protects vendors from the daily technology feature race. After all, we're only human! We also introduced Dr. Howard Gardner's notion that leaders achieve their effectiveness through the stories they tell and embody. Gardner further found that "the most basic story has to do with issues of identity."

Users of a technology product or services similarly identify with certain companies or products. More to the point, they identify with the people who make and sell those products and services. Companies are made up of people! It's more than what they do, it's also who they are. Enterprise technology executives may identify with the safety of a conservative company like Cisco or IBM, while more counter-cultural creative types might identify with Apple. Furthermore, the latter identify with not just with Apple, but specifically with its people and especially its leader who is the one who embodies the brand and its stories.

A brand is not just what you say it is! Just as a relationship is not what you say it is. It takes both parties to agree on what the relationship is all about. Otherwise the relationship is doomed to failure. A nameless bureaucrat in Cupertino or Detroit cannot single handedly make a brand happen. There are too many deep identity issues at play. When Coca Cola changed the flavor of its flagship soda product, Coke drinkers reminded Coke executives that they didn't just sell colored sugar water. They sold an identity wrapped in a soda drink. This was not something that executives could mess with at will. When Oldsmobile executives said "This is not your father's Oldsmobile" believing that they could create a brand by diktat, they were utterly wrong.

Apple is a case in point. The company went through an existential crisis in the mid-1990's not just because it didn't have the right products but because its brand was out of sync. Regardless of their management skills neither one of their two successive CEOs at the time (Michael Spindler and Gil Amelio) could bring the passionate counter-cultural artistic personality that was such a big part of the Apple story and its brand. Stories, people, symbols, and products all need to build on one another. In the discussion about leaders and stories above we mentioned that to be credible leaders need to embody the stories that they tell. Spindler and Amelio were at a disadvantage because to the Apple faithful they did not embody the stories embedded in the brand. Watching the monotonal performance of the company's leadership at the annual MacWorld applefest was too much for many of the faithful to bear. Only when founder Steve Jobs came back did the brand get back in sync. Its products, people, stories, and symbols were coherent again. Apple's brand was whole again.

Word-of-Mouse

We can't possibly stress the importance of word-of-mouth and word-of-mouse in the success of a high technology company. Word-of-mouth is one of the most powerful ways to help create a brand. Many managers mistake this for free publicity. Managers who misunderstand word-of-mouth (and its Internet equivalent word-of-mouse) and try to use it as free advertising may feel the backlash that comes from its true power.

You may not know what JibJab is. However, if you lived in the U.S. during the 2004 presidential elections you may have seen an animated cartoon called *This Land* that showed John Kerry and George W. Bush insulting each other to the tune of the eponymous Woody Guthrie song. That cartoon registered more than 80 million page views–basically all from word-of-mouse[71]. To put this figure in perspective, let's compare it to television viewership. The Super Bowl is traditionally the highest rated event on American television.

It is heavily advertised and highly anticipated throughout the whole four months of football season and has a history of 35 years behind it. The 2005 Super Bowl registered 86 million viewers, just slightly more than *This Land* had from pure word of mouse in a few days.[72] Months later, JibJab's *This Land* is still getting page views!

Companies like Facebook.com, Skype, and Google have been built mainly if not only through word-of-mouth and word-of-mouse. Take the case of Gmail.

When Google released its free Gmail email service to the world in April 2004, it didn't advertise and didn't even open it up to the world. The Yahoo! email and Hotmail services it wanted to compete against were mostly free and open to anybody: new users could just go to mail.yahoo.com or hotmail.com to sign up. Instead Google made it an invitation-only service. At a time when Google's IPO was on everyone's mind, Gmail was initially set up as an exclusive club. The company released its service to a few hundred employees who were given the power to invite a few friends. The latter, in turn, would be given invitations to hand out to *their* friends after using the Gmail service for a while. In other words, Google, recruited its own user base as champions of its new Gmail service. At one point, Gmail invitations went for $150 on eBay![73]

Is exclusivity so inherently powerful that anything becomes attractive if it's exclusive? Not always. In technology markets the product or service has to offer real value. It was instantly apparent that users of competing services were experiencing pain, like running out of storage and therefore losing emails and attachments. Amongst other things, Gmail offered for free ten to a hundred times the storage that competing services offered for a fee–thus solving this pain.

I belong to a Stanford University email list that usually serves as a way for alumni to communicate about current events, careers, and whatever topic is hot. For a time after Google released its Gmail service, this list buzzed with people offering and asking for invitations to join Gmail. There were so many email messages about Gmail that someone on the list asked that Gmail-related emails be stopped. Alumni responses to that email were instantaneous and clear. Here's a representative response from an email user to the whole Stanford email community:

"I've had my Stanford account for almost two decades and it has served me wonderfully. Yahoo took away free PopMail retrieval, and reading Hotmail through Outlook Express is painful. So my Stanford account has been the best thing since sliced bread. When my friends and acquaintances started sending me huge attachments I would go over my disk quota and lose email. Gmail was the blessing that came along to the rescue.

So, please keep on sending out the invites and the requests. This is a valuable service to Stanford alums from Stanford alums."

The lessons from Gmail are two-fold. The first one is that the product needs to be of substantial added value to customers. The Gmail example showed that this service became popular because it created measurably large customer value above what the incumbents offered. If there's a pain in the market that your product fixes, that's value. The second lesson here is that it word-of-mouse is an incredibly powerful tool to build a new product, service or company. When your own customers go out of their way to publicly recommend you you have the makings of a successful product. Gmail was a successful case of word–of-mouse at work!

Name Calling

Your product name and your company name are an important part of your communications strategy. If you are an entrepreneur in a startup company or have a new product in a new category, then you need all the help you can get in standing out from the crowd. Your name is the tip of your communications spear: the clearer and sharper it is the better it can penetrate the marketplace.

Your name is especially important in the early stages of the technology adoption lifecycle. When you only have a few seconds from a possible user or influencer, you want to say things briefly and effectively. Your name is your badge. You don't want your name to be insipid, boring, or cryptic. You want it to be memorable.

Quick! What does Altria do? What about Inprise? (OK, if you read Chapter 2, then you know about Inprise.) What does Enterasys do? Can you imagine a bunch of marketing MBAs sitting around a room thinking of the most obscure and confusing name for their company or product? Spending thousands of dollars for a consulting company to play name roulette putting together tech-sounding prefixes and suffixes?

Altria actually went out of its way to look for a name so the market would not relate it to its tobacco business. So that the market would *not* know who it is. The former RJR Nabisco wanted to stay away from its name and paid for a generic, boring name to literally hide away and escape publicity. This is what seems to happen within high tech companies everyday. Just like the "communications" full of buzzwords, many company names are obtuse and meaningless. Even otherwise successful companies make this mistake. Check out the following list of (real) products from (real) companies (Fig. 2). Can you match the product name with the category and the company? (The answer is below the figure.)

Name	Category	Company
Axim	Handheld Computer	Dell
Inspiron	Laptop PC	Dell
Inspire	Car	Honda
Geode	PC processor	AMD
NetRanger	Network Intrusion Detection	Cisco
RangerNet	Power Ranger Network	Tripod
Pavillion	Laptop PC	HP
Alchemy	MIPS processors	AMD

FIGURE 4.1 – NAMING A PRODUCT. MATCH THE PRODUCT NAME WITH THE CATEGORY AND THE COMPANY.

What's the difference between NetRanger and RangerNet? Could Inspire be a car or a type of knowledge management software? How about a new brain medicine? The answer to the name puzzle is that there is no puzzle. Each product name on the left column corresponds to the category and company on its row! Who knew that Alchemy was a computer microprocessor?

Compare the insipid names in the left column of Fig.4.1 with names like Salesforce.com, Netflix, Facebook.com, CraigsList, Visa, Oracle, or PeopleSoft. These names mean something functional or have the capacity to evoke stories, feelings, or identification.

Here are four recommendations (by no means all) to create a name for your product or company.

1- Use the founder's name

The founder is the best spokesperson and storyteller for the company. Founders embody the best stories and they can tell the best stories. They are the best way to create a relationship with customers, prospects, and influencers. Here are a few examples:

- Craigslist. How many great stories can you craft about Craig Newmark founding of this great company and turning it into one of the most popular websites on earth? Read chapter 1! And what a great spokesperson Craig is!
- Linux. How do you name your Unix brainchild if your name is Linus Torvalds? A name that conjures many stories!
- Dell Computers. When a young entrepreneur starts a business from a college campus in Texas, it engenders many stories and associations in the minds of the customer.
- Norton Computing. More than a decade after he sold his business to Symantec, Peter Norton still adorns the boxes of the PC tools category he helped create.
- Hewlett-Packard. A name that conjures stories of the two young entrepreneurs fresh out of Stanford sitting in their Palo Alto garage thinking of the next great technology measurement device.
- Siebel Systems. The salesforce software company from the ultimate salesman himself: Tom Siebel.

2- Use functional names

Smaller companies or companies entering new markets may want to use functional names for their companies and their products. Why? Because they instantly say what you do or who you are. No need for long explanatory paragraphs. You are your name. Your product is your name. Here are examples of functional names:

- NetFlix. Do you want to get your movies on the net?
- Salesforce.com, They must do technology for the sales force, right?
- Facebook.com. A net extension of the ubiquitous college facebook. And then some.
- LiveJournal.com. Functional name for online journals from the people who brought another brilliantly named weblog product: Moveable Type.
- PeopleSoft. When this company started, they focused on developing human resources software. Software for people.
- XM Satellite Radio. Yes, we know what they do!

3- Use evocative names

They're not directly functional but make you think of the people, stories, messages that evoke feelings about the company.

- Oracle. Where did the ancient Greeks go for information and wisdom? To the oracle of course!
- Visa. Don't you need a visa to give you access?
- YouTube. Post your video and "Broadcast Yourself" says this newest phenomenon of the Internet.

4 - Use the Zeitgeist

In German, zeitgeist means 'spirit of the times' and it denotes the culture of the moment. Although I like descriptive names, not all markets require them. I prefer MySpace or LinkedIn but some markets seem to prefer Orkut or del.icio.us. If you're in similar spaces use the zeigeist to work in your favor - but you should still remember that your name should be memorable above all and should work for you. Some examples:

- Froogle. Google's own frugal price comparison site.
- Friendster. Leverage the Napster name for social networks.

5- Use acronyms.

In enterprise markets, acronyms seem to give companies an aura of credibility. Use them whenever you feel you have to use a manufactured name. If you can find or use an industry standard such as RSA Security, MP3.com, DivX Inc, SOA Software or VOIP, Inc, use it. Otherwise, acronyms such as SAP, SAS, IBM, 3Com and AT&T are much better than meaningless ones such as Inprise, Enterasys, or Altria.

Rule 4 Summary – Have a Story. Communicate Clearly

Technology entrepreneurs face many challenges when getting the word out to the market about their new products or services. Prospects are increasingly busy. The technology underlying the product may be complex and therefore hard to summarize. There are many concurrent competitors offering similar products. Tech markets move extremely quickly. Speed of adoption may be essential to the success of your product or service.

The most effective growth strategy is to have your customers recommend your product or service to others. In order for customers to understand who you are and what your products do, you need to simplify the messages you communicate to them.

Winning companies use their communication strategies as a means of gaining and maintaining market leadership. They understand that leadership is about crafting and telling stories. Stories have the power to shape human existence. They can give meaning and a human dimension to abstract technologies. These stories build on old stories and themes that have delighted humans for thousands of years. They also use brief, clear, and effective messages travel fast and stick to the audience. They build brands that are coherent with the stories, the people and the products they build.

Your positioning strategy can provide you with a way to simplify your messages. You should be able to say what the company or product does or your value proposition in ten seconds or ten words or less. Your name is the tip of your communications spear. Don't use boring, insipid, contrived names. Use the founder's names, functional, descriptive, or meaningful names. If you have to manufacture a name, use acronyms or the zeitgeist.

RULE 5
IT'S A RISKY WORLD.
SELL CONFIDENCE!

"When people feel uncertain they'd rather have someone strong and wrong than weak and right"

-- *Bill Clinton*

"Confidence is contagious. So is lack of confidence."

-- *Vince Lombardi*

Sycamore was a networking gear company located in Chelmsford, Massachussetts. Soon after its October 1999 IPO its stock went up from $12 to $189, it had $1.5 billion in cash and cash equivalents in it balance sheet, its quarterly revenues were $149.2 million and it had earnings of $13.8 million.[74] Then the market got tough and the bottom fell out of the company. Information technology buyers seemingly stopped buying from anyone but Cisco Systems. Around June of 2005, Sycamore's quarterly revenues had dropped to $14 million (a 90% drop) and its stock stood at $3.40 (a 98% drop). The market valued the company at little more than the cash in its bank, and it faced delisting by the Nasdaq[75] Despite having nearly a billion dollars in the bank, the company could not build a viable business and could not even find a buyer after it put itself up for sale.

Sycamore is but one of thousands of companies that were hit hard during the technology purchasing downturn that followed the Nasdaq collapse. Layoffs were rampant and companies were shutting down left and right. Office space availability in Silicon Valley is one indicator of the vitality of startup activity. In the late 1990s office space was so tight that many landlords started asking for stock options from prospective renters. After 2000 Silicon Valley went from having no office space available to a vacancy rate of 20% -30% in some areas. Santa Clara, where Intel is headquartered hit 33.4

percent vacancy, while Mountain View (home of Google and Sun Micro) hit 29.8 percent.[76]

Technology buyers seemingly ran for cover. They started buying only from the tried-and-true companies. We have heard it many times before: "No one got fired for buying IBM." The saying seemed to extend to all category leaders: "No one got fired for buying IBM, Oracle, Cisco, or SAP."

Many smaller and innovative companies usually bemoan prospects for going with "inferior" technologies. During the purchasing recession there was a louder cry of frustration. Many smaller companies felt they needed to "educate the customer" to make the "right" choice. Many strategists and executives from these companies don't understand the true nature of purchasing cutting-edge products and innovations. They may fail to look at this process from the perspective of their prospective customer. They may not comprehend the many risks involved in buying technology products or services. The higher the degree of uncertainty in purchasing their products or services, the less likely they are to be acquired. As Bill Clinton said, "When people feel uncertain they'd rather have someone strong and wrong than weak and right."

Does this mean there is no chance for startup companies to succeed in tough markets? Hardly. Clickability was a small and innovative company that prospered in this tough purchasing environment. Based in San Francisco, Clickability licensed "Content Management Software" that customers used to build and maintain websites. Large companies such as Vignette and Documentum had been providing such software for years. What was new about Clickability was that it offered this software as a service. Instead of large, complex and expensive software installation and customization projects offered by its established competitors, they delivered their product over the web. This software delivery model was known as Software as a Service (Saas).

Clickability was able to consistently grow its business despite the many reasons that worked against them and other innovative tech companies. Not only was the IT purchasing environment then generally biased against small companies, but also the company's target markets included many of the largest and most conservative publishing companies in America. Clickability also competed with larger established players like Vignette and Documentum. Three uncertainty strikes against it didn't bode well for a small startup company. How did Clickability fare?

Despite all the roadblocks, Clickability grew from one to 150 paying customers in the 2001-2004 recession period. How did Clickability do it? They sold confidence. Company management understood that selecting and purchasing high technology products or services is a difficult and high-risk proposition for the potential buyer.

INNOVATION ADOPTION IS RISKY

When they adopt new innovations, your customers are taking different types of risks: personal risks, reputation risks, career risks, financial risks, technology risks, standards risks, company risks. Imagine that you work in a large corporation and your job is to choose a specific technology. If the technology fails, all fingers are probably going to be pointed your way. You may look bad for not choosing the safe "brand name" in the category, even if they offered "inferior" and more expensive solutions.

Technology may be difficult to understand, deploy, and use. Most mortals who don't have advanced engineering degrees or an active interest in the specific technology don't understand what lurks inside those new semiconductors with millions of transistors that have been pushed to their limit, any more than they know what the side-effects of brand new drugs or medical procedures are.

Technology products can also be difficult to test. How do you test a product like ZoneLabs ZoneAlarm, a virus protection software program? By unleashing viruses on yourself? How about Spyware products? Can you generate the malicious spyware code that grabs information from your computer and sends it across the net for who-knows-what purpose? Unlikely. Very few prospective customers have the internal resources to test most new high-technology products. In fact, even if they did have the cash, time, infrastructure, and skills to do it, they probably have better things to focus on!

Many new innovations are "experience goods." This means that the products or services need to be experienced before the user knows how good they are. Think about consulting services: how do you know how good a consultant is? It's hard to say upfront. You need her to work on a project and produce results you can appraise. In fact, it may even be hard at that point to determine how good her output is. You may need to execute on her recommendations before you know how good they are.

Users are taking many types of risks in adopting new technologies. Some of the risks include: financial risks (am I going to lose my investment in this product?), technology risks (is this technology going to work at all?), standards risk (is this going to be the winning standard?), execution risk (can this company do what it says it will do?), company risk (will your company be around next year?), health risk (what are the health side effects?), environmental risks (how am I polluting the environment?), legal risks (does this product comply with regulations?), and public relations risks (am I going to look bad to the world if I use this technology?).

Given all the uncertainties involved in adopting new innovations and technologies, is it any wonder people don't want to take undue risks on a new product or service? When the purchasing environment gets tough as it did the first few years of thiscentury, uncertainty levels go up, and many new companies cannot succeed because prospects will not take a chance on them, regardless of the product's obvious benefits.

The types of risks potential customers are faced with will be different according to the industry, technology use, context, and customer type. Uncertainty is best addressed by deconstructing and addressing all the separate components of risk. Understand what the customer is facing and build a strategy based on that understanding. Some types of risks are obviously interrelated. For instance, environmental risks might lead to health risks and public relations risks.

Financial risk

Am I going to lose my investment in this product? What other financial risks am I taking? Nike paid $400 million to put in place a brand-new supply chain infrastructure. What did Nike get for this kind of money? As soon as it deployed the technology, $100-million-worth of inventory went the "wrong way" and the company lost $100 million that quarter. Furthermore, because Nike was a public company, it lost $2.5 billion in market capitalization (20% of the total) in one fell swoop and caused endless class action lawsuits against the company.[77]

Surely few of us take that kind of financial risk. However, technology can be expensive to buy, deploy, use, and maintain. A study found that the average SAP supply chain infrastructure software installation cost is $14.5 million. [78].

Not only does the user need to buy your technology. She needs to integrate it with her existing infrastructure, which implies the further cost of hiring systems integrators. After everything is installed, users need to be trained in the use of the new products. This costs more money in both training expertise and also in revenue foregone while the training goes on. The average enterprise software customer may spend six or seven times more money in additional hardware, software, installation and customization than in the core software license they are licensing. That $1 million in licensing fees can easily turn into a $7-million project.

Furthermore, switching costs can be even larger. Switching costs can be defined as all costs that the user needs to incur in order to swap out of an existing product, process or way of doing things. In fact, for many products categories, switching costs increase with time.

Think about a database infrastructure. The more data you put into the database the more value it has and the more difficult it is to transfer the data elsewhere. The more application programs interface with this database, the higher the likelihood of business disruption if you swap out of it. Many databases house not only data but also embedded programming code (SQL statements) to manipulate the data more efficiently. As programmers and database administrators come and go, they write embedded code for business situations where there are repetitive functions that need it. This embedded code is seldom deleted when it's not needed anymore. The more embedded code the harder it is to understand what it actually does and which parts are needed anymore and the more difficult it is to rewrite. Attempting to clean up, recreate and rewrite all this code can be a time-consuming, expensive or just impossible proposition.

The cost of switching away from a database can be insurmountable. That's why a company like Oracle has such an incredible hold on customers once they commit to its databases (ask any Oracle user!). Are you still wondering why Oracle is such a cash-generating machine?

As the Nike example shows, the financial risks in adopting technology can be enormous. It took Nike years to get their supply chain infrastructure right and the price tag was reportedly around $3 billion[79]

Standards risk

Am I buying into the winning standard? Am I going to get stuck with useless technology? Several organizations are in the business of helping industry define standards. The Institute of Electrical and Electronics Engineers (IEEE) is one of them. Go to www.ieee.org and you will find dozens of standards from "Organics and Molecular Transistors and Materials (P1620)" to "Voting Systems Standards (SCC38)" being worked out by interested parties. According to IEEE, a standard is an agreed-upon published set of "specifications and procedures designed to ensure that a material, product, method, or service meets its purpose and consistently performs to its intended use."[80] It assures that products from different vendors will be compatible and will operate seamlessly with one another. Imagine having to worry about your toaster plug being incompatible with your wall outlet! International travelers know this feeling very well.

No one likes to invest in a product only to find out later that they will be left with a technology that will not be supported. Should your product be based on a standard that loses out in the marketplace this almost certainly means the loss of the customer's investment in a your product or technology.

Part of the reason Radio Frequency Identification (RFID) technology took so long to be widely adopted was that there were three incompatible standards. Who wanted to be the first company to spend the millions it took to upgrade its infrastructure only to find itself with an incompatible legacy system? "Three groups have proposals in contention before Brussels-based standards body, EPCglobal. Solo RFID specialist Alien Technology has proposed one, Royal Philips Electronics and Texas Instruments have collaborated on another, and smaller firms EM Microelectronic-Marin, Matrics, Atmel and several others have offered a third."[81]

I have a useless DVD backup unit that cost me $300. As I write this, many players are still attempting to set their own DVD standards. Look at your DVD backup unit. Is it DVD-RAM, DVD-RW or DVD+RW? The interesting thing is that this time we have three standards battling it out (instead of the usual two), although DVD-RAM seems to be an early loser. We have companies like Dell, HP, and Phillips backing the DVD+RW standard, while Apple, Hitachi, NEC, Pioneer, Samsung, and Sharp have backed the DVD-RAM and /or DVD-RW. The standards are all mutually incompatible and only one will likely emerge as the winner. This means that whoever buys into losing standards will have to use an incompatible standard until the machine dies or is sold for pennies on the dollar.

The DVD standards war is reminiscent of the Betamax (owned by Sony) vs. VHS (owned by Matsushita) battles in the 1980s. Millions of users got stuck with useless video cassette recorders once VHS won and became the category standard. As we saw in this battle, even the backing of a giant like Sony (with what many believed was a superior product) was no guarantee that a standard would win.

Sometimes the industry will agree on a joint standard that merges the competitors' technologies. For instance, in the late 1990s, there was a 56k-speed dialup modems war. On one side there was 56Kflex (Rockwell/Lucent), and on the other side X2 (USRobotics). Luckily for the market adoption process, 3Com, then a large and highly influential networking provider and a supporter of 56Kflex acquired USRobotics Both X2 and 56flex got merged into the new V.90 standard.

VCRs, DVDs, and modems are interesting and recognizable products, but they are also inexpensive, worth at most a few hundred dollars. Junking them will not hurt the buyers much. Now imagine an enterprise software infrastructure standard. Corporate software is expensive to develop and even more expensive to maintain. It costs anywhere from hundreds of thousands to tens of millions for upfront licensing and development costs. They usually have a way of hanging around many years beyond its supposed "useful" life. Faced with the 'Y2K' problem back in the 1990s IT managers started inventorying their software infrastructure. The numbers of COBOL programs that were uncovered and still running decades after they were written were unimaginable! People left them alone because they worked.

Imagine you are selling a business process management software (BPMS) infrastructure into corporate information technology shops. BPMS is a relatively new breed of software that allows organizations to map their business processes and create programs directly from there, as opposed to having several layers of people translate business requirements and then manually program for them, using any of a plethora of computer languages. BPMS projects start in the half-million to low-millions of dollars for relatively small projects. In 2004 there were two competing BPMS standards: BPML (business process manipulation language) and BPEL (business process execution language for web services).

Your prospect will look at the competing standards and wonder if she's buying the right standard. She might ask herself, "what if I buy the BPMS equivalent of Betamax?" This is a real risk that she and her organization may not be willing to take. She might be willing to take a chance for a few hundred dollars (Betamax or DVD-RAM), but for several million dollars the risk might be too high.

Technology risk

What are the chances that the technology will simply not work? Has it been proven under a variety of circumstances?

To understand this risk let's look at a life-and-death example.

In September 2004 a voice-switching and control system that was used to track airplanes in the Los Angeles Air Route Traffic Control Center automatically shut down, leaving air traffic controllers unable to talk with pilots. For 12 never-ending seconds 800 airplanes were on their own in one of the busiest air spaces in the world. There were five "incidents" where planes flew "closer than rules allow" to one another.[82] Furthermore, the backup system also failed to work "because of a software problem." Thankfully, there were no accidents, but the problem caused 600 flights to be cancelled and 400 to be delayed.

Under most circumstances lives will not be at stake when customers adopt technology. What is at stake when buyers take technical risks is their livelihood. , Plant shutdowns, payroll mistakes, and logistical problems are more likely – all of which carry high costs.

Execution risk

Another risk for technology buyers is whether the vendor will execute well. Do they have what it takes to deliver on a project given the unique characteristics of my organization? Even if a company has delivered a working technology for others, it may not mean they will deliver for you. According to the Standish Group, 90% of Enterprise Resource Planning (ERP) implementations were late, 178 % over budget and took 2.5 times as long as planned[83].

Throwing money at the problem will likely not solve the execution risk. Let's look at a U. S. Government example. The US Missile Defense Agency has reportedly spent more than $80 billion since 1985 to develop a defense system against incoming missiles. This technology is complex, involving a number of interrelated software and hardware systems working in unison. As soon as an incoming missile is detected, interceptors are supposed to launch to seek and destroy them. Testing has repeatedly failed. For instance, during a test in December 2002, the interceptor missed its target by hundreds of miles and burned up in the atmosphere.[84] The system failed again two years later (December 2004) due to "unknown anomalies." In a *New York Times* interview, U.S. Sen. Jack Reed said that "It reinforces the point I've been trying to make. This is a very complicated system that requires testing."

Company risk

The prospective customer will ask themselves whether they are buying into a company that will stay around and support your technology product or service.

Pandesic provided e-commerce applications based on SAP software that it hosted on its own servers. In exchange for investing in the development, maintenance, and hosting of portions of their IT infrastructure, it extracted a percentage of their clients' transaction revenues. The company was a joint venture of Intel and SAP, two of the top leaders in information and communication technology. It was endowed with $200 million in venture capital. Many CEOs felt safe placing their companies' business-critical processes and information in Pandesic's hands. Pandesic quickly gathered more than 100 clients that included many dot-coms and also relatively well-established organizations like the San Francisco Giants baseball team, the San Jose Symphony; and Beverages & More.

Pandesic didn't survive long. Technology buyers were left holding unsupported technology infrastructures. This was an interesting case because it was never thought of as a fly-by-night operation or even as a start-up company. Because it was backed by two of the most solid names in the business, Pandesic was born wealthy and famous. If Pandesic eventually made buyers look bad, how do you think they would feel about doing business with a startup company? Very afraid!

Legal risk

Your prospects and customers may be asking whether your product complies or helps the user comply with laws and regulations. What is the likelihood I or their company will get sued if they deploy your product? A VP of IT at a pharmaceutical company told me: "Sarbanes-Oxley is the one thing we're focused on. Everything else takes a back seat to Sarbox. We're not developing new business-critical stuff because Sarbox has to be done."

The Sarbanes-Oxley Act of 2002 (also called Sarbox or SOX) was the law enacted by the Congress in 2002 in response to the well-publicized abuses of executives at companies such as Enron and Worldcom. These executives misled the public in their financial statements to the tune of billions of dollars, causing both companies to collapse, lose tens of billions of dollars in market capitalization, and file for Chapter 11 bankruptcy. Sarbox demands that public companies keep relevant financial and accounting records for at least five years. Importantly, Sarbox makes the company chief executive officer (CEO) and chief financial officer (CFO) personally liable (with fines and imprisonment) for the financial information and disclosures published by the company. The VP of IT of the pharmaceutical company added that the orders to implement Sarbanes-Oxley "are coming directly from the CFO and CEO."

Managing (minimizing) legal risks has become an intrinsic part of personal and organizational life in the 21st century. The regulatory environment has changed constantly, with new regulations such as Sarbanes-Oxley (public corporations), HIPAA (health care management), and CFR 11 (clinical trials) becoming part of the corporate landscape in America and around the world. Issues surrounding liability risks have become paramount in technology purchase and deployment. Lawyers may see your technology as the "Full Employment Law for Lawyers" or as the "Lawyer Retirement Fund." What are the legal risks around your technology? What are the legal requirements your prospect want you and your product to comply with? Consider it from the perspective of the customer (not you) taking the legal risk of adopting your technology.

Implementation of new rules and regulations has fallen squarely in the hands of the information technology group.

Public Relations risk

Using a new technology may prove to be a public relations nightmare for a technology user, as Italian fashion designer Benetton proved in 2003.

Radio Frequency Identification (RFID) tags are tiny sand-size microchips that emit short-range radio signals. Because they are so small and cheap (a few cents per unit) they can be used by industry to uniquely identify individual products as they move through the supply chain. An RFID tag on a razor blade package would say something like: "I'm Gillette Mach 3 razor #400533412, built at the AB line in the Boston factory on March 12, 2004, at 9:56.21 a.m. EST." The benefits to the supplier of certain products are clear: they can perform automated inventory by scanning boxes as they move through the supply chain. Imagine being able to track the exact location of each razor blade as it goes from the factory in Boston to the Gillette warehouse in Chicago or Sydney to the retailer's warehouse (CVS, Walgreens, or Wal-Mart) in Appleton or Auckland to the exact retail store. In fact, since the RFID tag stays with the product the company could theoretically track it beyond the retail store into the buyer's office or home. This fact raised concerns about individual privacy rights. Imagine someone scanning your home (without physically entering) and finding out what magazines and books you read, what music you buy, what cosmetics you use and exactly what clothing you wear! George Orwell would have had fun writing about RFIDs.

When Phillips Semiconductors announced in March 2003 that the Italian clothing designer and manufacturer would use its RFID technology to track 15 million articles of clothing throughout its thousands of stores worldwide, it set up a public relations backlash that Benetton has not quite recovered from. *Wired* magazine invoked Tom Cruise's then recently released *Minority Report* movie in which anyone's eyes could be scanned anywhere by anyone for quick identification. The RFID would not be far from that.[85] Privacy activists demanded Benetton stop such an affront on individual rights, and even demanded that the public boycott Benetton clothing until they do so (www.boycottbenetton.com).

Within weeks, Benetton recanted and denied that they had any imminent plans to use RFID technology. They issued statements saying that it "is currently analyzing RFID technology" and that "no feasibility studies have yet been undertaken with a view to the possible industrial introduction of this technology."[86] But the damage had been done. Benetton became synonymous with RFID privacy concerns. The MIT Media Lab put together an RFID privacy workshop in November 2003 where it described the Benetton issue upfront–and how to avoid it.

Did Benetton, expect such a public relations disaster? It's hard to imagine that it did. Benetton has for many years worked to be a good social citizen by promoting racial and ethnic harmony as well as other socially responsible causes. Perhaps they thought this would insulate them from a privacy public relations flop. Other companies are clearly watching and are wary of taking this type of risk when adopting new technologies.

Career risk

Make the wrong decision on acquiring a new technology for your company, and your reputation within the department may suffer. You may not be assigned to exciting new projects. You may not be promoted as quickly. You may in fact be fired. However, if you had chosen to go the safe route, all of those risks would be minimized: you'd look smart, thoughtful, and "managerial." Those promotions and salary raises would be quicker in coming. Never mind that you spent more of the company's money on products that took longer to deploy.

The average tenure of a Chief Information Officer in corporate America is less than two years. Not what we would call a stable job. CIOs and technology buyers in general take career risks when they buy a new technology. The IT infrastructure is a patchwork of technologies tied together with "glueware." It kind of "works." Anything you add to that patchwork may make it exponentially more complex. The situation is so bad that many companies run decades-old pieces of software because they "work." No one wants to touch it.

I spoke with a senior technology executive of a multi-billion dollar consumer products company who said he would never touch his enterprise resource planning (ERP) infrastructure. He made sure I heard the word "never" several times. It worked as it was and there was no major need to touch it. So adamant was his company that they had not upgraded their ERP infrastructure in years. Even same-vendor upgrades were risky! Backward-compatibility is seldom 100%! This company would need to modify its programs every time it performed an upgrade.

After reading about Nike's disaster above, it's hard to blame him. Why should he take such a career risk?

How Clickability Wins Customer Confidence

At its core, every great company sells confidence. As a vendor, your job is to lower uncertainty as much as you can. You need to make your potential customers feel that they're going with a safe, low-risk solution. In other words, you need to make them feel confident that they're making the right choice. You need to make the product or service easy to buy. The easier to buy the product is, the easier it will be to sell

Confidence can take many forms: it can be safety in numbers, going with the leader (or potential leader), risk-assurance of a backup plan should the product fail, of getting their money back, etc. There are many things you can do to make the potential customer feel that she's making a safe choice with your product.

Selling confidence is more necessary (and difficult) when you have a new technology or when your company is small or new. When times are hard, we instinctively turn to safe, tried-and-true solutions. The collapse of the Nasdaq in 2001 turned the information technology purchasing world into such an environment. IT shops ran away from new or small vendors and went back to the large, tried-and-true providers such as IBM, SAP, Cisco, and Oracle.

Clickability was a small and innovative company that prospered in this tough IT environment Clickability grew from one to 150 paying customers during 2001-2004, one of the toughest IT purchasing environments in recent memory. How did Clickability do it? They understood the risky nature of the purchasing process. They had a great product but first and foremost they sold confidence. "We do our homework to understand the customer and their pain. Then we go overboard in our attempt to make them feel comfortable with our people, our company, and our solution," says John Girard, CEO and co-founder of Clickability.

There are several things that a technology vendor can do to overcome the perception of the inherent risks of innovation adoption.

Product tests

Clearly your product needs to work. More important, the prospective customer needs to believe that the product is going to work specifically for her. Functional risk might be allayed by having the product tested and results published. The more complex the working environment in which the technology is going to live the more you need to perform product tests. Independent third-party testing is a good way to start.

Prospective customers will usually place more trust in independent third-party tests and opinions than in verification vendors themselves provide. So vendors need to make sure they work with the leading product-testing organizations in their industries.

PC Labs, for instance, is one of the better known product testing outfits for personal computer software and hardware. Its results have been followed by millions of users throughout the years. Certainly, this type of testing works if your product is in a packaged-type product category. Newer categories or more complex types of products need to rely on other methods of lowering uncertainty. Back when distributors, analysts and the media would not give Apple Computers the time of day, the company decided to open their own retail stores to showcase their new products and innovations. They had several test machines where potential buyers could listen to and test these new machines. This hands-on experience turned out to be a great method of lowering the uncertainty of potential buyers in new Apple products such as the iPod.

Technology users have been "burned" many times by companies over-promising features, capabilities, and timeframes. "Be honest when your product is not a fit. In those cases just recommend someone else," says John Girard, CEO of Clickability. "Whenever they have a problem they will come to us first and give us a first shot at solving it."

Honesty may be a refreshing way to differentiate your company!

User testimonials

Few things make people feel more comfortable than knowing that others like them have used and are happy with a given product. The more complex and new a product is the more this is the case. Use real customer testimonials liberally in your marketing and sales literature. For instance, go to the websites of Salesforce.com and you will probably find a customer quote on the home page. Even a billion-dollar company like Siebel used testimonials. An example print ad featured Pierre Gagnon, President and CEO of Misubishi Motors North America. He was quoted saying "Siebel helped us realize a savings of $3.7 billion." A testimonial from the CEO and Chairman of one of the largest auto manufacturers in the world carries quite a bit of weight. What Siebel is saying is: "if he is willing to risk his reputation to endorse a third-party product then it must be really good, right?" It's all about selling confidence in Siebel!

If you sell a complex product you probably want to have "case studies" that detail the infrastructure of a happy customer and how your technology was used to resolve a specific problem. It's important to say how your product fit into the over-all infrastructure and why it would work with other complex situations.

Opinion leaders

In many categories, opinion leaders can make or break a product. An endorsement from an opinion leader can literally move markets. This is especially true with new products or categories.

There are opinion leaders in each product category. Finding opinion leaders and converting them to your cause is so important that I think it's a Fundamental Rule in and of itself (see Rule 9 Convert Champions not Deals). Here's one example of opinion leaders making a difference in the life of a product or company. If you make personal technology, some of the most followed opinion leaders are David Pogue, the technology editor at The New York Times, Walter Mossberg, of The Wall Street Journal, and Stephen Manes of Forbes. Whether your product is the Handspring Treo, Adobe Photoshop Album, or XM Satellite Radio, you can do much worse than getting a positive review from Mossberg or Pogue.

When, in 1992, Mossberg recommended America Online over Prodigy (which then had almost ten times the number of subscribers as AOL) it "really helped put AOL on the map," admits founder Steve Case. "It turbocharged our growth."[87] Sales of spam filter Mailblocs *tripled* the day after Mossberg endorsed the product in 2004. CNET's stock went up 33% the week after Mossberg endorsed this service, and XM Satellite Radio's stock went down 8.5% the day he blasted the poor design of their car radios.[88]

Customer references

Few things make people feel more comfortable than knowing that others like them have used and are happy with a given product. The more complex and new a technology is, the more this is the case. Use real customer testimonials liberally in your marketing and sales literature.

You need to use fresh, current references who are using your latest product. The more these references are like your prospect, the more impact they will make. That is, the more similar the business is and the more similar the situation you are solving is, the more the prospect will feel comfortable with your solution.

"It's not really valuable to talk to a happy user from three years ago," says Clickability CEO John Girard "We have our prospects call customers at several stages of the product deployment lifecycle."

Software development, like sausage and politics, can have an ugly, messy development and integration process. Prospects may wonder how your company will handle that process.

"We use references from customers who are in the customization phase. They are not even installed. The reaction we get is: "You mean in 8 weeks I can have a working technology like that? Wow!" The impact in terms of confidence in our ability to deliver is huge."

More than 80% of corporate IT spending goes to maintaining existing systems rather than purchasing new products and services. "One of the prospect's biggest fears is what is going to happen after the development team leaves. Who is going to take care of the inevitable technical glitches?" To allay that uncertainty, Clickability has the prospect talk to a reference customer who has been using their product for two or three months. That gives them the confidence of knowing what they are going to face at that point in time.

Serve tough customers

There is credibility in your ability to serve the "tough" customers. These are the individuals or organizations that are well known for their ability to be tough to satisfy. They are technically savvy, their infrastructure might be complex, they will push your products and services to the limits.

"If you pass the test for a Wall Street Journal or CNN, most companies will think your product will work for them," says Clickability's Girard. "It's not just that they are big, well known names. They have a reputation in the publishing industry for doing thorough technical analysis and testing and pushing vendors to really perform both before and after deployment."

Tough customer's businesses will help you get on the consideration set of others in the market. It can also change the conversation from product quality to deal quality.

Market share

Technology adoption is a social process. The majority of the market feels safety in numbers. There is an incredible virtuous cycle that accrues from being the market share leader. As you gain market leadership you gain more customers--which adds to your market leadership. If you're on the other side of the competitive fence, you'll see this as a "vicious cycle." The less market share you have, the more customers "jump fence," and the fewer new customers you get. This makes you lose even more customers.

"Now that our customer base has grown to 150 customers the sales process can be different," says Clickability CEO John Girard, "prospects feel confidence that we are a solid company with a solid product. They feel that if all these large companies run their businesses using our technology infrastructure, we can be a safe choice for them too." This doesn't cinch the deal by any means, but your company can get into the consideration set of "safe" solutions to buy for the prospective customers. Some of the technology, product and company risks are mitigated.

That there is safety in numbers is no secret to marketing communications professionals. Remedy has used this type of advertising for its "Service Management Solution." They mention the number of users (10 million) that access their product from their 9,000 installations worldwide. They mention their 312 alliance partners who can come to the rescue of the customer's infrastructure. Their goal is to lower prospect and user uncertainty–to make them feel that they are in good company. Just like "no one got fired for buying IBM." Remedy wanted the prospect to feel good that "no one got fired for buying Remedy SMS.

Interestingly, the Remedy ad campaign said nothing about the product itself. No bits, bytes, speed, or size. It didn't even say what the product did! Remedy was just selling confidence that the prospect would be in the company of thousands or millions of like-minded people.

Financial guarantees

Lowering financial uncertainty is sometimes a good confidence booster. This is especially true of products that are hard to measure or in new categories where a clear leader has not emerged. To alleviate uncertainty, some companies let you try the product for free for a certain period of time, say 30 days. After that time you can buy it or disable the product. Clickability offers its clients a money-back guarantee if their software and integration doesn't work as promised.

"We're so confident about our product that you won't pay anything until two months after you've used it," says CEO John Girard.

Have credible allies and partners

If your company is small, or you are in a new product category, the market may also judge you by the company you keep. If you have the ability to attract solid credible partners, that credibility may extend to you too.

A partner is someone who will vouch for you and introduce you to potential opportunities. A partner is not a logo on your website. The problem with many tech companies is that they fill up their websites and marketing materials with logos from "partner" companies who are not really partners. This may have worked in the 1990s, but prospective customers and the market know better now and have wizened up to this fact.

"Don't have your venture capitalist investors call a potential customer," says Clickability's John Girard. "They have no credibility anymore. A lot of technology buyers got really burned by VCs in the 1990s and they still remember." Many entrepreneurs also remember that VCs would push products from their other portfolio companies when making a sales call. "They are really over-rated as a sales tool," adds Girard.

Clickability uses customers as allies. "Our customers will call a prospect and say something like: 'I understand you're having this problem. We had a similar problem and here is how Clickability helped us,'" says Girard. This is of course a bold move because unlike vendors, customers have no obvious financial stake in whether Clickability wins a new contract. "We go overboard for our customers. Just like we do the right thing by them, we trust that our customers will do the right thing." This is selling confidence at its best!

Free trials

A free trial is a traditional way to lower the financial risk for the potential customer. They can use the product for a period and purchase it only when they're convinced that it will work for them. Note that this is not the same thing as a money-back guarantee.

Alphasmart has an evaluation unit program so teachers can test their education computers free of any charge. Free means free: Alphasmart doesn't even charge for shipping the computers. The company considers this trial program so important that it has two full-time dedicated people working on this program, and there are more than a thousand units on free trial at any given time. Some companies offer a free "light" version of their products and then ask you to pay money for the versions that are "loaded" with features. They may also offer that "free" version to individuals but ask corporations to pay for the "enterprise" version. ZoneLabs did that with their ZoneAlarm personal firewall, which resulted in more than 30 million downloads.

I acquired a new laptop computer to write this book. I wanted to transfer all my software, documents, and settings from the old computer to the new one. I found a company that promised to transfer everything to my new computer or I wouldn't have to pay anything. I downloaded their program for free and transferred all my files. Only after I was satisfied that it did what it promised did I pay the asking price. There were a few glitches, but after only a few hours I was up and running with my new computer.

That was well worth the price.

Simplify–contain complexity

The more complex, expensive, or newly developed the technology is, the likelier that things may go wrong in actual deployment. The longer the customization timeframe and the more pieces that have to be integrated, the likelier it is that things will go wrong. This breeds uncertainty about you and your product. You can increase confidence in your product or service by reducing its complexity.

Clickability delivers its projects in at most twelve weeks. This short timeframe improves the likelihood that they will succeed. Success brings with it confidence on the part of the customer that this vendor will deliver. This in turn brings more business to the company. A virtuous cycle is thus started with your ability to deliver on simpler better defined projects.

Be standards-agnostic (or compatible)

Your technology product should either be the standard, support the leading standard or promise to be compatible with whoever wins the standards race. This promise will instill confidence in the buyer that their purchase will not go the way of their Betamax library or X2 modems. Lack of standards will likely slow market adoption in a given market. No one wants to have to spend money maintaining a legacy system that is incompatible with new and improved technology.

When Alain Rossman started Unwired Planet in 1994, he had a vision of creating a Netscape-like browser for mobile phones. After developing the first working version of the protocol, he started shopping it to mobile companies like AT&T, Nokia, and GTE. Getting the dozens of manufacturers and service providers to agree on a standard proved to be a tough undertaking, but Rossman knew that for his company to succeed he needed to be compatible with whatever standard would win. Since he had created a protocol, it might as well be the one to win. Instead of battling it out he decided to publish his protocol, now called Wireless Application Protocol, or WAP, and put it in the public domain. Adoption took off and soon almost 100% of all mobile phones in the world ran WAP-compatible software.

Unwired Planet became phone.com which soon went public and became OpenWave. This company's software has been installed in more than 600 million phones and the company achieved $291 million in revenues in 2004, with a market valuation around $1 billion.[89]

Be an expert

Being an expert in the product category that you are selling instills confidence in the prospective customer. There are several mechanisms to convey expertise. As Nobel-prize winning novelist Gabriel Garcia Marquez said "No one will remember you for your secret thoughts!"

Speak at industry trade shows. Whether you are on industry panels or deliver a technical talk, speaking engagements are low-cost, high-impact ways to get you in front of the customer and prospect. They can see your knowledge and public persona and start creating a relationship even before you know it. When you speak publicly, talk about interesting topics. Don't just talk about the same tried-and-true and don't just push your product. "Bringing interesting topics positions you in a more creative light which makes you more attractive as an expert," says John Girard. By the time you approach them your personal expertise has already been established.

Publish white papers.-- they show your expertise to the world at large. This is especially important when your product belongs in a new category and prospects need to be educated on the subject. They implicitly trust your expertise to teach them what they need to know. Again, be careful not to turn white papers into just product propaganda.

Write for trusted publications. "You need to be where the prospects are," says John Girard. "You need to be in the magazines that they read. In our industry, *Editor and Publisher* is a small publication but everyone in our market reads it."

Start and/or be on the board of standards associations. "Being an expert places you above just being a product pusher," says John Girard, "it builds confidence that you know the big picture, and that today's products are just part of that roadmap."

Keep your promises

The American Heritage Dictionary defines confidence as *"trust or faith in a person or thing."*[90] You build trust when you keep your commitments. Starting with the small things you build confidence that your word and your commitments are important and that you will follow up and deliver. When you later promise the big things, like product suitability and project delivery times, you will have already built up trust and confidence that you will do what you say.

"Following up is simple but is very rare in the industry," says Clickability's John Girard. "If you say during a conversation that you will email a follow-up document by Friday, then do it!" Part of the process of establishing trust is having people take responsibility early in the process. As the company starts a conversation with the prospective customer, Clickability will introduce the "project manager." In truth, the project manager won't be needed until a deal has been signed and the customization project has started many weeks or months later. In practice, having a known person throughout the process creates continuity that is hard to achieve otherwise. It also introduces someone who is responsible for the company keeping its promises. This builds long-term confidence.

Communicate professionally

Larger and more established companies usually have a protocol for communicating with prospects and customers. These protols have been built over time and have been generally proven to "work." These professional communications, albeit frustrating sometimes, instill confidence that the buyer is dealing with an established company. Smaller companies and startup companies that communicate with prospects in more informal (read: unplanned and sometimes careless) ways may be missing a simple way to be perceived as a solid and professional organization.

"We have highly professional communications with our customers," says John Girard. "We keep detailed minutes of our conversations. This shows that we are actually listening." The company kept a master document with every single conversation between the company and the prospective customer. "The front section lists every single contact made: calls, meetings, points discussed, and conclusion. This shows how the communication has progressed." This document was attached to proposals. "Proposals have a way of going around their company and reaching folks we may not even know of. This detailed document frames our relationship and gives them context and historical perspective. It shows who has been involved and to what extent." It also shows that there has been progress from the first meeting.

An important element of communications is language. This may be obvious but many companies miss it. Your target market may have a vocabulary of its own, whether it is healthcare, engineering, or publishing-industry-specific. You need to learn this vocabulary and use it in your communications. It shows you're not just a neophyte but you do know your prospect's industry.

Be a leader!

Companies don't purchase technology–people purchase technology. Human beings instinctively follow leaders (many times to our detriment). If you want to be perceived as a leader then you need to be a leader. You should have integrity, confidence, and boldness. You should be trustworthy. You should have true strength born of convictions, and not be afraid to put yourself on the line for those beliefs. You should want to show the way.

"I believe that hosted applications will comprise the majority of new software licensing in 10 years. I say it in public without any doubts because I truly think that's what's going to happen," said Clickability's John Girard. "I give my customer my personal guarantee that they won't be sorry they chose us. We will do whatever it takes to gain and keep your trust. We will be there after the sale and after product deployment for you."

On November 2, 2004, some of Clickability's customers' websites received record number of hits. The highly contested United States presidential election was expected to be a tight race. I called Girard late that evening and he was at company headquarters working round-the-clock with his engineering team. He wanted to make sure his customers' websites didn't miss a beat while working under the heavy loads. His engineering team appreciated his leadership and his customers probably did too.

Hold open contests

In 1993 RSA Data Security was a small company in Redwood Shores, California that developed encryption technology. It was in the business of helping its customers keep their data secret. The RSA encryption algorithm promised to encrypt a text and render it illegible to all but the most committed and wealthy hackers. RSA Labs was comprised of several math PhD's whose only goal in life was to research and prove the security (or insecurity) of encryption algorithms. However, would you trust RSA's own laboratory to tell you how secure their algorithms were? If you were a large enough user, you would probably perform your own tests. What if you weren't? Who could you trust?

In 1993, RSA did what was then unthinkable: it invited everyone to break its algorithm. It published the encrypted text of the RSA-129 (consisting of 129 digits of text) and held an open, worldwide contest. The encrypted text looked like this: 1143816257578888676

69235779976146612010212967212423625625618429357069352457
3389783059712356395870505898907514759929002687954354[91]

Hackers of the world unite! The company offered to pay $5,000 to the first person or group who could break it. What ensued was a global race with groups from Russia to France to Australia spending countless hours and computing resources to decrypt the RSA text. The beauty of an open contest like this one is that the winners will communicate exactly what kind of resources it took them to break the code. In this case, it took 600 people in more than 20 countries 8 months and 5,000 MIPS (million instructions per second) of computing power to decipher the text.[92] To do this, they had to connect thousands of volunteers' computers around the world to use their spare computing power. Was RSA management self-destroying? Not at all. The way the RSA encryption works, if you extend the encryption "key" a single digit, it would double the security, if you extend it two digits, it would quadruple it, and so on. After the code was cracked in April 1994, potential users knew that it would take 5,000 MIPS to break RSA-129, which could be extended to 10,000 MIPS to break RSA-130 and 20,000 MIPS to break RSA-131.

An open, public contest did more to sell confidence in RSA's technology than any of its own employees could possibly have. Partially as a result of these contests, RSA was widely adopted as the security standard for financial institutions around the world. Electronic voting companies take note!

The prescriptions discussed above, some of them quite simple or obvious, taken together should go a long way to help you instill confidence in your prospects and customers.

RULE 5 SUMMARY: IT'S A RISKY WORLD. SELL CONFIDENCE!

Technology products may be difficult to understand, deploy, and use. They may also be difficult to test. Many new innovations are "experience products," which means that the products need to be experienced before you know how good they are.

Users are taking many types of risks in adopting new technologies. Some of the risks include: financial risks (am I going to lose my investment in this product?), technology risks (is this technology going to work at all?), standards risk (is this going to be the winning standard?), execution risk (can this company do what it says it will do?), company risk (will your company be around next year?), legal risks (does this product comply with regulations?), and public relations risks (am I going to look bad to the world if I use this technology?).

Considering all these uncertainties involved in adopting new innovations and technologies, your main job is to sell confidence. The higher the risks involved for the customer, the more you need to work on selling confidence in your company and product's ability to solve the customer's problem. The more complex the product, the smaller your company, the more difficult the integration into the existing infrastructure, the more uncertainty there might be in your ability to deliver. Whatever you do needs to lower customer uncertainty about your technology product or service.

Some of the actions you need to take may include third-party product testing, using customer testimonials, gaining the endorsement of opinion leaders, serving "tough" customers, giving financial and other product guarantees, having credible allies and partners, offering free trials, being standard-agnostic, simplifying the product or service delivery project, keeping your promises, being an expert, and most important, being a leader.

RULE 6
CONVERT CHAMPIONS NOT DEALS

"If there's lots of technology, we won't understand it."

- Warren Buffet

"It is not raw numbers that we've gone after; it is those key people who would attract a network of users."

- Konstantin Guericke

LinkedIn was a provider of an online business network based in Mountain View, California. It was founded in May 2003 at a time when there were dozens of other companies offering some type of social or business networking. Two and a half years later it had grown to about 4 million registered users. This number made it the leader in a category that had grown to include more than 50 players[93]. The company had no sales department and a marketing staff of two people. They had never paid to promote its service beyond hiring a small public relations firm to generate publicity. A full 97% of LinkedIn users joined as a result of a direct personal invitation from other users. Only 3% have joined by going to the website and registering without an invite (possibly because they read an article or heard about it from a colleague).

LinkedIn, like most technology-based businesses, had users who championed its cause. "During the critical first six months 8% of the users have brought in the other 92%," said co-founder and Marketing Vice President Konstantin Guericke. "They were what we call 'Power Inviters.'" While the numbers were satisfying, it was the quality of the users that gratified the company management. "It is not raw numbers that we've gone after; it is those key people who would attract a network of users."

The story of how LinkedIn went from being a late entrant into its marketplace to being the acknowledged leader is described later in this chapter. It is a story of how a bright set of founders used several smart strategic marketing rules to pull their company ahead of its rivals. Importantly, they were determined from the beginning to use champions as a strategic asset.

Technology product or service adoption is a social process. Buyers look at others for guidance before adopting new technologies or for validation that they have made the right purchasing choice. This is especially true of technologies that are hard to evaluate or innovations that challenge the status quo. When decision-making conditions are tough, potential users look to experts' advice, and at what their peers are buying and using. By investing their money in influential users and opinion leaders, technology companies can multiply their chances of success. These "champions" can further leverage the vendor's marketing and sales dollars by serving as guiding lights to the marketplace, encouraging others to adopt the vendor's specific technology or standard. By lowering customer uncertainty, champions can also help accelerate adoption speed. As we will see later in this chapter, Paypal's whole product partner, eBay, was its main champion. LinkedIn's "power inviter" users were the company's champions. Starmine's champions included media such as Forbes and Yahoo! Microsoft's new product champions included software programmers. Look around your company and you may find champions in the most unlikely places.

Let's review some concepts and tools that are available to the product strategist before coming back to how LinkedIn used them to create a winner.

ADOPTION OF INNOVATIONS IS A SOCIAL PROCESS

When in doubt, human beings usually look to others for guidance before making decisions. The newer and more complex the new product, technology or innovation, the more we're in doubt and need reassurance. Furthermore, there are so many new products and service categories to choose from! Even if we wanted to do research before purchasing every new item we buy, there's not enough time in the day to do it properly. Uncertainty seems to rule our decision-making life.

Have you noticed how the more packed a restaurant is the more it seems to attract patrons? What about the converse: the emptier it is the fewer people want to go there? One of my favorite little restaurants in San Francisco is a Chinese eatery in the Chinatown district called *House of Nanking*. It's always packed. Day in and day out there's a line of people who are willing to endure heat, cold and rain in order to eat there. What makes this even more interesting is that there are other restaurants next door that are mostly empty. They are clean and inviting. Furthermore, there are literally dozens if not hundreds of restaurants just around the corner. There is a similar (albeit magnified) phenomenon in high technology markets.

Here's the conundrum: a full restaurant gets fuller and an empty restaurant gets emptier. How do you turn an empty restaurant into a full restaurant? Clearly, at some point the House of Nanking or PayPal or LinkedIn had no customers. They were empty. How did they go from empty to full? More to the point: how do you get a market to adopt your new tech-based product?

We look for leaders and experts to help us make decisions. We talk to our friends or peers and read newspaper reviews to decide what movie or concert to go to. We read *Consumer Reports* before buying a high-definition TV. We see what performance artists are wearing as guidance to buying our clothes. We look closely at bestseller lists and movie reviews and opening numbers.

TECHNOLOGY AS MAGIC

Arthur C. Clarke, who wrote more than 70 popular science and science fiction books and the screenplay for the Academy Award-winning film *2001: A Space Odyssey* said that "any sufficiently advanced technology is indistinguishable from magic." An exaggeration? Hardly! Warren Buffet is arguably the most successful American investor of the 20th century. Starting with $10,000 in 1956 his 30% stake in Berkshire Hathaway (a fund he still runs) has grown to $43 billion, making him one of the world's wealthiest people.[94] He has amassed this wealth by buying into companies like Coca Cola, Gillette, and Capital Cities/ABC. He has six clear acquisition criteria for the companies he acquires. One of those criteria is that he won't buy technology companies. He says: "If there's lots of technology we won't understand it." This despite playing poker with his friend Bill Gates.

GE's Global Research Center, home of Nobel-Prizewinning scientists and groundbreaking inventions like the MRI (Magnetic Resonance Imaging) and Solid State Lasers used to be called the "House of Magic." Technology is by definition complex and getting more so. A version of Moore's Law, which famously states that the complexity (or price/performance) of semiconductors doubles every eighteen months, seems to apply to many areas of technology these days: semiconductors, networking, light emitting diodes, software, genetics, or biotech. Semiconductors grew by about 1,000,000 times in complexity the last two decades and were predicted to grow by the same amount over the next two decades. Nathan Mhyrvold, Microsoft Chief Technology Officer, has said that software expands until the growth is limited by Moore's law.[95] The Windows operating system, already bursting at the seams with tens of millions of lines of code, was still growing in size by more than 30% per year!

New pharmaceuticals and medical treatments are no different from integrated circuit (IC) technologies in this respect. Consumers don't understand what about them makes them work, what the potential side effects are, and how they compare with existing cures. They hear horror stories about side effects: will it improve my heart problems but burn my liver? How will it work with other medicine I'm using? The news reports about Vioxx, the arthritis pain medicine that Merck recently recalled because the drug had been shown to double the risk of heart attacks and strokes in long-term users. According to CNN, "adverse reactions to prescription and over-the-counter medicines kill more than 100,000 Americans and seriously injure an additional 2.1 million every year."[96] Is it any wonder many people are afraid to adopt new prescription drugs, especially from smaller companies?

Our PCs are populated by an endless stream of ever more unintelligible programs: virus protection, spam filtering, wireless networking, spyware, adware, and channel encryption. Most users don't understand what these programs do or how they do it anymore. Making decisions on what to buy and who to buy it from is very difficult and risky. This is especially true of innovations. What's this new new thing? Why do I need it? Who can I buy it from? Will it work with what I've got? What damage can it cause?

Many vendors don't make it any easier on tech users. I recently uninstalled a spam protection program only to find out that it was still attached to my email software program. I couldn't get rid of the darn thing! Resistance is futile!

This is why choosing what technologies to adopt is hard for most mortals. As the world gets more complex, we have less and less time to do proper product research. We feel we have lost control. The explosion of the web means that the information to base our decision on is there somewhere. The problem is that it's hard to find the right information and to trust the source of the information. Uncertainty rules the day when adopting into a new product category. How do we make decisions?   We look for sources of certainty.

Think back to the restaurant in San Francisco's Chinatown. Most new customers there went there for one of four reasons:

1. They read about it in a travel guide or restaurant review (a trusted source).
2. A friend told them about it (trusted source).
3. They saw the crowd and assumed it's a good (or at least safe) place.
4. They looked in the window and saw customers they identified with who displayed signs of gastronomic happiness.

Notice that in all of the above cases, prospective customers looked at what others were doing or saying before making a purchase decision. In the first two cases, they appealed to trusted sources, in the third case to the collective intelligence or the safety of crowds, and in the last case to happy peers. The decision-making process for technology adoption is not very different from the above. Whether we're looking to adopt a new Business Process Management System or a virus protection program, we look at what others are doing. At best, we assume they must know what they're doing. At worst, there is safety in numbers. Psychologists call it "Social Proof."

SOCIAL PROOF

Buyers look to others for guidance before adopting new technologies or validation that they made the right purchasing choice. This is especially true of technologies that are hard to evaluate or innovations that radically challenge the status quo. They look to experts' advice, and at what their peers are buying.

Think about it. We all know someone we call when we need advice on what to buy. Digital cameras? My friend Alex just bought one after extensive research. I'll ask him. Spam filtering? Cindy down the hall is always tinkering with such programs. Vitamins? Fred takes them; let me ask him!

Every group has influencers and opinion leaders that many members look up to, reference, or trust before making a technology adoption decision. Identifying and converting your target segment opinion leaders can be one of the surest ways to wider adoption. It's a much better use of your marketing dollars than blanketing the whole segment with promotional material. Who are the opinion leaders in the market segment you are targeting? There are probably a few dozen of them in each market segment. They might be the analysts, media columnists, industry pundits and academics, industry leaders, standards group leaders, opinionated individuals, and writers. Examples of opinion leaders include Walter Mossberg of The Wall Street Journal and David Pogue of The New York Times, newsletter pundit George Gilder in networking technologies, and Linux creator Linus Torvalds for open source technology.

Marketing to champions and opinion leaders is not a high-tech specific strategy. Take the wine industry. Consumer uncertainty reigns supreme in the wine business. There are thousands of brands with tens of thousands of unique variations in their wines. Not many of us can tell the earthy spiciness from the longer finish, the depth and complexity from the sweet-to-acid balance. Even if we made an effort to know our wines, guess what? It is all going to change next year! We have to repeat the process again! How do we choose? We ask the expert! American wine critic Robert Parker probably exerts as much influence in the wine industry as any individual does in any other sizeable global industry. Popularity and prices of wines from

Napa Valley to Bordeaux to South Australia are determined by Mr. Parker's wine ratings.

Music also has its opinion leaders. For instance, music critic Ben Ratliff of *The New York Times* exerts huge influence on what succeeds in jazz in the United States.

Finding and influencing opinion leaders is so important in high tech because of the inherent speed of high-tech market development. Multiply high uncertainty and high speed and you get high tech consumer angst. Markets develop so quickly that successes as well as mistakes get magnified. Mistakes can mean a quick death. Have your product endorsed by key opinion leaders and you have incredible wind behind your back to build life-giving market momentum. Lose that endorsement or get a negative one and you have much more work to do to convince a skeptical marketplace.

Let's look at two important concepts that will help us realize why speeding up market adoption of your product is so important in technology: critical mass and network effects.

CRITICAL MASS

National Geographic Traveler magazine runs a photography contest every year. Keith Belows, the magazine's editor, wrote in December 2004 that "just three years ago...90% of our photo contest entries were shot on film. This year? About 20%."[97] Digital photography technology had been improving for a couple of decades but hadn't made a major dent in the film business. Sometime after reaching 10% or so of the market, it achieved critical mass. It then took only three years for this technology to topple film and dominate the market.

Critical mass is the point beyond which adoption of an innovation is a self-reinforcing process. Before your product reaches critical mass you focus on generating demand. Once critical mass is achieved user adoption can just explode. Your company would then focus on fulfilling demand--a totally different ballgame! This is the process that fills up the restaurant and helps keep it that way. Conversely, innovations that fail to achieve critical mass can fall into a death spiral-- the process that empties the restaurant and helps keep it that way. Once the market achieves critical mass the adoption uptick can be astonishingly quick. It took LinkedIn 15 months to attract its first million users, 6 months to attract the next million and then 4 months for the next millionth user to sign up.[98]

You have probably heard that this or that tech product has "viral" qualities. The reason is that behavior of markets is very similar to the growth of viruses and bacteria. After long and seemingly slow growth, a market achieves critical mass and user adoption just explodes – demand seemingly feeds on itself. The mathematical curve mapping that behavior is called the "S-curve." (This curve is also used for mapping technology price/performance improvement).

Time	New Bacteria	Cumulative Bacteria Count	% ot Total Capacity
0	1	1	1%
1	2	3	2%
2	4	7	4%
3	16	23	13%
4	32	55	32%
5	64	119	68%
6	32	151	87%
7	16	167	96%
8	4	171	98%
9	2	173	99%
10	1	174	100%

FIG. 6.1 – BACTERIA GROWTH NUMBERS

The dotted line in Fig. 6.2 is the "S-curve". It represents the sum total of all bacteria. The solid curve underneath it is the "Bell-curve" or new bacteria. These curves are used to represent the technology adoption lifecycle. The "S-curve" would represent all market adopters while the "Bell-curve" would represent new adopters. Notice that in the beginning the curves rise slowly. Look at the percent of Total Capacity column in Figure 6.1. It is the equivalent of the percent of the market who have adopted a product or technology. It takes three time cycles to move up to 4% market adoption. Time cycle equivalents would be quarters, years, or decades. Over the next three time cycles market adoption just explodes. First it triples to 13% and then it bursts up to 32% and finally doubles again 68% market adoption. In just three time cycles two thirds of the market adopts the technology. Then it rises smoothly over five time cycles to reach 100% market adoption.

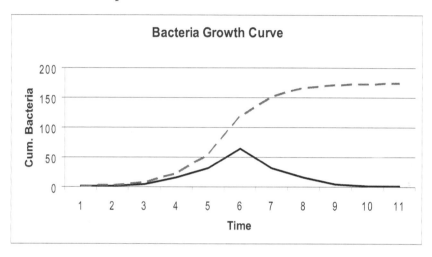

FIGURE 6.2 – BACTERIA GROWTH S-CURVE

The Microsoft Internet Explorer vs. Netscape Navigator fight is an example of how these vicious and virtuous cycles work. In 1995 Navigator was the de facto standard-setter and leading web browser. Navigator still had near market dominance (90%+) when Microsoft unleashed version 2.0 of its Explorer browser in 1996. By the time Microsoft came out with version 4.0 in October 1997, Netscape still had 72% of the market vs. 18% for Microsoft (and 10% others.)[99] For Netscape it was downhill from there. Microsoft had not just caught up technically; it hit critical mass. Microsoft garnered tremendous momentum and by the middle of 2000 its share was above 65%–vs. 30% for Netscape [100]–on its way to garnering more than 90% of the market–versus less than 5% for Netscape.

NETWORK EFFECTS

To understand network effects, think of the telephone in its initial days. One telephone is basically useless. If there's a second telephone user, then you can call one person. Once a third user adopts, then each existing user can call two people. By the time a tenth user joins the network, each user can call nine other people, and the total combination of possible calls is about 90. Once the millionth person joins, there are just under a trillion (exactly 999,999,000,000, if you really want to know) possible phone calls. Note two things: the first is that each time a new user adopts the telephone the value of the network increases for existing users. Secondly, the value of the network increases exponentially. The formula is calculated to be around $N^2 - N$, where N is the number of users.

The issue with the telephone network is that every single user needs to be using compatible technology standards. Anyone who is not is shut out of the network. Other technologies for which network effects apply include fax machines, email, and operating systems. Network effects are the main reason you might be stuck with a Windows PC (whether you like it or not) and can't swap it for a Macintosh. Most software and hardware companies develop only for the Windows platform, not for the Mac.

This means that network effects almost guarantees a winner-take-all market. That's why you see so many high technology companies with products and services that have huge market share: eBay, PayPal, Microsoft, Cisco, and Oracle, to name a few. Network effects may also mean that a specific standard (not a product) is the winner. In the 1980s and 1990s there were many different private email standards, such as Compuserve, Minitel, and AOL. The winner, however, was the public Internet email system based on Internet Messaging Access Protocol (IMAP). While there was one email technology standard that won it all, no individual company did. The reason was that the winning protocol was an open, not proprietary standard.

HOW LINKEDIN BUILT A WINNER

When LinkedIn was started in May 2003, its founders had a tough nut to crack. There were more than two dozen companies within the business networks market that they wanted to enter. The founding staff made a decision that they wanted to focus on business networks market rather than "social" networks. The latter field was already too crowded and companies such as Friendster.com were growing their membership into the millions. The business network field had many entrants but no clear leaders. Ryze.com was thought to have the most members (40,000). LinkedIn's founding team thought that neither Ryze.com nor any of the other competitors was anywhere near the critical mass or the momentum to run away with the market. They thought that no one was providing the value that would attract businesspeople to sign up to an online network.

How did LinkedIn go from a horizontal tool to an Internet site where business people could find value and conduct business? Marketing Vice President Konstantin Guericke was a LinkedIn co-founder and was a member of that original strategy team. The question that Guericke and the LinkedIn strategists wanted to answer was: How do we develop a service that is valuable enough to a business audience for them to come and register and find attractive enough that they will invite their business peers, associates and friends to the network? The team went to work

To answer this question theLinkedIn team had to consider three aspects of a network:

1. Growth: the size of the network–how many members have joined the network. This is what externally most people measure. You need to have a critical mass of members so the network is useful.

2. Usage: how often the network is used. Are members using the network every day or once a month? What are they using it for? You want to have high usage members, that is, members who respond to a reasonably high number of inquiries generated by other members in the network.

3. Revenues: how much money is the company making from the network? Needless to say you want high revenues and margins.

These three aspects of a network can sometimes be in conflict with the goals of the company. At the end of the process the company wanted to build a sustainable business with high revenues and margins. That means it was looking for a large number of users who would make high use of the network. The company would therefore prefer to have a member that invited 30 people who would use the network a lot than 1,000 members who did not. The desirable members are those for whom relationships matter and for whom an online service would facilitate trusting business transactions that they already performed offline (introductions, hiring, business deals). They were turned off by "networking" and the online equivalent of gladhanding. The use of the network for gladhanding would further prevent users from adopting an online network. Of course, when you start a network, you don't have this problem.

The company decided that it would focus on each one of the three critical aspects in three stages:

1. First it would focus on growth, and work to create a network that could achieve a critical mass of members.
2. Then it would focus on usage, and work to create a higher-value network for high-usage members.
3. Finally, it would focus on generating revenues from the network.

Breaking down the evolution of the company through the network lifecycle was a great first step. Not many tech companies include a strategic vice president of marketing when first designing its product or service. However, a healthy dose of experienced paranoia about high tech evolution led them to assume the competition had gone through a similar analysis. LinkedIn resolved to do to launch their enterprise quicker and better. They understood that the nature of networks is such that there could only be one winner. Everyone else would be shut out.

The original question then became: how do we create a network service that will generate growth (the first step above) without diluting the future value?

They decided that they would start by focusing geographically in a business area they all knew well: the San Francisco Bay Area/ Silicon Valley. Things move very fast in this area: ideas, technologies, products, people, and money come and go before most of us have had the time to digest lunch. Engineers, business managers, salespeople, investors, consultants, recruiters and other service providers, are usually on the lookout for new opportunities. Was there anything that was common amongst these diverse groups? LinkedIn management concluded that entrepreneurship and jobs were the staples of the business conversation in Silicon Valley. The next big thing always seemed to come from a new company, whether it was Cisco, Intel, Yahoo!, or Apple. These companies were the ones who would provide the job and wealth opportunites that many were after. "Entrepreneurs start the companies that generate the jobs that people are looking for," said Guericke. "If we could attract the entrepreneurs to our site, they could attract the people who were looking for new job opportunities." The latter would in turn attract the job recruiters who were looking to connect with both the hot new companies who were hiring, as well as the employment seekers.

Recruiters would probably derive huge value from the ability to get candidate leads and check references. Recruiters get paid a hefty commission for finding engineers and managers--up to the equivalent of about three months of the employee's yearly package. Recruiters would probably pay dearly for the ability to both post job opportunities and for quickly and effectively finding employees and getting them hired.

How would the company find the recruiters who would adopt this network? According to Guericke, in 2003 there were an estimated 160,000 job recruiters in the U.S. This market was quite fragmented, since recruiters specialized in narrow fields like medical staff recruiter, financial services recruiters, software developer recruiters, and so on. Guericke and the product strategy team thought that recruiters would follow job seekers, who would in turn follow entrepreneurs.

Attracting entrepreneurs was then the key to the growth of the network. But finding them is hard. What are most entrepreneurs looking for? Capital to start or grow their startup companies. In Silicon Valley this usually means venture capital. The answer seemed to be getting clearer: LinkedIn needed to attract venture capitalists (VCs) to its network. VCs are easy to identify and find. There are lists of them. For instance, the National Venture Capital Association website (http://www.nvca.org/members.html) has the names of dozens of VC firms and links to their respective websites, which in turn have the names of their general partners prominently displayed.

The new question became: how do we attract VCs? How do we create value for them?

Just like the recruiters mentioned above, venture capitalists are in the people business. For instance doing due diligence on potential investments is an important part of the VC workflow. Due diligence involves fact-checking assumptions about the business plan, people, and opportunity that VCs are looking into. This means they have to check the backgrounds of the executive team they want to invest in. They haveto check their assumptions about markets they usually know very little or nothing about. They need to talk to industry or functional experts, and hire consultants to help them review the assumptions of the company business plan, review the underlying technology, patents, and so on. All this work involves finding and talking to people. The ability to help VCs find these people so they can perform due diligence quickly and effectively would be very valuable to them.

Venture capitalists also have outsized influence in Silicon Valley. They are seen as experts in the industries they invest in–even when they have no experience working in those industries. Their words are spread by the media as gospel. They are invited to industry panels, entrepreneurship events, and academic meetings. Furthermore, many VCs receive hundreds if not thousands of business plans every year. Most of these plans go unread. The only way most VCs will even consider reading one is if it's recommended by someone within their network. VCs can pull in this network, which in turn can bring in the entrepreneurs network, which in turn can bring in job seekers and everyone else. Venture capitalists, in other words, could be the perfect champions for LinkedIn's network.

Both Venture capitalists and job recruiters would find the network extremely valuable and would likely pay to use it. LinkedIn decided that they would build a product to attract two main audiences: Venture capitalists and job recruiters. VCs would be its main champions. Entrepreneurs would go where VCs are. Job seekers would go where entrepreneurs are, and job recruiters would go where job seekers are. The team went to work.

Finding Your Champions

Champions can help you grow your business faster and further. They multiply your marketing efforts and give you credibility. Champions can make a huge difference in technology markets that move quickly. Who can be your champion and where can you find then? Just as LinkedIn did, finding and converting champions should be an integral part of your product development and marketing strategy. Look around you. Champions can be found in many places within your business ecology, including users, partners, media, newsletter editors, and leading practitioners. For instance, leading practitioners are important champions. General Electric's Healthcare is a $14-billion division that produces medical imaging, diagnostics, monitoring, and information technologies. They mainly sell big-ticket items to large hospitals. Hospital purchases tend to be influenced by well-published medical researchers, especially from leading medical institutions like Massachusetts General, Mayo Clinic, Johns Hopkins, and Stanford. GE Healthcare has a board of advisors of exactly this type of doctors who help the company develop new technologies, products and services. This group of "luminaries"[101] act as both an early-customer sounding board for GE's products, and later as experts and opinion leaders.

Users

Many of your customers will be promoting your products directly or indirectly. Directly by actively telling others what the product is and why they should buy it; indirectly by being reference customers and helping to generate a critical mass. Think about it, would you trust what your peer or friend who uses a product or service you are considering adopting says, or what the vendor says? In today's world, people would likely discount many claims made by vendors. People instinctively trust their peers and friends. That's precisely why they're friends! They instinctively trust their opinion leaders. That's precisely they choose to follow them! Product users are the best champions a company can have. They can recommend your products within their companies, professional groups, and peer networks. As we saw in the case of LinkedIn they can also attract a whole network of users.

Microsoft has invested in an army of insiders who act as Microsoft champions within their companies. Microsoft is by far the world's largest software development company. One of Microsoft's greatest assets is its Microsoft Developer's Network (MSDN). MSDN is a multi-billion dollar infrastructure that Microsoft has used to support and encourage millions of developers around the world who are developing software that is compatible with and dependent on Microsoft. MSDN provides education, tools, software samples, downloadable programs, and nearly everything MS programmers need to run their IT shops. By giving full support to MS programmers, Microsoft has created a cadre of customers who go beyond just using their products. These programmers champion Microsoft products within their companies, throughout their personal and professional networks, and to their clients and partners. Microsoft could not hire better salespeople if they tried.

Leading practitioners

In any given industry there are practitioners that are early adopters of technology. They may work at companies that are fairly open about sharing--or even boasting about--success stories. They are not shy about saying what technologies or processes they used to achieve advantage over their competition. They go to trade shows and conferences and speak at panels. More conservative (or late) adopters will look to these leading practitioners before considering adopting a new product or service.

When Alphasmart was a small startup educational computer company working to get the word out, they seeded about a dozen free evaluation units to select industry leaders. This was an extremely successful program. Industry leaders such as David Thornberg used to talk about the Alphasmart Dana computer at many national and international education conventions. He truly believed that this was an important technology for educating children. This publicity was priceless at a time the company had no money to pay for it.

You should go to trade/industry conferences frequented by your target customers. Look at the speakers list and find them there. Furthermore, look at the proceedings from the last year or two to find leading practitioners of years past. They may be working on new projects and therefore on the lookout for new technologies. They may also have changed jobs and be looking for the next big thing to help their new organization and get on the road again.

Partners

Your partner can also become your number one champion. In 2005 Paypal was the Internet payments industry leader. Founded in 1998, they entered a market that had seen a number of e-payments technologies such as DigiCash, CyberCash, and Mondex fail. Several technology consortia like Visa and MasterCard's Secure Electronic Transactions also failed to gain any traction. Paypal soon became the standard payment mechanism by finding not just a channel partner but a mighty champion: eBay. The online auction king promoted the payment system to its millions of users and Paypal soon became the standard form of payment for eBay users everywhere. These users in turn took Paypal everywhere else online they went, and this form of payment became the standard for person-to-person online payments. Paypal became so powerful in this market that eBay's later efforts to develop and promote its own payment system (BillPoint) as an alternative all but failed. In 2002 eBay gave up on BillPoint and decided to acquire Paypal and its 45 million account holders for $1.5 billion.[102]

Media experts and industry analysts

Starmine found champions in both the traditional and the online media. Starmine was a leader in the financial analyst measurement software category (see Chapter 3). Founded in 1998, it entered a tough market with many competitors with longer histories and deep funding. It quickly established its presence in the financial services industry with its "Bold Estimates" predictions. CEO Joe Gatto was so confident that his software would predict surprises in earnings announcements that he started publishing them beforehand. *Forbes* magazine started featuring them in September 2000, and Starmine soon became a magazine staple. Not only do Starmine's target customers read *Forbes*, their customers' customers also read it! With *Forbes* as its champion Starmine soon gained other powerful media that not only uses its software but which in turn act as champions for yet more prospects. Talk about influencing a target from several angles: no sooner had *Forbes* published Starmine's data than Yahoo Finance and the San Francisco Chronicle started carrying Starmine's earnings surprise predictions.

There are opinion leaders in each product category. Finding media opinion leaders and converting them to your cause can be a huge shot in the arm for your company. For instance, if you make personal technology products, two of the most followed opinion leaders are David Pogue, the technology editor at *The New York Times*, as well as Walter Mossberg, of *The Wall Street Journal*. Whether your product is the Handspring Treo, Adobe Photoshop Album, or XM Satellite Radio, you can do much worse than getting a positive review from Mossberg or Pogue. When, in 1992, Mossberg recommended America Online over Prodigy (which then had almost ten times the number of subscribers as AOL), it "really helped put AOL on the map," admits founder Steve Case. "It turbocharged our growth."[103] Sales of spam filter Mailblocs *tripled* the day after Mossberg endorsed the product in 2004. CNET's stock went up 33% the week after Mossberg endorsed this service, and XM Satellite Radio's stock went down 8.5% the day he blasted the poor design of their car radios.[104]

Newsletter and weblog editors

Many high-tech pundits (and self-appointed pundits) write newsletters. Some of them are sent for free–via email, while others have paying subscribers. When George Gilder recommended Excellera in his *Gilder Technology Report* on February 17, 2000, the company's stock (XLA) shot up from 32 to 48 within hours. Three days later it stood at 68, and in March it hit 111.[105] Surely, the winter of 2000 marked the height of the stock market bubble and as of this writing XLA was a penny stock. Still, the mere mention of the XLA stock by Gilder's newsletter moved the market to triple the price of a stock within a few weeks. Newsletter editors can have huge influence with technology purchasers, media, and investment markets. Companies that may have been too risky to do business with, may suddenly become certified "safe" because an opinion leader like Gilder praises it in his report. Of course, as a company manager your goal is to achieve market leadership, not to pump your company's stock. God knows, there are too many executives, directors, and venture capitalists who have crossed ethical or legal boundaries between company building and stock hawking, and too few have landed in jail instead of the corporate boardroom. That said, the truth is that investors, pundits, buyers, media, and policymakers have become more intertwined. Sometimes you don't know where one ends and the other begins. Because of this permeability of spheres of influence, it is important for you to have champions across the board. In technology markets many of these pundits are respected as opinion leaders and move markets.

Academics

Champions and opinion leaders have the ability to bring bigger market champions to companies large and small. You may find your champions writing, teaching, or doing research in academia.

Alien Technology co-founder and former CEO Jeffrey Jacobsen was a guest lecturer in my high tech strategy course at Stanford University in 2002. As much as he loved to speak in my class, he called me twice that quarter to reschedule his presentation due to meetings in Boston. What was he doing there? I found out when the press release went out months later. Alien Technology was a company that made RFID tags–microscopic versions of the sales tags found in your books, audio CDs or shirts. For Alien Technology to succeed as a company, RFID tags had to be adopted across a supply chain large enough to need not just millions, but billions of tags. As a startup company, Alien didn't have the resources to convince hundreds of companies to adopt its technology. Someone else did: Gillette. When Alien got a purchase order from Gillette for 500 million RFID tags[106] the world took notice. What was remarkable about this purchase order was that it came early in the lifecycle of this technology and made Alien an instant leader in the category. Alien got not just a customer, but also a champion.

How did Alien gain the credibility to talk to, let alone sign up Gillette? A champion in academia: Massachusetts Institute of Technology. Alien worked closely with MIT's Auto-ID Center to create an open standard for RFID tags. That gave tiny Alien a seat at the same table as giant Gillette–which is headquartered in Boston not far from MIT. Gillette was a top supplier of Wal-Mart, which in turn was the largest retailer in the United States, with just about $258 billion in sales in 2003, or about 2.6% of the whole US economy. When Wal-Mart decided to use and require the use of RFID in its supply chain infrastructure, Gillette was ready to recommend Alien as a key supplier. One of the most influential information technology users on earth soon highlighted tiny Alien for hundreds of the largest IT buyers in the world. Finding a champion in academia helped Alien find bigger champions who helped the company become a market leader.

Industry analysts

Industry Analysts are an obvious place to find champions. Analyst influence is of two kinds: first, they directly influence buyers when they endorse specific products, technologies, or standards. Secondly, they influence other influencers; for instance they are quoted by the media when they write about the space. Given the panoply of new technologies, products, and services and the fast change in the industry, and the high stakes involved, many buyers look to these specialists and experts for advice and guidance. A whole industry of analysts has developed around the need for technology product advice. In information and communication technologies (ICT), some of the most influential companies include IDC, Gartner, Forrester, Meta, and Giga. Their analysts generally specialize in specific markets and technologies and develop frameworks that can help facilitate their understanding. Some of them develop forecasts that extrapolate industry growth into the future.

Gartner's Magic Quadrant, for example, is anticipated with hope and apprehension by legions of technology vendors who depend on good ratings for their sales success with more conservative buyers. A high mark means getting additional deals and a poor mark can mean longer phone calls to prospects explaining why analysts "don't get it" or why their latest product overcomes the analysis shortcomings. The "sweet spot" is of course to be on the upper right quadrant, where the vendor is classified as a "leader" in both "completeness of vision" and "ability to execute" (whatever that means!). Remember, the market likes to go with the leader and the opinions of these analysts do matter. For smaller vendors converting these analysts can provide an additional boost in their quest for market leadership. While some analysts have lost credibility, they still exert remarkable influence amongst many buyers, especially the more conservative ones.

RULE 6 SUMMARY: CONVERT CHAMPIONS NOT DEALS

Buyers look at others for guidance before adopting new technologies or validation to assure themselves that they are making or have made the right purchasing choice. This is especially true of technologies that are hard to evaluate or innovations that challenge the status quo. They look to experts' advice, and at what their peers are buying and using.

Technology markets have characteristics that make it important to achieve market leadership quickly. Network effects basically guarantee winner-take-all markets. Second place in a network means being shut out of the network. Understanding the importance of generating critical mass is critical for the tech strategist. Given these dynamics in tech markets, it is important that you gain market leadership as quickly as possible. Champions can help you do this.

Champions come from many sources and they may change over time. Technology companies multiply their chances of success by investing their promotion money in key users and opinion leaders,. These "champions" can further leverage the vendor's marketing and sales dollars by serving as guiding light to the marketplace and encouraging others to adopt a specific technology or standard. By lowering customer uncertainty, champions can also help accelerate adoption speed.

LinkedIn is a provider of a business network that successfully made use of the tools in this chapter to achieve market leadership. They developed a service that would attract champions who would generate increased demand and eventually critical mass. They understood the importance of network effects and used it to beat dozens of other companies that aspired to the market leadership prize.

RULE 7
CHOOSE THE RIGHT PARTNERS.
MANAGE THEM WITH CLARITY

"An alliance should be hard diplomatic currency, valuable and hard to get"

- Walter Lippman

"My words establish contacts by being spoken and create isolation by remaining unspoken"

- Ludwig Wittgenstein

F5 Networks was a Seattle-based provider of Application Delivery Networking products that made Internet-based applications (from companies such as SAP, Oracle, and Siebel) run faster, safer, and with decreased downtime. When F5 Networks started its partnership program in early 2001 the company's share price was in the midst of a dizzying slide from above $100 in early 2000 to its crash-landing at $3.75. Its revenues were moving sideways ($108.7 million in 2000 and $107.4 in 2001), but its net income sank from a positive $13.7 million in 2000 to a loss of $30.8 million in 2001– a swing equal to about 40% of its revenues. Prospective customers, who had built excess computing and communications capacity in the late 1990s, became more demanding of their information technology suppliers. The purchasing environment had become hostile. F5 needed help.

Fast forward four years. By the end of 2005, F5's stock had climbed by an order of magnitude back to 56, its annual revenues had more than doubled and were on their way to $251 million, and its net income swung back up to $61.2 million. How did F5 do it? With a little help from their friends. During that time "we became embedded in our partners," said Vice President Jim Ricthings. Certainly, the market had recovered and the purchasing environment became less punishing, however that was not enough to account for their dramatic recovery. In 2005, F5 Networks's partners contributed about 50% of the company's product revenues, up from less than 40% the year before, and from single digits four years before that. Much of the improvement in F5's financial and market position was due to its partnership programs. F5 created the right partnerships and managed them with clarity.

BodyMedia was a company in Pittsburgh, PA, that made wearable body-monitoring technologies and products. Their products, worn like armbands, collected physiological measurements such as heat flux and heart rates in patients outside the clinic environment. This enabled monitoring of a patient's patterns up to 24 hours a day (instead of just for a few minutes during a doctor's visit). But despite a clear need in the marketplace, stellar technology, and a crack founding team, they had trouble gaining market traction and raising venture capital.

In 2003 BodyMedia management decided to change its strategy, making partnerships the cornerstone of the company's business model. For the foreseeable future, BodyMedia would only develop products and enter markets with select partners. The latter would provide the market knowledge that BodyMedia needed to complement its product development skills. Just a year later, in 2004, BodyMedia, which had fewer than 20 employees, was able to strike partnership deals with multi-billion dollar companies like Roche Diagnostics and Apex Fitness group. By partnering for the right reasons, BodyMedia was able to successfully penetrate markets that would otherwise have been out of its immediate reach.

HOW BODYMEDIA AND F5 NETWORKS PARTNERED TO WIN

What made F5 Networks and BodyMedia's partnerships work so well? Mainly two things:
1. They partnered for the right reasons.
2. They managed the partnership with clarity.

Partnering is as fundamental and essential to the success of today's high tech company as any other function of a company. Middleware software vendor BEA Systems' partners brought in 40% of its revenues in 2003. "This includes systems integrators like Accenture Ltd. and BearingPoint Inc., hardware vendors such as Intel Corp. and software vendors such as Documentum Inc., Siebel Systems Inc. and E.piphany Inc."[107] F5 Networks got 50% of its product revenues through partners in 2005. Siebel Systems' partners brought in 75% of its licensing revenues in 2001. BodyMedia brought in virtually all of its revenues from partnerships in 2005. These are substantial portions of any company's revenues. While the "right" percentage of revenues to be derived from partnerships varies, it is safe to assume that a successful partnership program can make the difference between winning and losing the battle for market leadership. Maybe even the battle for the company's very existence.

The rest of this chapter will delve into some of the "right" reasons for partnering and how companies can manage partnerships successfully. First, we start with the basics: what a partner really is and therefore what a partnership should be.

What Is a Partnership?

"Partnership" may well be one of the most abused (or misused) words in Silicon Valley. If you are to believe the slew of company speeches, promotional material, websites, or press releases, it seems like most technology organizations have a partnership with everyone else in Silicon Valley. Both smaller and larger companies contribute to this confusion.

In the 1990s for most Silicon Valley technology companies engaging a partner meant writing a press release. Little else would happen after announcing these "partnerships." Company management then wondered why the partnerships floundered and immediately went on to engage other "partners" on similarly fuzzy terms. Some partnerships did work for a while and then faltered when the original business development managers left. Institutional knowledge of the relationships resided in the brains of these engagement managers.

Very few companies had formal partnership programs. Even fewer could remember what the main purpose of any given partnership was in the first place.

Business development managers at some major companies were compensated according to the number of partnership deals they closed. The deals' terms were so mushy that even the company's own contract attorneys had a tough time understanding what the purpose of the deals were. Once the contracts were signed and the press releases were out the door, the "business development" managers were off signing other companies. Who could blame them? They were paid by the number of deals not the eventual success of the "partnerships." Companies hoped a few of these deals would be successful so they could claim, in hindsight, how smart they were in signing them up. Similarly many executives of smaller technology organizations would happily tell you that they had not just a "Partnership," but a "Strategic Partnership" with industry leaders, like Cisco, Intel, and IBM. If you looked at the communication materials from the larger companies you'd see that they didn't even mention these smaller companies.

Where was the disconnect? Lack of communication? Probably in the definition of partnership itself. Partnership is oftentimes confused with "relationship." A partnership is a type of relationship, but not every relationship is a partnership. Relationships run the gamut from transaction-based to the more permanent. What separates the former from the latter are the goals shared, the degree of mutual commitment, the governance principles established, the amount of resources invested by each party, and the degree of intimacy involved. Your company may have a relationship with basically anyone it does business with. The organization might have a transactional relationship with a company such as Office Depot, Federal Express, or Intel. You purchase a service or product, pay for it, and go back to work.

To paraphrase Walter Lippman, a partnership should be "hard diplomatic currency, valuable and hard to get."

F5 sells 85-90% of its products through external distribution channels. That is, organizations like value-added resellers (VARs), distributors, and other third-party agents and brokers move most of F5's boxes. This means that F5's distribution strategy is an essential component of its corporate strategy. Are all of its distributors strategic? Or, for that matter, are any of its distributors also partners?

Might they just be outsourcers of a logistical function in which F5 does not specialize?

Ingram Micro represented 19% of all of F5's business in the June-end quarter of 2005. This is a high number for F5. Should Ingram not do its job well, F5 would certainly suffer. Does this make Ingram a partner? Not necessarily. This may just be a high-revenue distributor for F5. We need to dig deeper into the relationship to see where the partnership might lie. You have a partnership with a company with which you work closely–uncomfortably close together, even intimately–to accomplish a mutually shared goal. The degree of intimacy between companies is one way to measure a partnership.[108]

There is a continuum that starts with a transactional relationship, like purchasing a router or memory upgrade kit, all the way to a merger where two companies become one. In between you may have gradations of relationships: transactional exchanges may morph into relational interactions, which can grow into some type of alliance, which can develop into a partnership. The strongest type of partnership would be a company acquisition or merger. Fig. 7.1 is a simple way to visualize the "Relationship Continuum."

Relationship Continuum[109]

Transactional: at its most basic level a relationship entails just a straight exchange of goods or services.
Relational: this type of relationship involves continued interactions over time.
Alliance: companies share some business goals.
Partnership: involves interdependence and a high level of management, legal, financial, technical, operational, and marketing commitment.
Merger: partners become "one."

FIG 7.1 RELATIONSHIP CONTINUUM

When you hear someone say they have a "partnership" with Intel, think about the relationship continuum in Fig 7.1. Do they think Intel and the company are "interdependent"? In most cases that's unlikely. Given Intel's more than $30 billion in annual revenues, the partner would need to be quite large to be interdependent. They could be dependent on Intel, but not the other way around. Microsoft, however, would fit the bill as a partner with Intel, as would HP or Dell.

Does this mean no small company can partner with Intel? Not at all. We can also look at a partnership from the point of view of a product category. If your company is addressing a potentially huge (or "disruptive") opportunity that a large company sees as strategic, your small company is a good candidate for partnership with the big boys and girls. For instance, at the turn of the millennium Intel was working on a new wireless product strategy for a standard called WiMax, which was planned as the next generation of the then existing WiFi (wireless fidelity) standard. Revenues from WiMax technology were comparatively negligible, given Intel's more than $30 billion in revenues. However, Intel has staked a large claim in the wireless arena. If your company could turn itself into a key to making Intel successful in that new category, then you could say that you were partners with Intel, despite the low impact you might have on the company overall. You could even say you were a "strategic partner"!

Craigslist, for instance, could have been viewed as a strategic partner of eBay when the latter decided to purchase a 25% stake in the former in 2005. Craigslist was then an 18-person company (with about $1 million in monthly revenues), while eBay's revenues were about 1 billion dollars per month. At the time, eBay saw the whole "community" category as a key strategic growth area. How strategic? eBay founder Pierre Omidyar himself joined Craigslist's board of directors to learn as much as possible from the leader in the category.

PARTNERING FOR THE RIGHT REASONS

Many companies feel that they need to fill the "Partners" tab in their website with an impressive-looking list. They know that this might "sell confidence" and impress investors, prospects, and the media. It hardly matters that these "partners" might be contributing little to their success in the marketplace. It looks good in the press release, but that's not enough. About 80% of joint ventures and 70% of acquisitions fail to add shareholder value, according to author and management consultant Chris Zook.[110] How do you improve your chances of partnering for success? Winners start by partnering for the right reasons. These reasons change according to the many internal and external factors that make high tech strategy so dynamic. Generally speaking, a company should partner when that is the most optimal way to help it accomplish its mission. In high technology markets gaining market leadership is the name of the game when deciding to engage in a partnership. This is especially true in market categories where there are network effects–that is, winner-take-all markets.

Below is a list of some of the best reasons to form a partnership, though this is not exhaustive. Most of them are reasons for partnerships that help a company win an existing market or enter a new one, and therefore overlap. For instance, if a company wants to enter a new market, it may want to do so by taking its own products and then partnering to develop a whole product, or it may want a partner to create a joint product.

Partner to create the whole product

Customer needs are getting more complex and high tech markets are developing faster and faster. Your company needs to win customers and market share as quickly and effectively as it can. Creating and delivering the whole product to your core target market can be the best way to gain market leadership and it may just be the most important reason for a high tech company to develop a partnership. This is especially true in the early stages of the adoption lifecycle.

When F5 Networks started its partnership program, most of its sales were directly to customers. From the customer's point of view, F5's Application Delivery Networking products (as well as the competition's) were not standalone products. They were part of a "whole product" or service. Customers saw F5 as an element in the provision of key applications from companies such as SAP, Siebel, and Oracle. In other words, the customer was not just buying F5's core product; they were buying a way to enhance the larger whole product. Conceptually, F5 had to be "embedded" in the larger application. Once F5 management realized this, it became obvious that they needed to partner with the big application providers. Partnering in this case meant that they should develop and test technologies together, and that they should bring their customers together to create a joint customer base. As mentioned before, by the end of 2005, partners contributed about 50% of F5's product revenues.

In many cases, partnering is the only way for you to win in the marketplace. If F5 had not created its partnership programs, it is hard to see how they could have doubled their revenues or achieved the market penetration they did. It may not have been possible to penetrate so many large accounts, integrate F5's software into their infrastructure, train the end users to use its products, and grow revenues 100% in such a competitive marketplace. F5's partnerships lowered the perceived risk level for prospective customers to adopt its products. For instance, Siebel Systems officially supported only one company for its Siebel 7 platform: F5 Networks. This meant that Siebel and F5 had worked together to integrate their products and test them together in both laboratory and real-life situations. By partnering right and being part of Siebel's whole product, F5 could truly sell confidence!

Partner to enter new markets

Entering new markets is a key strategic skill for growth companies. Making decisions as to which markets to enter and how and when to enter them can make the difference between winning and losing the battle. Partners can help a company enter and win in new markets. This is especially true when a company is entering markets that it does not know well, such as international markets. It is also true when it wants to enter a new market with a brand new product line (which is always a more difficult undertaking).

BodyMedia's corporate strategy is based on partnering to enter new markets. The company focuses on creating a technology platform that can be uniquely modified to address the needs of many market opportunities. When the company decided to enter the European market, they started in Italy and signed up Sensormedics Italia, a medical equipment distribution company. Sensormedics started out as a simple distributor, and as their successes with the BodyMedia products accumulated, Sensormedics became more immersed in the opportunity. Sensormedics and BodyMedia became engaged in product development work for the European market. Sensormedic went from being a mere local distributor to a partner intimately involved in all market activities. Sensormedic helped BodyMedia enter a new market by creating a new whole product. It educated BodyMedia staff on the particulars of European health care systems, helped develop new products, helped find distributors across the continent, train them, and coordinate sales, customer service, and marketing activities.

Partner to create joint products

BodyMedia CEO Astro Teller knew that the company's wearable bio-metric monitoring system could be used in the fitness market. As brilliant as his team was in developing technology, he knew that he needed a partner to develop and market products for this market. He found it in Apex Fitness Group. In 2004 Apex was providing products and services to more than a thousand health clubs in America and had revenues in excess of $500 million dollars. The two companies collaborated in developing the bodybugg, a wearable monitor that tracks calories burned, body temperature, and other exercise data that can then be uploaded to a weight-management system on the web. Apex provided the customer and market knowledge that BodyMedia needed to develop a successful product. Furthermore, Apex had the brand name and distribution channel to place the bodybugg at gyms and retail stores where exercisers could test and buy the product. In return, BodyMedia provided the technology and development savvy to create a product to generate incremental revenues within Apex gyms nationwide.

Was this strategic for Apex? Apex was a hundred times larger than BodyMedia in terms of revenues at the time. Normally, when the difference in size between the companies is this large, the quick answer would be no. In this case, the answer was yes. Apex needed to differentiate itself in a marketplace that was highly commoditized. It needed to offer value to its customers beyond the traditional fitness products and services that the industry offered, and it needed to transform the way the industry did business. As of November 2005, about half of the Apex Fitness Group's valuable homepage (http://www.apexfitness.com) real estate was taken up by services around the bodybugg. There was no doubt about the product's importance to Apex! Both the larger company and the smaller one benefited from sharing their different yet complementary expertise.

In late 2005, Intel CEO Paul Ottelini announced the creation of a joint venture with Micron Technology to make NAND flash memory for consumer products such as iPods.[111] Why would the leading semiconductor company in the world want to partner with a former competitor? Sometimes the best–or only–way to enter a new market is through partnerships. IM Flash Technologies, as the new venture was called, "enables us to rapidly enter a fast-growing portion of the flash market segment," Ottelini asserted. The flash memory market was then dominated by Samsung, which had more than 50% of the market. Each company invested an initial $1.2 billion and committed to at least another $1.4 billion to help the new venture succeed over the next few years. To further assure that they would get a healthy toehold in this market, IM Flash Technologies signed a $500-million deal with Apple Computers to supply NAND memory for the fast-growing iPod product line. The deal was signed before the first chip rolled out of the new venture's facilities. Intel partnered to enter a new market with a new joint product.

Partner to gain market share

Partnering to gain and increase market share is a good strategy if market share can lead to market leadership. High market share is a prerequisite for but not an assurance of market leadership. In fast-growth markets it is not always clear what the final rules of the game will be, so engaging in partnerships to substantially increase market share is usually the correct strategy. However, in mature markets with low switching costs or barriers to entry, market share may not translate into market leadership. Many companies may make the mistake of partnering to gain market share in battles that both are losing. If they're both slipping separately, it's not clear they won't continue to slip together. In this case, the likelihood of success and therefore justification for partnering is diminished.

Take HP. Both HP and Compaq were in a long-term losing battle for market share with Dell Computers. The Dell juggernaut seemed to be unstoppable. Its units sold and revenues had risen inexorably almost since the company inception. Just in the years between 1995 and 2001, Dell grew its revenues from $5.3 billion to $32.2 billion, and its net income rose from $260 million to $2.2 billion[112]. Compaq had acquired former giant Digital Equipment Corporation and got mired in integrating two companies that were totally different in character. Compaq had also acquired "big-iron" company Tandem and was at a loss as to how to integrate it into its business. Having been distracted from its core PC business, Compaq lost the battle for market share to a far more focused company: Dell.

HP saw a chance to increase its market share by acquiring a still-struggling Compaq in 2001. From the beginning it was not clear that just winning marketshare was positive for HP. Walter Hewlett, one of the company's largest individual investors, the son of one of the company's legendary founders and a director on the HP board thought it was a bad strategy. A legendary board of directors' war ensued. Battling Mr. Hewlett was the acquisition's main advocate, CEO Carly Fiorina and the (remaining) board who approved the deal. In the end HP investors cast more than 1.7 billion shares and voted 51.5% to 48.5% to merge the two companies. HP got a temporary bump in market share by merging two companies with sliding market shares. However, they did so in a product category that was mature and had low switching costs, and PC customers continued to switch easily from HP and Compaq to Dell and others. Dell soon regained leadership and again became unstoppable.

Partner to protect your competitive position

Gaining market leadership is the main goal of the partnering exercise. However, sometimes a significant source of that market leadership may be at risk of failing or falling into competitive hands. Worse, your core business may be at risk. If this is the case, partnering may be a good way to protect your core business or competitive position.

In 1996, Apple was having a terrible time building a next-generation operating system. At the time, having a next-generation O/S was fundamental to the very existence of the company. After years attempting to build one on their own (code-named Copland), the company gave up and went out to the market to license someone else's. Apple negotiated with several suitors, including Be and Next. Both these companies had been started by former Apple executives. They had both developed next-generation operating systems that seemed to fit Apple's technical needs. Ultimately, the company decided to acquire Next for $400 million.[113] In doing so, Apple brought in not just an operating system to save its technology platform but also its most strategic and hard-to-replicate resource: Steve Jobs, Next founder and former Apple CEO and cofounder.

In the fall of 2005 Google was the leading search engine in the world. Its main competitors at the time were Yahoo! and Microsoft. AOL represented a significant percentage of Google's revenues, accounting for $382 million or 12% of its 2004 revenues and $422 million or 10% of Google's January-September 2005 revenues.[114] At the time both Microsoft and Yahoo! became interested in partnering with AOL to get some or all of that business. While still growing fast, Google had to protect its AOL flank. The company management knew that they didn't "own" this business: in 2002 Google had replaced Overture as AOL's main search engine. Overture was later acquired by Yahoo! who was also attempting to partner with AOL in order to get back that business. The fall of 2005 saw a beauty contest amongst Google, Microsoft, and Yahoo!, all of whom wanted to partner with AOL to gain its piece of the search market. In December 2005 Google announced that it would invest $1 billion dollars to acquire 5% of AOL.[115] It was a stiff price to pay, but Google had to protect its competitive business.

SUCCESSFULLY MANAGING PARTNERSHIPS

So you have partnered with the right company, and you have also partnered for the right reasons. Congratulations! You're way ahead of the curve. Albert Einstein said that success was 1 percent inspiration and 99 percent perspiration. In order to make your partnership succeed you need to manage it with well. It's perspiration time. Think of your partnership as a standalone business, and you will realize that it needs many of the same resources and tools that make any business successful. And then some.

Managing a partnership is difficult for several reasons. You have no direct authority over your partners. Their companies may have different goals, missions, and strategies from yours, so they march to a different drummer. Cultures may differ. Some companies have highly formalized processes while others are quite informal. Some companies have aggressive cultures while others are more relaxed. Some companies have a longer time horizon while others have a short-term view of the world. These are differences that may or may not be compounded by differences in languages, legal systems, and time zones.

How do winning companies manage these differences? The answer is, with clarity.

Winning companies don't leave success in partnership open to misinterpretation and miscommunication. Below are some of the many dimensions of setting up and managing a partnership. Each aspect needs to be defined and agreed upon upfront in order to make your relationship more successful.

- Clear partnership definitions and responsibilities
- Clear goals and objectives
- Clear communication mechanisms
- Clear management and governance structure,
- Clear resource investment and wins for all
- Clear intellectual property rights
- Clear term of commitment

Let's look at each individual item on the list.

Clear partnership definitions and responsibilities

First of all, you need to define your place in the universe. Who am I and who are you? What do I do and what do you do? What type of a relationship do we want to have? What level of involvement? What type of product or service should each party contribute to the relationship? Where do we engage together–locally or globally? These are the questions that need to be answered upfront. F5 Networks, for instance, offered two types of partnership programs, The F5 Advantage Alliance Program, and the F5 Advantage Reseller Programs. In turn each of these programs had several subsets based on the goals and performance of their partners and allies. For instance, the Advantage Alliance Program had three different types of partnership modes, and each of them has clear definitions as to who does what.

1. iControl Alliance Partner : This was geared to industry-leading application software vendors like SAP, Siebel, and Oracle, to fully integrate and automate their solutions with F5 products via F5's iControl programmatic interface.

2. Technology Alliance Partner: This allowed for a lower level of involvement, i.e., third-party technology providers who wanted to make sure their products interoperated with F5's products.

3. Solution Developer Alliance Partner: This facilitated independent application developers, value-added resellers, and systems integrators in developing applications using F5's products.

Each of the above types of partnerships was geared to a different type of company, and each one offers a different level of integration and involvement. For partnerships to be sustained, there should be clear definitions of the type of partnership, evaluation criteria, qualification requirements, certification requirements, responsibilities, and general guidelines. The more clearly you define each other's responsibilities and duties, the better you can manage your relationships.

Clear goals and objectives

What are your individual, organizational, and mutual partnership goals? Why are you engaging in this partnership? Each company, as well as departments and individuals within those companies, pursue many activities that are important to their business. Winning partners do not hide their goals or assume others already understand their objectives. Write down what the objectives of the partnership are. Be as specific as you can and make sure that the other party understands you. Clear goals give everyone within your organization, as well as that of your partners, goals to target. Along with having clear goals comes clear tracking and management of success. "We have quarterly revenue goals with our key partners and we manage to those numbers," said F5's VP of Business Development Jim Ritchings. There's quite a bit of work to arrive at those figures, so goals tend to be a combination of the strategic and the tactical. "We follow leading indicators such as go-to-market interactions and field interactions." These are the measurements that point to future revenue numbers.

Here are a couple of guidelines to make your objectives more achievable:

- The fewer the objectives the more achievable they are. You may want to have one main objective and no more than two or three supporting objectives. For instance, the main objective of a partnership might be to become market-share leader in your industry. Supporting objectives might be to build the whole product by a certain date, and to develop future versions together.

- The more specific the objective the better. You should know when you are there. For instance, once you have decided that market share is your main objective, decide how you define market share. Is it in terms of the number of units shipped? Total revenues? Number of accounts that have installed it? A clear definition helps all partners create supporting operating procedures to achieve those objectives.

Many partnerships are multifaceted and are built with a multi-year goal in mind. You may be building a new semiconductor, developing a new software infrastructure or taking a new pharmaceutical drug to market. These are all long-term commitments that take many players from multiple divisions of the different partners to complete successfully.

Clear management and governance structure

A management and legal framework might be very important for the relationship to be successful, especially for a complex and important business endeavor. If you think of the relationship as a standalone business you can start clarifying this framework. When starting a business, you ask yourself who is going to manage it, how the revenue is going to be generated and divided up, how the budgets are going to be set, and what types of legal contracts you need to set up and run the business. While not all partnerships need all this level of complexity, it seldom hurts to cover your bases. Here are some of the questions that you may want to think about when establishing and managing a key partnership.

- How is the relationship going to be managed?

- What is the commitment from management? How many hours per week/month/year?
- How are conflicts and differences of opinion going to be managed and resolved?
- What recourse do companies have in case of a dispute?
- What about issues of competition? Are there any non-compete requirements?
- What are the legal bases of the partnership?
- What are the disclosure requirements?

BodyMedia CEO Astro Teller says, "All our partnerships have a project manager on both sides. They are in charge of managing all aspects of the partnership. Their name and email address is published so anyone from either company can reach them with any project questions. They're responsible for managing the development of the product from conception to market, and then they are in charge of marketing activities." The project manager invests himself or herself in the technical market aspects of the product. This manager invests in building personal relationships with the partners to understand them more deeply and solidify the relationship on that level. He or she gets involved in a range of activities, from testing the product with actual users, to looking at revenues and margins.

Clear communication mechanisms

Communication is key to making any relationship work. Many people and companies neglect to work on this upfront. The clearer you are about how to communicate with your partners the better your chance for success. Clear communication will enable you to catch mistakes earlier and set appropriate new courses of action.

When Security Dynamics, a Boston-based company, acquired RSA Data Security, a Silicon Valley company, the differences were stark. RSA was a classic Silicon Valley company in terms of culture: egalitarian, informal, open, and agile. Security Dynamics brought a more hierarchical, formalized, closed, and slower type of culture. RSA strategy meetings were about brainstorming and finding the appropriate course of action. The staff would come up with recommendations that would bubble up to the CEO, who made the final decision. Security Dynamics strategy sessions were more about communicating a previously decided course of action.

A lack of clear communication mechanism between the two companies made this relationship difficult. Setting up these mechanisms beforehand can help avoid misunderstandings due to cultural, legal, historical, linguistic or other reasons. Some of the questions you may want to think about upfront are:

- How often should the parties meet? For instance, you might decide that engineers will have one 30-minute phone meeting every week.
- Who will attend the meetings?
- How many face-to-face meetings will there be?
- What should be discussed? What's off-limits?
- What documents are going to be produced? Budget? Legal? Patent? Status Reports?
- What third-party documents need to be communicated?
- Who is responsible for writing and editing them?
- Who is responsible for checking them?

"When the product is in the marketplace, we meet with our partners once a week," says Astro Teller. "Usually this is a project manager meeting, and they check on mostly business but also technical issues. They review unit sales, revenues, margins, adoption issues, and status of marketing programs. We also touch on non-routine issues to make sure we prevent problems before they happen. We are a small company, so we make sure we keep communications honest and open. During the product development phase we don't generally wait for the weekly status meeting to communicate. Developers need to communicate on an ongoing basis and we make sure that they can do that."

Clear resource investment and wins for all

Define clearly who is going to contribute what and when. You will need people, money, time, and other resources invested over time to make your partnerships work. Whether it is equipment, engineering resources, marketing development funds, intellectual property, or customers, it's important to clarify who contributes what resources upfront and as the relationship progresses. Ask yourself the following questions and craft a matrix of the answers–for each type of partnership:

- What is the price of entry?

- – What are the ongoing fees?
- – How many people from each partner?
- – What are the training and development investment needs?
- – What are the marketing development funds needed?
- – What are the resource commitments from all parties involved?
- – How are revenues going to be divided up? Who gets what when?

"We both share skin in this game," says Astro Teller. "We also design the relationship to be profitable for all sides according to the success of the product in the marketplace."

A partnership is not real unless all parts have a clear win at the end of the rainbow. The way that companies define a win may differ. One company may be interested in revenues, while the other one wants the unit market share, market exposure, or learning experience that the partnership would provide. What's important is that they define what constitutes a win for each. This is important for all parties since good partnerships can only survive if all are winning.

Clear ownership of intellectual property rights

If a tech partnership is even mildly successful, it's likely to generate valuable intellectual property rights for its parties. Intellectual property may take the form of new technology (whether patentable or not), copyrights, trademarks, trade secrets, business process and other skills. An important question to answer upfront is: who is going to own these intellectual property rights? How are they going to be divided and distributed amongst the partners? Just how important is intellectual property ownership? Covering all the bases can be important to the future success not only of your partnership but also of your company.

Back in 1970, a Japanese company called Nippon Calculating Machine Corporation (later Busicom) engaged a one-year-old little-known Silicon Valley company called Intel Corporation to help develop a microprocessor for its 141-PF calculator. For $60,000 Intel developed the 4004, a 4-bit processor that ran at 0.1 MHz.[116] Busicom owned the intellectual property for the 4004 chip but failed to notice how brilliant the technology was.

The Busicom calculator, introduced in Japan in 1971 had limited market success. The company engaged in price-cutting tactics and soon started bleeding cash. Busicom gave the intellectual property for the 4004 back to Intel in late 1971. The 4004 begat the 8008 which begat the 8080. The Intel 8080 was the microprocessor chosen by IBM when it designed its first PC back in 1983. The rest, as they say, is history. Intel has, of course, become one of the most successful companies in high tech history and one of the most valuable companies on the planet.

Looking at another example, F5's leaders, in order to encourage market adoption of its products, decided to publish an Application Programming Interface (API) called iControl. This API makes it simpler for programmers to write software that communicates with F5's products. It also makes intellectual property ownership issues cleaner. Partners can write and own things like plug-ins, test cases, and even whole application programs that are compatible with F5 products, while the latter keeps ownership of its underlying software and hardware. The API creates a clean separation of IP ownership.

BodyMedia partnerships create new technology, products, services, and data. Covering their bases on all these fronts is essential to the success of the company. BodyMedia partnerships can generate millions or billions of bytes of user data. An important question is who owns these data? For instance, BodyMedia created the BodyBugg Calorie Management System as part of its partnership with Apex Fitness Group. When customers use the BodyBugg, they generate streams of data that they can later analyze to assess and monitor calorie usage. Once you compile these data for hundreds or thousands of users, interesting patterns may emerge that turn the database into an extremely valuable asset. Who owns these data? The user? Apex? BodyMedia? "We work very closely with our partners and they are usually several times our size," says BodyMedia CEO Astro Teller. "We always make sure that intellectual property rights ownership issues are covered in detail in our agreements. We cover not just the patents and technology ownership, but also things like data ownership and usage rights, market exclusivity rights, and platform usage rights. We are clear on who owns what and how and where it can be used, and for how long. We can't afford not to be clear on this."

A company partner like Apex, for instance, might own the data generated by the users of the products it sells into the exercise and fitness market. However, BodyMedia would demand to have a copy and the right to use the data at an aggregated (not individual) level. This would permit the company to continue to develop new and better algorithms and to find new patterns in the data that may or may not be related to the Apex field-of-use. Since BodyMedia's other partners might be generating data from diabetes management or cardiac treatment users, the company might find hidden relationships between all the diverse data sets.

As in the case of network-based products, these "network-externalities" will eventually make everyone in the network better off. BodyMedia's algorithms improve and its position at the center of the network becomes more powerful. At the same time, Apex and its users will be able to get additional value from the data and algorithms. If BodyMedia does not have rights in the fitness data, its value in the network will diminish, as will the value of each individual partner.

Clear term of commitment

Things change quickly in the high tech world. Your partner may get acquired or his business strategy may change, the regulatory environment may change, or the importance to you of the partnership may change. It's impossible to predict the future. What you can predict is that not everything will go according to plan. You will want to anticipate some of these issues and build contingencies for the benefit of all parties.

If the project is disbanded before termination, what's the price to be paid by the different parties, and for what reasons? How do you deal with product recall issues? Who supports the product that's released into the marketplace? Who owns what intellectual property? While you can't predict how long a partnership will last, you should try to deal with "breakup issues" upfront.

Even in the scenario where everything goes according to plans, the partnership project will need to have a termination point, perhaps with an option to renew. Once the project is disbanded, it is vital to know what is expected of the parties going forward.

BodyMedia was a young company that went through an early termination of a strategic partnership. Roche Diagnostics was one of BodyMedia's major early partners. A $5 billion company with established brand name and sales and distribution power, Roche worked with BodyMedia to develop sensors for weight loss program patients. Roche invested millions in time, people and money to produce and market their joint product, called HealthWear. After early adoption success in the marketplace, Roche Diagnostics went through an internal upheaval in 2004 unrelated to the HealthWear program. The U.S. Food and Drug Administration had been investigating the company (as well as other large pharmaceuticals), which changed the risk profile of its management and staff. They could not take any risks on new products, especially on offerings that did not promise to make the company the billions of dollars to warrant the risks. The importance of the HealthWear program first went to nil, and then to negative. Roche Diagnostics even recalled the units that were successfully being used in the marketplace. It was a blow to BodyMedia's financial and market aspirations, but luckily management had crafted a partnership with clearly defined intellectual property ownership, including the product and the data. So both companies walked out unharmed, and BodyMedia retained ownership of a product that it can market with other prospective partners. Clear breakup agreements saved both companies from further trouble.

RULE 7 SUMMARY: CHOOSE THE RIGHT PARTNERS. MANAGE THEM WITH CLARITY.

Partnership strategy has become one of the key elements of corporate and marketing success. Today, markets move ever faster, customer needs have become more complex, and companies must focus and specialize more than ever. Partnerships are sometimes the only way to fill the gaps and meet these challenges. In high-tech, the right partnering strategy is essential to a company's success. Companies like F5 Networks and BodyMedia have gone from serious trouble to market leadership as a result of winning partnership programs.

Two factors in these companies' strategies stand out:

1. They partnered for the right reasons.
2. They managed the partnership with clarity.

In high technology the most important reason to partner is to gain market leadership. Partnering to create the whole product may be the best way to achieve leadership. This is especially true in the early stages of the technology adoption lifecycle.

Once you have established a partnership, you need to manage it well. Clarity is the key to making partnerships work. It is essentuial to define and communicate upfront the partnership's objectives, milestones, management, and contingency plans.

RULE 8
DESIGN PRODUCTS AND SERVICES
THAT ARE EASY TO ADOPT.

"Simplicity is the ultimate sophistication"
- Leonardo Da Vinci

"Everything should be made as simple as possible, but not simpler"
- Albert Einstein

In 1996 Netscape burst into the world consciousness, forever changing the face of the information and communications technology world. Within months, more than 50 million people were using Netscape's web browser (Navigator) to auction on line, get news, and trade stocks--including Netscape's own!

Skype Technologies is a Luxembourg-based Internet telephony company. Just one year after it was founded in 2003 it had more than nine million users[117], who had used 1.2 billion minutes of Skype-to-Skype internet phone calls. A year after that, more than 100 million copies of its software had been downloaded and its users had logged more than nine billion minutes. Skype learned and used the same principles that helped Netscape achieve ultra-fast market adoption. By September 2005 the company's software had been downloaded 163 million times and it had 54 million registered users, three million of whom were on the phone at any given time. Revenues in 2005 were estimated at $60 million and were expected to grow to $200 million the following year. Just around two years old, the company was acquired by eBay for an estimated $2.6 billion.[118]

When Apple launched the iPod in late 2001 there were many digital portable music players on the market. Yet, despite being years late entering the market, Apple Computer's iPod became one of the most successful products in consumer electronics history. By the fall of 2005 Apple had sold more than 20 million iPods and had grabbed more than 90% market share.

What enabled Netscape Navigator, Skype telephony, and the Apple iPod to be adopted that quickly? Is there a principle that we can learn from these and other successful products and services that you can use to help your product achieve a faster market adoption than it would otherwise? Yes: these products were designed to be easy to adopt.

How Skype Built a Winner

Once a year I fly to Auckland, New Zealand, to teach a two-day workshop on "Strategic Marketing of High Technology Products and Innovations" to executives and mid-career professionals. In March 2005 I had just mentioned to my class how I had a conference call that morning from Auckland with one brother in San Francisco and another one in Miami. That conference call cost me nothing. A sales executive shared with me and his classmates that he spent about an hour each day talking to the company's new regional representative in Vietnam. These calls were made using Skype's PC-to-PC Voice over IP (VOIP) technology and they all cost exactly nothing. The advantages that Voice-Over-IP (VOIP) or "Internet telephony" technology provided over the existing alternatives were so overwhelming that it was clear to everyone in the class that VOIP was here to stay.

How can you achieve faster market penetration? That's a question that is on the minds of many technology CEOs, executives, and product strategists. One of the most fundamental tasks in high tech markets is designing products that are easy to adopt. This is particularly important in tech markets because achieving rapid market leadership is fundamental to a company's success. To illustrate this I'll compare two companies that started with the same VOIP technology and designed products that achieved vastly different adoption curves: Skype and Vonage.

As of May 2005 Vonage had around 600,000+[119] users, while Skype had more than 50 million.[120]. What accounted for the almost 100-times difference in the adoption rates of these two companies' products? The answer from some analysts might be that this is an unfair comparison since these companies do not belong in the same category. I went to Vonage's website and was directed to some interesting research. The UBS Investment "Telephony and HSD Update for 4Q04"[121] was a 17-page document that sliced and diced the Voice-Over-IP (VOIP) competitive landscape and technology adoption curve. This UBS report mentioned Skype exactly once. The "BroadbandTrends.com" TrendSetter Report for May 2005[122] defined a "VOBB" or Voice over Broadband category where Vonage has captured "35% of the 1.2 million subscribers at the end of 2004." Skype is not mentioned at all in this report. I talk about ignoring competitors who "are not in your category" in Rule 8. Suffice it to say that products within a category do compete with products in several other categories. Ignoring or denying them may cost you your company. For instance, Kodak's film business was decimated by digital cameras. Sure, film is in a different category, but denying that film competed with digital photography technology cost Kodak billions in revenues and market capitalization and cost tens of thousands of their employees their jobs.

There are many reasons why Skype and Vonage have achieved vastly different adoption rates even though they both use the same underlying technology. One of the most important reasons is "trialability." When designing a product or service, ask yourself: how easy is this product to try? Can you try before you buy? What's the impact of a trial on the end user? What are the risks to him or her personally or to the company they work for? The first time I used Skype I was at home in San Francisco talking on the mobile phone with my brother who was in Florida. We simultaneously downloaded, installed, and registered the Skype software on our respective PCs. We then hung up the mobile phones and continued our conversation using Skype. The whole process took less than 10 minutes.

Additionally, there were no risks in trying this service. Both the software and the service (the phone call itself) were free, so there was no financial risk. It took only a few minutes to install and try so there was little risk in terms of complexity. To set it up there was no infrastructure to build, nor was there any infrastructure to rip out. I could keep using my landline telephone for as long as I wanted. If we didn't like the new technology, we could just uninstall the software from our PCs and move on. No damage done. It really doesn't get easier to try a technology than this!

Could Vonage match that? While the underlying technology (VOIP) was similar to Skype's, Vonage had designed a different product. They ask their prospective customers to rip out their existing land line phone and replace it with Vonage's. This is a relatively large leap of faith for most people. Whatever issues many people have with their telephone company, we know that our landline phone service is pretty reliable. I have made (and received) phone calls from Houston during a tornado and from Los Angeles during an earthquake. When my DSL equipment died during the California energy blackouts of 2002, I went back to dialup mode and it worked beautifully (albeit slowly). I went online to find out about the extent of the blackout (not bad), emailed my family to let them know I was OK, and went back to work. Skype was easier to try and to adopt than Vonage, and that was the main reason for the huge difference in adoption rates between the two companies.

APPLE'S IPOD AND THE BIRTH OF THE COOL

D&M Holdings, makers of the Rio digital portable player, anounced in August 2005 that they would exit the business[123]. Rio was one of the pioneers and an early leader in the MP3 player market. This announcement was not really surprising as the Apple iPod had won it all in the category. According to the NPD Group, Apple's market share had steadily increased, surpassing the 90% mark in some areas[124]. NPD Group estimated that companies like Rio and Creative had each a bit more than 2% each (yes, that's two percent each!).

Why did the Apple iPod, a very late entrant to this market, win the digital portable player contest? Some people said it was because the Apple iPod was "cool." Many marketers love fuzzy, undefinable terms like "cool." In thinking about cool, I recalled a brilliant 30-page essay written by Rick Moody in 2004 titled "Against Cool."[125] In an appendix, Moody quotes high school students who define the term as "when you have lots of money and great clothes," and also that "cool is whatever you think it is." Sure there is a "cool" factor attached to some technology products, but I'm wondering if it comes *after* rather than *before* the product is a success. That is, the product is a winner first and then it becomes cool–precisely because it's a winner.

Apple has always had a penchant for "cool." It's part of the company's zeitgeist. Was the Apple Newton a "cool" product? How about the Apple QuickTake digital camera? Clearly Apple's "cool" did not make either one of these products a success. How many other categories has Apple really dominated? The Macintosh computer, as cool as it is, has held no more than a 2.5% market share for two decades. Let's not forget that not long ago, Apple was near bankruptcy, saved by Steve Jobs coming back to run the company and a $150 million cash infusion from Microsoft. Apple's cool had not produced category winners until the company evolved its latest media-centric strategy that revived the company and produced the iPod. Clearly "cool" will only take you so far. MP3 players were pretty good before the iPod came out. The Rio won many design and innovation awards. The Rio even looked (gasp!) "cool"! And yet, the Rio and its many sister products never made it big.

My first experience with the iPod was helpful in understanding the reason for Apple's success. I unwrapped the iPod box, charged the iPod batteries and installed the accompanying software on my Wintel PC. I ran the iTunes software program and set my options and preferences. I inserted a CD of the SFJAZZ Collective (*Inaugural Season Live 2004*) in my PC's CD player. In four minutes iTunes had copied all its contents and started playing the first track on the PC. A couple of minutes later I plugged my headphones into the iPod and was listening to the SFJAZZ rendition of Ornette Coleman's 1959 classic "Lonely Woman."

I had just walked back from a San Francisco Giants baseball game and was feeling content because the team had won its second game in a row (a feat in an otherwise sub-par baseball season.) I felt like playing Tony Bennett's "I Left My Heart in San Francisco." Stopwatch in hand, I ran iTunes on my PC and quickly went to the integrated iTunes store, registered as a user, gave Steve Jobs my credit card number, searched for the song, paid my 99 cents, and downloaded it. What took the longest? There were a couple of dozen versions of the song so I had to choose one. Did I want the "MTV unplugged" version or the "CBS Classics" version? (Wait! Tony Bennett has an MTV unplugged CD? Is Tony Bennett cool now? Really?) I was humming along with Bennett just 10 minutes after I started this process. Mind you, this was the first time I ever used this piece of software. The experience was totally seamless. The iTunes Store was one with the iTunes Player, which was one with the iPod hardware.

Life before the iPod and iTunes combo was a bit different. While the portable digital music players themselves were functional, the process of getting and playing the music was a bit onerous. You had to use software and hardware from different companies. If you wanted to transfer music from a CD, you'd use Microsoft Media Player or equivalent. Then you would manually transfer the files to the MP3 players via parallel ports–a slow and tedious undertaking. If you wanted to download music from the web it was a similarly multi-step process. This all assumed of course that you could find and legally purchase the music.

Not long before I used my iPod, I had transferred a music CD to my PC using Microsoft's Media Player. I got a folder with file names like Track 01, Track 02, and Track 03. Organizing the music was not easy. When I wanted to hear the music, it played the tracks randomly. Nothing wrong with "shuffling" the tracks–when I want to hear it that way. Shuffling Puccini's *Turandot* opera didn't sound quite right. The iPod won because it designed a product that was easy to adopt. In its category it was literally the first plug-and-play product. Apple was the first company to build not just a digital portable player but the "whole product"– every piece of software, hardware, and service needed to enjoy the music listening experience. Before the iPod it was very difficult to start listening to music. The early digital portable players still offered great advantages over Walkman-type CD players. That's why many people bought and used them. Still, they were not designed to be easy to adopt. Rio and other companies saw their product as being the player only. This is usually fine for the very early adopters who don't mind dealing with transferring files by hand or dealing with the idiosyncracies of these products. However, these players needed to evolve, to include other sofware, hardware and services that were not part of the core product (the music player).

Steve Jobs and his Apple product developers understood what the early entrants missed: listening to music is an experience. They designed a whole product that would encompass the whole experience: from transferring music from CDs to PCs to organizing them, and from downloading music from the Internet and paying for it. Apple even built an ecommerce store to make sure there was music available legally and cheaply for its users. Apple's designers built the software to take care of all these steps: transferring music from and to CD's, downloading, playing it on your PC (or Mac), choosing playlists, and finally downloading it to the MP3 player. Every part of the music listening experience was built into the iPod product.

Apple sold its one millionth iPod in June 2003, just about 18 months after its first release in November 2001. Apple had released the iTunes store for the Mac in April 2003. But sales really took off after the company launched the iTunes music player and especially the iTunes store for the PC. While sales of the iPod were good, one could argue that they had flattened during the April to Septermber 2003 period; Apple sold 304,000 units in the April-June quarter, and 336,000 during July-September. The company launched the iTunes player and the iTunes store for the PC in October 2003, which completed the whole product. Sales more than doubled that quarter (Oct-Dec 2003) with 733,000 units shipped, and went up by an order of magnitude to 4.5 million units during the same quarter (Oct-Dec) a year later.

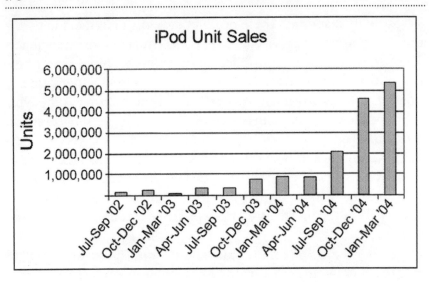

FIG. 8.1 – APPLE IPOD QUARTERLY UNIT SALES[126]

By making the iPod easy to use and adopt, Apple opened up to a whole new marketplace for the category and ran away with it. By September, 2005, the company had sold 22-plus million iPods and half a billion downloaded iTunes songs--achieving nearly total dominance in both categories. Apple had won it all. Cool!

HOW APPLE DESIGNED THE IPOD AND BUILT A WINNER

One of the most important concepts for the entrepreneur and high tech product strategist to master is the "Whole Product (or Service)." The company needs to deliver the customer's product, not the vendor's. Fig. 8.2 shows the traditional way to represent the whole product, in the form of concentric circles. Your product is at the center and it's called "Generic Product" or "Core Product," simply defined as "what you ship in the box." Around the core product you can find concentric circles that represent more expanded customer views of the product. The expected product is the minimum configuration to achieve the buying objective. Notice I say "buying," not "selling." It's what the buyer thinks she's buying. Every product or service is different of course, but the expected product might include things like cables, installation, and web support. The augmented product is the above fleshed out to achieve maximum buying objective. Again, every product is different, but the augmented product might include things like 24/7 phone support.

The outer product ring is traditionally called the potential product. This encompasses room to grow with ancillary, third-party, after-market, and future-oriented products and services. The customer looks under the hood and makes a decision that the company will be around for a while, that it's going to support this product and the channel, that it's going to invest in standards, technologies, and an upgrade path.

Delivering the whole product doesn't mean you have to manufacture every single piece. It means that with a combination of internal and external resources you put everything together in a way that the user finds relatively seamless. Another example is the Blackberry, one of the most successful products in the personal digital assistant space. In this case, the company chose to lease the wireless service from the mobile phone companies, and build the rest of the whole product itself. The interesting thing about this approach is that you look at the product or service from the potential customer's perspective. Here are three things to remember about the whole-product approach:

1. The customer is buying the whole product, not just the generic (core) product!

2. The outer rings are essential to the purchasing process, not bells and whistles.

3. The generic (core) product may be sufficient for early adopters -assuming the product category is in the early stages of the technology adoption lifecycle. This was clearly the case in the portable digital player market before the iPod moved in. However, as the category moves into later stages of the adoption lifecycle the outer rings increase in importance. As the elements from the outer rings collapse into the inner rings, new elements come to be part of the outer rings. As I write this, podcasting capability has probably gone from being part of the outer ring to being part of the whole product that Apple includes in the iPod/iTunes product.

The Apple iPod/iTunes whole product (figure 8.2) is centered around the iPod (its core product). On the immediate outer ring it includes the basic components such as capability to seamlessly import music from CDs, legally purchase it online, all the cables, headphone, software and hardware to make the listening experience easy, simple, and pleasurable.

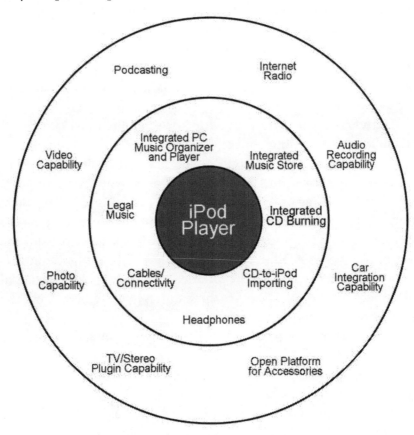

FIG. 8.2 – THE IPOD/ITUNES WHOLE PRODUCT

The "outer ring" shows other capabilities that may not be absolutely necessary for the buyer's immediate purchasing needs. Many buyers will look at what the future of the platform might bring and want to know about other capabilities that the company offers today or might offer in the future. That ring will also become part of the inner ring in that near future so the company needs to keep adding value to stay competitive and expand its markets.

When you develop your product, make a list of all the elements you would need to build the whole product. Make sure that from the user's point of view you are not missing any elements and that it all integrates and works seamlessly. Furthermore, you may want to assign someone to be specifically responsible for both delivering each and every piece, and for integrating it into the whole. You may also want to hire a usability manager, whose job would be to make sure the product is easy to use and that everything works seamlessly together. Finally, have potential users test the whole product again and again until you know you have it right.

HOW TO ACCELERATE THE ADOPTION OF YOUR PRODUCT

Netscape Navigator, Apple iPod, and Skype's telephony were successful products with phenomenally fast adoption rates. They all went from product launch to tens of millions of users in a few years or even a few months and added billions of dollars of market value to their respective companies. The adoption of these products follow principles that can be learned and used by any product strategist. In fact, many of these principles have been known for more than half a century.

The adoption of innovations field started in the 1940s when Dr. Everett Roger and his team wanted to learn what factors accounted for the adoption of new agricultural innovations like hybrid seeds, weed spray and fertilizers among farmers in Iowa. This landmark study introduced the conceptual framework that Rogers and others have generalized over the next two decades to produce what today is known as the technology adoption lifecycle. It is certainly interesting that many of the same principles that govern the adoption of Smartcards or Internet telephony also govern the spread of water-boiling for health reasons in a Peruvian village, to the teaching of modern math in Pittsburgh, to growing miracle rice in Bali.[127]

How adoptable is a new product? How do you accelerate the adoption of a product you already have in the pipeline. Here's a matrix that summarizes many of the issues a technology product strategist needs to consider when designing a product for quicker adoption. I will start with an example (smartcards) and then go over the principles that govern adoptability and what you can do to help your cause.

To introduce the adoptability framework, let's look at a product that has had a long trajectory and a difficult adoption path in the United States: smartcards.

Can smartcards Win the Battle?

I began working in the data security industry around 1996. I then read several reports that that year would be the "year of the smartcard." As I discussed these reports with my boss Jim Bidzos who was then the CEO of RSA Data Security, he asked me to look at reports from previous years. I did exactly that and found that 1995 was also the "year of the smartcard," and so were 1994 and 1993. It seemed that smartcards were the technology of the future and they would always be.

A smartcard is a pocket-size card with integrated circuit chip built in. It can have memory to keep information (such as personal identification, financial data or health information) and/or a logic chip to process that information (to keep it private).

While smartcards have made inroads in countries like France, they have not been very successful in the US market. Are smartcards doomed to be the "technology of the future" forever? Let's find out. Let's rate smartcards for adoptability.

Fig. 8.3 shows the adoptability matrix for smartcards. There are ten attributes to consider (such as trialability and observability). Two columns show the ratings and a brief comment on the rating. We rate each attribute on a -5 to +5 basis. A rating of +5 means that adoptability is so easy it's a slam dunk. A rating of 0 is neutral, that is, it's no better than other alternatives but also no worse. A rating of -5 means that it's a value-destroying or nearly impossible adoption path.

Attribute	Rating (-5 to +5)	Comment on Rating
1 - Substantial value improvement	1	Smartcards offered no major increase in benefits over other existing technologies. For instance, magnetic strips offered "decent" security for ATM networks. Other uses may vary.

2 - Compatibility	-1	The smartcard requires a special purpose reader. Whatever the use of a current machine: credit card payments, ATMs, PC authentication, they needed to add a chip reader to each machine to read a smartcard.
3 - Complexity	3	Understanding smartcards is actually quite easy.
4 - Trialability	1	The user needed to add a smartcard reader and software to try the smartcard. Not difficult, but also not trivial.
5 - Observability	1	The benefits are not obvious.
6 - Communicability	1	Communicating the value of smartcards depends on each specific use and is not obvious.
7 - Customer Risk	-1	Since a hardware and software infrastructure needs to be installed, there is some financial and technical risk involved.
8 - Incumbent reaction and power	2	Probably not high since there is no one incumbent. Smartcards compete with different products in each target space.
9 - Competing emerging technologies	0	Fingerprint authentication, retina scan, face recognition, magnetic strip cards, and many more.
10 - Clash with prevailing beliefs, laws and regulations	1	Depends on the use. Financial services is a heavily regulated industry where infrastructure companies need to comply with existing regulations or create new ones.

Fig. 8.3 − Adoptability matrix for smartcards.

Assuming that the above number are fair assessments on the technology, it looks like smartcards rate low in substantial value improvement (over existing and competing products) and extremely low in compatibility. Basically they don't seem to offer the compelling increase in value that would help overcome the major risk, expenses or infrastructure surgery that would be needed to make it easy to adopt.

Given these low ratings, it's fair to ask what made this product successful in some countries like France. The answer is that this was a technology product legislated by the government.[128] Once the government showed the way, the French banking industry and organizations like France Telecom built an infrastructure, ordered millions of smartcards and distributed them to users throughout the country. Thanks to the government, smartcards became the standard, didn't have to compete with any other technologies and gained a whole development ecosystem that built new applications for specialized markets (such as health, security, and mobile telephony cards).

Let's look at each adoptability attribute and then come back to other applications of the adoptability matrix.

Substantial value improvement

Does the new innovation represent a substantially large increase in benefits over the existing alternative? Is the new way of doing things so much better that the customer would never consider going back to the old ways after adopting your innovation? Value of course resides in the customer. Many vendors mistake features for value (see Rule 3).

When word processing software running on personal computers first came out it represented a huge improvement over the electric typewriter. When you typed on a typewriter a minor typographical error or any modifications implied having to rewrite the whole page again. Liquid paper was an interesting innovation that helped to deal with minor typos. But word processing allowed you to rewrite the document as many times as you wanted, save it for later editing, and send similar documents to many people to edit and approve with only minor effort. The value of word processing software was orders of magnitude above that of the existing paradigm. The return on investing in word processing software was huge. The world never looked back. The typewriter industry crashed and PC Word Processing became a multi-billion dollar industry for decades.

Netscape Navigator's web browser opened the world to a whole new way of doing things. Finding information on the web was orders of magnitude quicker and less expensive that the existing alternatives. Suddenly, prospective buyers didn't need to order paper catalogs. They didn't need to go to the library to access company information for investment purposes. Product comparisons became much easier. The value of all this information at the user's fingertips was vastly greater than whatever people used before the web.

Michael Powell, then the Chairman of the Federal Communications Commission, said "I knew it was over when I downloaded Skype." He was of course referring to the existing telephone companies. "When inventors are distributing...a program to talk to anybody else, and the quality is fantastic, and it's free - it's over. The world will change now inevitably."[129] Skype's substantial value creation was clear.

Compatibility with existing infrastructure

Can your product or innovation be inserted into the current infrastructure fairly easily? What kinds of changes or additions to the infrastructure are needed to use your product or service? Do you need to create a whole new infrastructure?

Netscape had a remarkably fast adoption curve. In order for a product like Netscape Navigator to be quickly adopted, potential users needed to have access to a personal computer, as well as a modem and a phone line to access an Internet Service Provider (ISP). By the time Netscape Navigator came out in 1996, the personal computer industry was mostly mature. Most American users already had a PC and industry revenues mostly came from replacement sales rather than new users. Basically everyone had a phone line. Modems were also a standard accessory on most new and existing PCs. Adding a modem to the PC infrastructure was both cheap and easy. In 1996 there were thousands of Internet Service Providers (ISPs). Most of them were local ISPs with a few routers, but giants such as AT&T, UUnet and AOL had blanketed the nation with their service. In other words, web browsers fit in easily within the then existing infrastructure. If any of those infrastructure pieces hadn't been in place, Netscape could not have had the phenomenal success they had. Either they or someone else would have had to build that missing piece—which would have delayed the adoption curve.

Skype smartly made use of the existing Internet infrastructure for its voice-over-IP products. By the time this company was founded there were a billion Internet users worldwide. Netscape and others had blazed the Internet trail that Skype used to achieve its meteoric rise. They had the basic infrastructure needed to run VOIP software. Furthermore, Skype's end-user software is modeled on Internet Messaging user interface. This has made it easy for IM users to transition to VOIP: instead of typing to "chat," they just talk to chat. It's back to the future of chat! They have lists of friends, get a popup message when one of them goes online, and can talk privately or in groups.

Hydrogen cars offer a contrast in adoption. It is generally agreed that hydrogen-fueled cars have many benefits over gasoline cars: they are easier to maintain, environmentally safer, and cheaper to manage. The value to individual drivers and especially to our society is pretty clear. Why then don't we see a lot of them on the road? Because we need to create a whole new infrastructure to service these cars: we need hydrogen "refineries," hydrogen "gas stations," safety standards, regulations, and so on. This requires a massive effort that impedes and limits the speed of adoption. There might be several ways to solve this adoption problem. The first one is to create a local infrastructure. For instance, a coalition within the San Francisco Bay Area could build such an infrastructure within that geography that would propel the industry locally. Another solution could be a transition path; in other words, hybrid cars. Hybrids would allow for an easier and more orderly transition to a new type of product (hydrogen cars) while still allowing the existing infrastructure to be used and upgraded. Even a transition of a decade or two would be faster than attempting to sell a pure hydrogen car upfront. Either way, the fact that hydrogen cars cannot readily be plugged into the existing infrastructure has made that technology tough to adopt.

Satellite television is an innovation that makes use of the TV infrastructure that most people have in their living rooms. There's no need to make massive changes in lifestyles, infrastructure in order for satellite dishes to be adopted. Just install a dish where the antenna used to go, point it to a satellite nearest you, and off you go. Contrast this with the need to build tens of thousands of hydrogen "gas" stations across the country to make hydrogen cars work. "Companies do not have to put in their own power plant or water system or sewerage pipes. Why? Because there are modern networks already in place and they can take advantage of them so they can focus on whatever they do," said Salesforce.com CEO Marc Benioff.[130]

The tech world has seen an untold number of new data storage standards. A small list of the better known ones would probably include Betamax, VHS and DVD for movies; 8 inch floppies, 5 ¼" "mini floppies," 3 ½ "micro floppies," and CDs for PC data. Each time a new format was introduced a whole new generation of hardware had to be adopted–and existing investments discarded. This dynamic slows down the adoption of the standard as users have built up a library of content in the then prevailing format. Think of the owners of all those collections of LP records. They had a hard time making the transition to CDs. Similarly, it took years to get rid of the old VHS tapes to make the transition to DVD players. (In fact I still see tapes at the local rental store, which means there must be a lot of people still using them!) As soon as we were comfortable with our DVD players, along came the major labels with two new digital standards to replace it: DVD-HD supported Toshiba and NEC and Blu-ray Disc (BD) supported by Blue-Ray Disc Association (BDA).

As I wrote this book, these two groups had braced themselves for a Betamax vs. VHS type of war. They both promised that the new standard would be backward-compatible with existing libraries of DVD's. This would make it easier for users to preserve their movie library investments when adopting either standard. The DVD-HD group had actually done the BDA one better in terms of being compatible with the existing infrastructure. When Universal, Paramount, New Line Cinema, and Warner Bros announced shipment of the DVD-HD format they said that these disks would carry movies in both formats: DVD and DVD-HD. "The discs contain two layers, an upper DVD layer with a capacity of 4.7GB and a lower HD-DVD layer with a15GB capacity."[131] This dual-format disc would allow users to build a library of content that is compatible with the HD-DVD format at no incremental cost to them *before* they buy a new HD-DVD player. Then Warner Bros hedged its bets by also supporting Blu-Ray, saying it would ship movies in both formats.

Complexity relative to alternatives

How complex is your technology or innovation? How does it compare to the existing paradigm? How does it compare with alternatives? Note that complexity is defined or perceived by the user not by the vendor! The easier it is to understand and use a technology, the easier it is to adopt.

Business Process Management Systems are software infrastructures that let information technology departments model the way a particular organization does business, and generate software code that runs the way the company processes work. Many companies, small and large, inhabited the BPMS space for years. Gartner, an information technology research and analysis company, counted more than 30 players in the BPMS space.[132] These companies were not just chasing the next billion-dollar marketplace[133], they were chasing the next killer app. The ancient dream of bridging the gap between information technology and business users would finally be solved!

The benefits of a BPMS solution had been widely touted for years. Well respected authors, researchers, and consultants Howard Smith and Peter Fingar, both of whom worked for the multibillion IT consulting firm CSC, published a book calling BPMS technology nothing less than the "Third Wave" of business process, and "the breakthrough that redefines competitive advantage for the next fifty years."[134]

As I write this, despite all its promises BPMS adoption has been slow to take off. There are probably several reasons, but one of them is its complexity of implementation. BPMS technology has traditionally required users to map the flows of documents, people, and document from end to end. This is a useful but complex task. To further underline the complexity of the technology, the BPMS conversation is still in the early-adopter stage. In 2004 Smith and Fingar published an article that still explained business processes in terms of Pi calculus.[135] This made for interesting reading, but anything explained in terms of calculus is probably too complex for the mainstream user.

Contrast this with Netscape Navigator or Skype. A software program can hardly be easier to use: download, install, run, and get the benefits. No complexity to speak of, nothing to explain, no user manual, nothing to change. Just add water.

Maybe the BPMS space was where the MP3 player was right before Apple entered with its iPod and iTunes whole product. Some would say that it is not fair to compare a $300 consumer electronic gadget to a far more complex enterprise software product. That would miss the point and the learning experience we can get from looking at what Apple did right to emerge from the pack. Once Apple simplified the music listening experience with the whole product that included Apple's iPod and iTunes it became similarly easy to use relative to all competitors, within and outside the industry. The iPod was not just the heir to the portable digital music category. It was arguably the heir to the broader portable music player market pioneered by Sony in 1979 when it first came out with its eponymous Walkman. The Walkman product line had been one of the most successful consumer electronic products of all time, having sold sold more than 300 million units.The iPod was as easy to use as the Walkman while offering value orders of magnitude higher.

Trialability before buying

Can your product be tried or used before purchase? Buyers are taking risks when buying a new technology product. You need to help them by minimizing those risks.Many traditional industries have learned this and have made it part of their standard offerings. The more the prospective customer can try or use the product before purchase the easier it is to adopt.

Zone Labs was a PC security company located in San Francisco (acquired in 2004 by Checkpoint Software). Their main product, named Zone Alarm, was a firewall that prevented malicious entries into the user's personal computer. This was a technology product whose innards were inherently hard to understand. Despite this complexity, the product achieved a high rate of adoption. The way Zone Labs achieved it was by offering an entry-level product that had tangible value: Zone Alarm. This product was free of charge and could be downloaded from the web and installed in a matter of minutes. The user could also get rid of it by easily turning it off if they didn't like it. To generate revenues, ZoneLabs also developed the "Zone Labs with Antivirus" version for about $24.95 and the "Zone Alarm Pro" for about $49.95. The company generated high trialability with the basic product and then, if the user liked the basic product they could always upgrade to the next level of functionality. The retail industry has long ago learned the value of making it easy for the prospective buyer to try before they buy. Electronic superstores like the *Good Guys* offer 30-day money back guarantee if your purchase doesn't work as advertised. Some car dealers will let you drive a car and even take it home for a few days to see if you like it. The more buyers can try a product and see how it works the more willing they will be to purchase it. Apple took a cue from this model when it released its iPod music player. The company set up iPod hearing stations at its retail stores around the nation. Potential buyers could see how easy the iPod was to use and could listen to the sound with high quality Bose headphones.

Macromedia was one of the most successful software companies of the Internet era. Its "Flash" player was downloaded by tens of millions of users around the world and became a standard for showing short videos on websites ranging from large publisher NYTimes.com to tiny independent movie house UpForGrabsMovie. com. Macromedia's success is partly due to the ease with which it lets potential users try its products. Macromedia developed several products that became leaders in their categories including Dreamweaver, Director, and ColdFusion. These and nearly two dozen products aimed to serve the website designer enabled Macromedia to reach $400 million in revenues and a company valuation in excess of $3 billion in 2004. Part of the company's success was due to the ease with which customers can try new product offerings. In early 2005 they listed 23 products on their website (http://www. macromedia.com/downloads). All of them could be downloaded for a trial period or for free. I repeat, all of them. (Macromedia was acquired by Adobe in a transaction valued at $3.4 billion). [136]

Observability of results

Can the user observe or experience the results fairly quickly? Skype telephony benefits are easily observable. You can download the software for free, install it easily, and within a few minutes you can make phone calls–also for free. After I downloaded Skype for the first time I used it to call Singapore. The whole experience was seamless and took only a few minutes. It was not surprising that this product had spread like wildfire.

Penicillin was the world's first massively adopted antibiotic. The successful adoption curve was mainly drawn by the rapidly observable results of using the drug. Families of sick patients, doctors, government representatives, military officials, and nearly everyone else could see how penicillin saved lives and stopped disease in its tracks within days or even hours. The results were clear, measurable and observable to the naked eye. Soon after its first large-scale use word was out and the whole world was using penicillin. The multibillion dollar antibiotic industry was born.

Netscape Navigator also rated high on the observability scale. Millions of websites were available immediately after installing and running the product. The user could do research, trade stock online, buy a DVD, or auction that old juicer within minutes. They could observe real and quick results.

Mass communicability

As we have seen elsewhere in this book [See Rules 4 and 6], technology adoption is a social process. The easier to communicate, understand the uses and benefits, and show the product or service, the easier its adoption. You also need to enable users to talk about your product easily, so they will repeat your message quickly, succinctly, and memorably. Think about a product or service, a movie or a restaurant, a wine or a gadget you have recommended. You have probably found it easy to communicate what the product does and how you enjoyed its use. I have probably turned dozens of users on to Skype. I don't get any financial benefit whatsoever when I do this. I just say "free phone calls to anywhere in the world." How hard is that to communicate? It's only eight words. It's easy to communicate the value with a tight message.

Contrast that with communicating the uses and benefits of Business Process Management Software. It's not easy at all!

Customer risk when adopting

The smaller the economic, personal, or career risk involved, the easier it is to adopt a new technology. The more you mitigate such risks the easier the product adoption. (See Rule 5 for many examples). Netscape Navigator was a very low risk proposition, starting with the fact that it was free, plus no cost to switch from competing products-so there was no financial risk. It also didn't do any damage to the personal computer and could be uninstalled without traces, so there was no technical risk.

Incumbent reaction and power

The more threatened the established players feel about your new technology, and the more power they have to disrupt adoption of your product, the more they might work to slow it down or co-opt it. They can use their distributor or supplier relationships as well as legal, political, financial or other types of power to preserve their businesses and give them time to react to your threat.

XM Satellite Radio (XMSR) was a satellite-base radio station. It could beam hundreds of radio stations to compatible digital radios anywhere in North America. To users, satellite radio technology offered crisper sound, more programming variety, larger geographic reach and commercial-free programming. Think cable TV for automobile radios.

As soon as XMSR, its competitor Sirius, and a handful of other satellite radio companies were founded the incumbent radio station industry representatives (National Association of Broadcasters) mounted a political campaign against it to disrupt its success[137] They saw what satellite television had done to regular television stations and even cable broadcasters and did not want that scenario repeated in the radio business. They successfully lobbied the US Congress to pass law after law to protect the incumbents against the seemingly inevitable shift to digital radio. For instance, Congress waived the obligation of radio stations to pay royalties to performers for the songs they played. They also could use airspace for free. Satellite radio companies had to pay royalties to performers (tens of millions of dollars a year for XMSR), and they had to pay $200 million for the right to use the spectrum. The Federal Communication Commission (FCC) cut the number of allowed providers to two (XMSR and Sirius), cut the number of channels they could carry in half by shrinking its airspace, and made it illegal for them to broadcast locally. These additional expenses for and restrictions on the product or services made it more difficult for providers to offer a more valuable product and increased their cost of doing business. A higher price and a less valuable product would in turn make the adoption of their service slower than it could have otherwise been.

Competing emerging technologies

The more competing emerging technologies, product categories, or standards with fairly similar benefits, the more difficult it will be for consumers to adopt yours.

Technologies don't have to be exactly alike to compete with one another. Smartcard vendors don't just compete with other Smartcard vendors in the world of access authentication and security. They compete with iris, retina, fingerprint, face, vein recognition, and other biometric authentication technologies. Satellite radio also faced competition from several existing technologies like standard AM and FM radio. It also competed with emerging technologies like Internet radio and even players like Apple's iPod/iTunes. At first this may not be obvious, but think about it: if you can store thousands of your favorite songs on the iPod and play them both at home and the road, then you may just not need satellite radio at all. This may be a reason why XMSR and Sirius have spent hundreds of millions of dollars in producing unique non-music programming. Sirius, for instance, signed a multi-year deal with "shock jock" Howard Stern for $500 million, and XMSR signed a $650-million contract with major league baseball.

New technologies that enable and strengthen Internet radio in the automobile also are detrimental to the adoption of Satellite Radio. Technologies such as mobile phones and wireless communications technologies such as WiMax may fall into this camp.

Clash with prevailing beliefs, laws and regulations

The more your product or service clashes with prevailing culture, beliefs, laws and regulations the more difficult it will be to have a fast (if any) adoption curve. The Segway "Human Transporter" provided an interesting case in point. The Segway was a two-wheel battery-powered scooter-like vehicle that travels up to 12 miles per hour. Dean Kamen, creator of the Segway, claimed this vehicle would revolutionize human transportation. Venture capitalist John Doerr predicted that the company would reach $1 billion in sales faster than any other product in history.[138] Segway units would retail for $4,995, which meant they would need to sell anywhere from 200,000 to 400,000 units to reach that goal. (Depending on the margin they offered to retailers.) A factory capable of producing more than 40,000 units per month was built in Bedford, New Hampshire. Even before the Segway was launched in December 2001, the company mounted one of the most successful publicity programs of the last decade. The media seemed to go into a whirl early 2001 as soon as the first news about "Ginger" (its code name) "leaked" out. Soon, there was talk of a large sum given to an author to write a book about its development. Patents for the product's innovative technology prompted non-stop chatter and media anticipation. The Segway showed up in popular television shows like "Cramer" and "Good Morning America" and on the cover of mainstream magazines like *Forbes* ASAP. Even President George W. Bush and his father, former US President George H.W. Bush were widely shown riding Segways.[139]

The Segway publicity would qualify as a brilliant new product communications campaign. Soon everyone was talking about it. Success seemed to be around the corner. However, a problem arose as soon as Segways were released to the public. From Hawaii to California to Florida there was widespread opposition to allowing a 70-pound vehicle moving a human at 12 miles per hour on sidewalks and pedestrian areas. Some said the product needed to be heavily regulated and that it belonged with the motorcycle category. All the while the company insisted the Segway belonged on the sidewalks. Segways were soon banned across the country. The company had to shift gears and get into the legal lobbying business in many states, cities and towns across the United States. This legal backlash resulted in an extremely slow adoption curve. Twenty-one months after its introduction, the company had reportedly sold only 6,000 units[140], and almost three years later the company was still waging legal battles for the vehicle to be legally accepted across the country. "We're lucky no one has been killed on one of these things but it's only a matter of time," said Timothy Toomey, Chairman of the General Court's Joint Committee on Public Safety in the state of Massachusetts. "These Segways travel at 15 miles per hour. Fifteen miles an hour! Do you want that on your sidewalk? I certainly don't, and the overwhelming majority of Massachusetts residents don't either," Toomey said.[141] Segway had clashed with prevailing beliefs and regulations.

Another major issue against a fast adoption rate for Segways was lack of trialability. Consumers are used to try our means of personal transportation (cars, trucks, motorcycles, bicycles) before buying. It is risky for most consumers to spend about $5,000 on an unknown new product category without a thorough test drive.

DESIGNING NETSCAPE NAVIGATOR FOR ADOPTION

Now that we have explained the attributes that might make a product or service easy to adopt, let's revisit the framework and use it to rate other products and services. As mentioned before, the ratings are on a -5 to +5 basis. A rating of +5 means that adoptability is so easy it's a 'slam dunk.' A rating of 0 is neutral, that is, it's no better than other alternatives but also no worse. A rating of -5 means that it's a value-destroying or nearly impossible adoption path. A score of +5 means it's "perfect"; it should not be easily given. You should be as honest as possible in rating each attribute. A marketing team, or, if possible, a third-party team, should be in charge of rating the product for adoptability (it may be honestly difficult for someone who has been developing a product to be objective about these ratings). They should have actual customers or prospects help them rate the product. Certainly the earlier in the product design process the less expensive and painful it will be to modify.

Another important point is that this matrix should be used with specific applications (uses) and customer segments (users) in mind. This is similar to the "Customer Segment Discovery" idea that we introduced in Chapter 1 (Fig. 1.2). Unlike that framework, adoptability is not about adding the ratings for the different attributes. A small change in just one attribute might significantly improve the adoptability of a product.

Netscape Navigator had an unusual virtually "perfect storm" of ratings that made it possible for this product to achieve widespread and quick adoption.

Attribute	Rating (-5 to +5)	Comment on Rating
1 - Substantial value improvement	5	Surfing the web opened up huge new possibilities for individuals and businesses.
2 - Compatibility	4	To run Netscape Navigator you needed a PC, phone line, and a modem, all of which were in widespread use.
3 - Complexity	5	Understanding the concept of downloading and running. Navigator was fairly easy for PC users.
4 - Trialability	5	Navigator was extremely easy to try. It was free. Downloading it was easy and relatively fast, as was the installation. The user could also run it and try it immediately, from home or the office.
5 - Observability	5	Millions of websites were available immediately after installing the product.
6 - Communicability	5	Communicating the value of Netscape and the web in general was fairly simple.
7 - Risk	5	The product was as risk-free as they come. It was free, nonintrusive, didn't need additional software, didn't damage the infrastructure, could be uninstalled if the user didn't like it.

8 - Incumbent power and reaction	5	The most powerful incumbent at the time Netscape launched Navigator was Microsoft. Initially they either underestimated or ignored the Internet, so their opposition to Netscape was minimal. Later, Microsoft's reaction was swift, brutal and deadly.
9 - Competing emerging technologies	3	There were competing technologies like AOL, Compuserve and Minitel. All of them had closed user bases and cost much more than Navigator (which was free).
10 - Clash with prevailing beliefs, laws, regulations	4	The Internet was a fairly unregulated and open community at the time.

FIG. 8.4 – ADOPTABILITY MATRIX FOR NETSCAPE NAVIGATOR

Looking at the above table how does your product stack up? In order to improve your product's chances at being adopted, you want to work to improve the ratings on as many attributes relevant to your market segment as possible. In going through this process, you want to have frank discussions with your customers and potential users. Ask them what's holding them back from adopting. Test whether you're communicating the value of the product well. Talk to engineers and see if the product can be broken up into smaller bundles. Can you have an entry-level version that's cheaper and has most of the interesting value? Can you have a risk-free limited-time version?

RULE 8 SUMMARY: DESIGN PRODUCTS AND SERVICES THAT ARE EASY TO ADOPT

Why do some products take off while others have a hard time doing so–despite their evident value? Designing products and services that are easy to adopt may be the key to gaining market leadership. Given the speed at which technology markets move, you may not have the time to recover from designing a slow-to-adopt product.

Skype telephony and Netscape Navigator were two products that were extremely easy to adopt. Apple iPod was a late entrant into the portable digital music player market-- but it ran away with the market, achieving market shares in excess of 90%. Apple won because it created a product that was easy to adopt. This chapter introduced two tools that the product designer and product strategist can use to help design an easily adoptable product.

The first is that of the whole product. The entrepreneur needs to look at the product from the user's perspective, and to ask what all the elements are that a user will need to adopt this product. She needs to put them together with a combination of internal and external resources. Thus once Apple launched the iTunes music player and iTunes music store, the iPod took off and never looked back.

The second tool is an "Adoptability Matrix" to rate products and services against specific adoptability attributes, such as value improvement, compatibility with existing infrastructure, communicability, complexity, and trialability. This framework may enable your marketing and product development teams to measure and prioritize investments, and to make the product or service easier for prospective customers to adopt.

RULE 9
YOU'RE DOING WELL.
CONGRATULATIONS.
NOW CHANGE OR DIE

"It is not the strongest of the species that survive, nor the most intelligent, but the one most responsive to change."

- Charles Darwin

"Change before you have to."

- Jack Welch

In 1997 Apple was near oblivion, its stock languishing in the single digits near 10-year lows. Its main product line, the Macintosh computers, had been stuck around 2%-3% market share of the personal computer category year after year for a couple of decades without any hope of increasing those numbers. Apple's financials were bad and getting worse: its 1997 revenues were $7 billion (down from $11 billion in 1995), and its losses amounted to $1 billion (down from a profit of $400 million in 1995)[142] Many pundits discarded the company as a has-been; a one-time wunderkind who had seen better times. The future looked bleak unless something radical happened inside or outside Apple.

Fast forward to 2005. In 2005, Apple was riding high again, having transformed itself into a consumer electronics media company. Its stock had soared to a split-adjusted 120, which gave the company a valuation in excess of $50 billion. By comparison, consumer electronics giant Sony Corp, owner of Sony Music and creator of the Walkman, Trinitron, and some of the most successful consumer electronic products of the twentieth century, had a market capitalization of $33.6 Billion.[143] Apple's 2005 fiscal fourth quarter revenues and earnings were $3.68 billion and $430 million while heading for revenues that were twice those in 1997. All these numbers were company records. Apple was flying higher than it ever did. The same pundits who had discarded the company were hailing it as the future of the consumer electronics industry. CEO Steve Jobs was once again called a creative genius.

APPLE: FROM MAC TO IPOD

How did Apple do it? It re-invented itself. Apple changed its strategy and committed to a new media-centric strategy. It also changed its product-centric business model and changed it to a new business model that relied on both product sales and media content sales as sources of revenues.

Change is hard sometimes. The iPod entered a crowded market. At first sales of the iPod were relatively slow. Two years after Apple released the iPod, the market still did not seem to believe the new strategy. Apple's stock moved sideways between June and December 2003, hovering between about 10 and 11 (split-adjusted prices). Many uncommitted board members, investors and company managers would give up at this point. It took Apple about two years to get its iPod/iTunes whole product right. (See Chapter 8 and Fig. 8.2 for a detailed chart of the iPod whole product.)

But the company was committed to the new media strategy and had more to come. Apple launched the iTunes player and the iTunes store for the PC in October 2003 and the company never looked back (see Chapter 8 for more details). The iTunes store, where customers could download music, did not just redefine Apple, but the whole music industry. Apple did not just change its strategic choices but also its business model. It wanted to make money not just on iPod hardware sales but also on music content revenues. By February 2006 just two and a half years after launching iTunes on the PC, Apple customers had downloaded and paid for a billion songs from this store.[144] Any money Apple made reselling music, video or contet would be incremental revenues. A fifty percent margin would give Apple a nifty half billion dollars in revenues that it would not have generated under its old business model. Apple had achieved a remarkable feat: as of September 2005 it had a 90% market share in the digital music player category, and 82% of the US online music download category. Could it get any better than that for Apple? Yes. Of the 20 million iPod users, 10 million had opened accounts with the iTunes Music Store. "And they come with credit cards," said Apple CEO Steve Jobs.[145] These credit-card-holders were downloading (and paying for) 1.8 million songs per day from the iTunes store.

Apple is a great reinvention story. The iPod and iTunes were part of a strategic transformation of the company that recast Apple into a consumer electronics and media-centric company instead of a general personal computing company. However, many companies don't change, even when they have to. High tech history is littered with the remains of companies who could not or did not change their strategy.

In 1984 MicroPro was one of the darlings of the early PC application software space. It was also the largest PC software company in the world–larger than either Microsoft or Lotus. Its main product, WordStar had 75% of the PC word processing market[146]. As difficult to believe as this was, they lost the leadership to upstart WordPerfect who came "out of nowhere" to gain 50% of the word processing market by late 1990. What did MicroPro do wrong? It was too slow to notice what was happening around the company. It didn't keep up with customer expectations. It sat on its market lead and treated it as a cash cow to be milked for years. This strategy may work for a cola drink, shaving cream or cereal company, but not in fast-moving high tech markets.

Now, you would think that WordPerfect would learn the lessons from MicroPro and be totally paranoid about change, nimbler competitors and listening to the customer, right? Wrong! After becoming the market leader in the category, they repeated the very same mortal mistakes that had sunk MicroPro. They became comfortable. They stopped innovating. They did not change. They stopped listening to the customer. They promptly lost their market leadership to Microsoft.

Having a great technology, valuable product or even a large market share does not guarantee that you will stay on top of the high tech heap. Winners can take it all–but they can also lose it all. Companies like Netscape, Ashton-Tate and Lotus were clear leaders in their respective product categories–with high market shares and loyal user bases. Microsoft came in and supplanted each one of them. Ashton-Tate, for instance, was once the leading maker of PC database software. In late 1986, it had shipped its millionth copy of its best-selling $795 dBase product.[147] To put this number in historic perspective, Apple computer shipped its millionth Macintosh in late 1987–a full year later. Ashton-Tate grew to be one of the largest software companies in the world before it became too bloated to compete and had to sell out to Borland in 1991. Oracle and Intuit, on the other hand, have been able to successfully withstand Microsoft's frontal assaults for years. Apple lost and then came back by winning in an emerging and leaderless product category.

As the Internet exploded onto the mainstream in 1996, America Online first tried to resist it. AOL wanted the world to stay within its comfortable, closed, and proprietary software, content, and access world. Back then, AOL provided everything: email, content, chat, browser, and the physical network infrastructure. In addition to developing software and content, it had to own and manage the routers, switches, and communication servers that its users needed to access AOL using their home telephone. Yahoo!, on the other hand, provided search, email, and content and let the Internet Service Providers (ISPs) provide the access to its website.

AOL's communications access infrastructure made sense in a pre-Web era. However, that portion of the business had quickly become a commodity. Large companies like AT&T and WorldCom provided net access (in addition to voice phone services) while well capitalized companies like UUnet and Earthlink focused solely on building and growing the network access and management business. Furthermore, barriers to entry into the business had gone down so thousands of smaller ISPs sprouted throughout the land. As expected, this multitude of competitors drove availability up and prices down. Access used to be a valuable source of competitive advantage but by 1996 it had turned into a drag on AOL's finances and competitive focus. This competitive reality plus frequent service outages brought about by its own inability to manage the growth of the physical network helped the company accept the inevitability of the changes in the world order brought by the Web. The company relented. In 1996 the company changed its business model. Instead of charging by the hour it started offering a monthly subscription price around $19.95, closer to market expectations. In 1997 AOL sold its network access business to WorldCom for $1.2 billion in order to focus on the content side of its business.[148] These strategic changes allowed AOL to become nimbler and more focused on content product development and marketing. AOL would soon become the number one player in its category. AOL went on to triple its membership going from nearly five million in 1996 to17.6 million members (and revenues of $4.8 billion) in 1999.[149]

From Great to Naught

In February 2005 AT&T sold itself to former AT&T spinoff SBC, ending what for much of the twentieth century was considered by many to be the world's premier company. AT&T had built the most sophisticated and reliable telephone infrastructure in the world and for decades reaped the benefits of being a national monopoly. Its Bell Laboratories created technologies such as the transistor, the laser, and the Unix operating system that spawned whole new industries. At its peak, it employed 1 million people and reached a market value of $190 billion.[150] Why did AT&T slide into oblivion? Because the world changed and the company didn't change with it.

The hallmark of the technology industry is that everything changes–quickly: technology innovation, product innovation, business model innovation, customer expectations, supply chains, competitive capabilities, distribution channels, partnership goals not to mention changing appetite by venture capital investors and globalization. There are so many moving parts in a high tech business and they are all moving so fast in so many different directions, it's hard to believe anyone can keep up. But keep up they must.

Sometimes the "paradigm" or "world order" shifts, and what used to be a source of competitive advantage turns into disadvantage. The concept of "paradigm shift" has been abused in the Silicon Valley lexicon, but it's important for the product strategist to learn. Thomas Kuhn popularized the concept in his seminal book *The Structure of Scientific Revolutions*[151]. In a paradign shift the familiar (old) way of looking at things is swept aside by a brand new and radically new one. The shift from mainframes to minicomputers was one such shift, and the subsequent shift from minicomputers to personal computers represented yet another. There was a subsequent paradigm shift when the epicenter of computing went from the PC to the Internet.

Digital Equipment Corp. (DEC) was a great company that came into power because from the balance of power largely shifted from mainframe providers to more distributed minicomputer vendors. In both worlds, however, computer companies derived strength from vertical integration, where DEC, IBM, and others provided everything from the operating system to the microprocessor running the computers. As the personal computers paradigm took hold, the balance of power changed again. The world of information technology became more specialized. Personal computers were put together with products from a diverse spectrum of companies: operating systems companies, application companies, microprocessor companies, hard disk companies, monitor companies, and so on. Vertical integration became a source of competitive weakness instead of competitive strength. DEC couldn't change to compete in the new paradigm. In the 1990s the company started selling off parts of the company to fund its losses until it sold what remained of itself to Compaq in 1998.

There are many reasons why companies can't or won't change. One reason is that new paradigms start brewing even while companies in the existing paradigm are growing – sometimes very fast.

The growth of PCs in the late 70s and early 80s was exponential – but still the industry was rather small compared with a company like DEC. The company had yearly revenues around $4 billion in 1982. As table 9.1 shows, the top 10 PC software companies *put together* had a grand total of $345 million in 1984 – about 1 month of DEC revenues.

Company managers and directors, concerned with managing a workforce of 100,000 people, quarterly earnings, and current competition may not pay much attention.

#1	Micropro International	$60,000,000
#2	Microsoft Corp.	$55,000,000
#3	Lotus	$53,000,000
#4	Digital Research	$45,000,000
#5	VisiCorp	$43,000,000
#6	Ashton-Tate	$35,000,000
#7	Peachtree	$21,700,000
#8	MicroFocus	$15,000,000
#9	Software Publishing	$14,000,000
#10	Broderbund	$13,000,000

Fig. 9.1 – The top 10 PC software companies by revenues in 1984.[152]

Furthermore, at the time, DEC employees and management had an aura of invincibility. I lived in Boston around in the mid-1980s and I recall many conversations with DEC managemers who truly believed that they were going to surpass IBM any day as the world's top computing company. In his book "The Innovator's Dilemma," Harvard professor Clayton Christensen has brilliantly chronicled what happens when technology companies want to move up the food chain and move away from the market.[153] Microsoft, Compaq, Intel and their microcomputing ilk were not even on DEC's radar screens. By the time DEC stumbled and these companies were more powerful than DEC was it was too late. .

Another problem in fast-growth environments is that once the rules are clearly known and you are not on top, it's probably too late for you to win or even play the game. Only those who can adapt quickly enough and thoroughly enough can make the transition to market leadership in the new paradigm "By the time a technology becomes obvious to most of your customers or most of your peers in the industry or most of your employees, it's too late for you as a company to participate [and benefit from selling]" said Cisco CEO John Chambers.[154]

HIGH FLYERS - DROPPING LIKE FLIES

Let's take a different look at the top 10 PC software companies (by revenue) in 1984 (Table 9.1). Most of us probably don't recognize most of the names or even remember a time when Microsoft hasn't been the largest PC software company on earth. Nor would most of us recognize the name MicroPro, let alone know that it used to be the largest PC software company in the world. Back then, however, MicroPro's yearly revenues ($60 million) were larger than Microsoft's ($55 million) and Lotus ($53 million.) Notice that in 1984 Microsoft was just marginally larger than Lotus ($55 million vs. $53 million), and only one of five or six companies that were within a relatively narrow revenue range. VisiCorp was number five at $43 million–just about 20% smaller than Microsoft. Nine out of the top ten software companies in 1984 are nowhere in sight today! We have heard that nine out of ten startup companies won't make it but the thought that ninety percent of the very largest PC software companies in the world will disappear might be tough to swallow indeed.

Clearly, high tech is a hazardous marketplace – where the mortality rate of even companies that are successful enough to get to the top 10 is huge. This table is also an indicator that in many high tech markets winners take all. Microsoft went public in 1986 at a split-adjusted stock price of $0.08 (yes, that's eight cents) and has subsequently grown to be the largest software company on the planet with revenues of $40 billion per year and a market capitalization of $250 billion. Today Microsoft is larger by an order of magnitude than any other PC software company in the world – even great companies such as Symantec and Adobe are barely larger than $2 billion in revenues.

High tech product planning requires dealing with a set of pressures and timeframes not seen in more mature industries. It is not just because your own industry is changing, it is because everything is changing – fast.

If you are in the technology business or even if you just do business with tech companies, your competitors, suppliers, partners, and customer capabilities can transform themselves rapidly. They may go through what former Intel CEO Andy Grove calls "10x" change–an order of magnitude change.[155] Furthermore, these changes may be occurring simultaneously. The implication of fast-changing moving parts is that high tech strategic planning is as dynamic as systems planning, where products and companies change fast and often unexpectedly.

High tech product strategy is thus more like a living, breathing organism than a document you shelve after you develop it, and only revisit once in a while. All aspects of this organism, from product execution to strategy, are closely interlinked. There's too much at stake for a tech strategic planner to blink. Change is the order of the day. In the high tech world markets come and go right before our eyes. Whole product categories are created and destroyed by new generations of innovative products, services, technologies, and business models.

Change Before You Have to

The influence and transformational power of high technology can be as powerful and devastating outside of high tech markets as it can be within. Many companies that have a hard time competing within their own categories can be jolted and their very existence threatened by far away high tech innovation tsunamis. Combine changes in more than one technology category and the unintended, unforeseen, or unexpected consequences can be devastating across industries. Kodak, Siebel Systems, American Airlines, AT&T are just a few of the leading companies that were jolted by technology changes. Kodak never thought until quite late that a combination of imaging, mobile phone companies and chip providers would transform its business forever. Even in the midst of a worldwide recession digital cameras have gone through several generations of performance improvement and miniaturization that pushed their sales numbers past the existing analog camera industry. Unlike mature markets, all this nonstop performance improvement has come while costs have actually plummeted. Nikon, a company that was synonymous with film photography has abandoned film to concentrate on digital cameras.[156] Today's leaders in camera sales have names like Sony and Canon. By the time you read this, the leader may just be mobile phone manufacturers like Nokia and Samsung!

How about heavy-duty capital-equipment-based industries? The influence and transformational power of high tech in other industries is as powerful and sometimes devastating there too. American Airlines (AA) has spent billions of dollars to build the most powerful reservation system in the world. For decades, this system was a huge competitive advantage for AA, and helped it become one of the largest airlines in the world. Yet, startup airline JetBlue was able to get up and running in no time and with next to no upfront investment in information technology. How did it do that? Because of companies like Navitaire that rent instant reservation systems. Partly as a result of this shift in industry economics, JetBlue is profitable, while AA has been in and out of bankruptcy proceedings for years. This is not just about American Airlines and JetBlue. The whole airlines industry has been transformed as a result of changes in information technology. Dozens of low-cost airlines have sprung up around the world during the first few years of the twenty first century: RyanAir in Ireland, Click Mexicana in Mexico, Freedom Air in New Zealand are just a few examples.[157]

The ability to rent software without putting up a huge infrastructure has been made possible by a new breed of companies that provide Software as a Service (SaaS). Salesforce.com and Clickability are companies that have benefitted from this new business model (see Rules 2 and 5). Siebel Systems did not quite adapt to this new world. Siebel itself had benefitted from the shift from client-server computers to Internet-centric computing in the 1990s. Its revenues grew from $39 million in 1996 to 2 billion in 2001, and then went into a sharp decline for the following four years, before Siebel sold itself to across-the-highway rival Oracle in late 2005.

MIGHTY IBM CHANGES

Even mighty IBM had to massively change to stay in business. In the early 1990s IBM was reeling. In 1993 its net income was a negative $8.1 billion on revenues of $62.7 billion and its stock hit went down to twenty-year lows (hovering around an adjusted price of 10.[158] The IBM PC had turned into the Wintel PC as nimbler companies such as Microsoft, Compaq, and Intel successfully challenged IBM and wrestled control of the "IBM PC" architecture away from its creator. IBM was becoming increasingly irrelevant and there was no end in sight for its misery. Not long before IBM had been considered the most powerful company in the information technology world. It dominated many profitable segments: mainframe computers, personal computers, storage, database–you name it, IBM dominated it. But the company was in trouble. The world had changed and they hadn't. No one in the high tech world was or is immune to change.

IBM's 2004 net income was $8.4 billion on revenues of $96.3 billion and its stock was in the low 80s (eight times the price it was in 1993). The biggest change in that transformation was IBM's new focus on services. Between 1993 and 2004 IBM's hardware revenues went from $30.6 to $31.1 billion and its software revenues went from $11 to $15.1 billion while its services revenues went from $9.7 to $46.2 billion.

IBM turned itself around by going back to its customers. The company felt the customers' pain and built a business that was able to both create value for them and capture value for the company. The IBM organization that used to push its big iron computers above all (hardware represented about half its revenues in 1993) recreated itself by becoming consultants to and partners of their customers (services revenues were almost half of revenues in 2004). They started recommending whatever worked for the customer– Linux or Microsoft operating systems, Cisco routers, Siebel software, Oracle databases, even if they were competitive with IBM's own products. What emerged from this transformation was a stronger company, in touch with the needs of the marketplace.

Why even smart media executives sue little girls

While high technology industries are all about change, they are littered with the remains of companies whose executives tried to deny the new. The interesting thing is that these same companies probably became successful as the result of massive changes in the environment or paradigm shifts. Psychology provides us once more with a way to look at what happens to us when confronted with massive change or the loss of the old – a common thing in high tech markets.

In 1969 Elizabeth Kubler-Ross wrote her groundbreaking book "On Death and Dying," in which she introduced the "Five Stages of Grief." This conceptual framework has been subsequently expanded to many instances of catastrophic loss. Let's use Kubler-Ross's stages as we follow music industry executives as their world was transformed by irreversible changes in technology.

1. Denial

Ken Olson, one of the most influential entrepreneurs and CEO of Digital Equipment Corp. said famously in 1977, "there's no reason why individuals should have a computer in their home." DEC was a high flying darling of computing at the time, the equivalent of Microsoft or Cisco in the 90's or Google today. DEC didn't make the transition to a world dominated by the Personal Computers. Denial of the new is powerful and overwhelming. It happens to the most brilliant minds around.

Denial is one of the most powerful coping mechanisms in the human psyche. It is also a large impediment to change.

There are many ways to deny the loss of business for an executive. They may think it the loss is a bump on the road. It may be a temporary setback due to the economic environment, the weakness of the currency (international sales don't count as much), the strength of the currency (we can't export as much), a slowdown in spending due to weather, or whatever they can come up with. Another way to deny the new is to say that the new technology is not nearly as good as your existing product. The market will not put up with such shoddy products. This is what many technology company executives will say. Kodak's CEO Daniel Carp said "I saw my first digital camera 20 years ago."[159] That technology was certainly not then ready for the big time but it would come back to haunt Kodak's bread-and-butter film business later. Many everyday technologies including Linux, Java, XML, and personal computers have been dismissed in the past as "not good enough" by many smart people. Yet, each one of them has been transformative on its own right. Furthermore, when they are put together by a company like Google, you may have the most powerful information technology infrastructure in the world.

Finally, a way to dismiss the power of a new product, service or category is to classify it as a fad. As I started writing this book some categories such as blogging, podcasting and social networking were classified as fads. They all defied their critics. Technorati tracked 5.2 million blogs in 2004 and 21.2 million in November 2005. LinkedIn broke the million-user mark in 2004 and quadrupled that in 2005. These are hardly fads. Even with these kind of numbers, these technologies were sometimes dismissed as features of larger products than categories on their own. Podcasting was also viewed as a fad rather than a threat to traditional broadcasters.

Were music industry executives in denial about the power of technology to transform their industry? Personal computing technologies had the ever-improving capability to disrupt the music industry for a couple of decades before Napster. A PC with a CD backup unit could easily copy a perfect copy of a recording and play it back on a CD player. Mass distribution was still not easy. In the mid-1990s encoding technologies such as MP3 (or MPEG3 for Moving Pictures Expert Group level) made it easier to shrink the size of a music file by at least a factor of 12 thus making it easier to store and download it. Any order-of-magnitude (ten times or 10x) change in an important dimension has potential to disrupt an industry. The arrival of the Internet made mass distribution of MP3 music files possible–albeit from a central location. Add to this equation the development of MP3 music players, both in hardware and software forms and it was now possible to easily copy, mass distribute and listen to music from the comfort of any individual's personal computer or portable music player anywhere.

Where were the music labels in 1997 as this technology convergence was taking place? Some of them, like Capitol Records, started to play with Internet technologies. In early September it unveiled a website to allow fans to listen (but not download) British pop group Duran Duran's Barbarella for free over a two-week period. Other labels were not there yet. "Some labels, such as Sony Music and Time Warner's Warner Music, have launched online ventures where consumers can order albums to be shipped through the mail. Others have been hesitant to set up direct sales on the Internet for fear of alienating retailers."[160] The extent of their Internet work was to promote sales of physical CDs through traditional retail stores. Even Capitol Record's Barbarella website was a way to do that.

When peer-to-peer technologies arrived, all the necessary technologies needed to transform the music industry had arrived. Nineteen-year old Shawn Fanning put it all together and founded Napster in 1999. Boston, Massachusetts-based Napster quickly became the leading music downloading service in the world. Within a year, it had more than 28 million users freely downloading and swapping music files to their PCs. The transformation of the music industry could not be denied anymore.

2. Anger

The Recording Industry Association of America (RIAA) represents the traditional music labels like Seagram, Universal Music, Sony Music, EMI Group, and Warner Music Group. The RIAA promptly started suing little boys and girls (like 12-year-old Brianna LaHare) who were downloading music to their personal computers. "Nobody likes playing the heavy and having to resort to litigation," RIAA president Cary Sherman said in a statement. "But when your product is being regularly stolen, there comes a time when you have to take appropriate action."[161]

The second stage of the loss-grieving process is anger. Managers then become angry. The anger is first internal, blaming employees, and then external, blaming the world. They point fingers at the newcomers. They call the new products, services, or entrepreneurs ungodly, un-American, evil, illegal and un-whatever. How angry do they get? They may get lawsuit-happy. Incumbents blame everyone, even little girls and boys, and try to get via lawyers what they can't do through proper product development and strategy.

Managers may call for protection against "unfair" competition from new startup technologies. The radio broadcast industry has repeatedly done this against the new satellite radio players like XM Satellite Radio and Sirius. The incumbents did their very best to cripple the young industry even before it was really born not by competing directly but by lobbying the U.S Congress.

3. Bargaining

The third stage of the loss-grieving process is bargaining.

Managers then promise to do anything to cure the loss. They promise to work harder and ask others to do the same thing. They negotiate hard to get back to the way things used to be. They can't deny that the genie is out of the bottle, but they work hard to put it back in. Notice how American Airlines and other "traditional" airlines keep promising after every major round of layoffs that this is a productivity improvement or cost-cutting measure that would do the trick in their fight with "new order" companies such as Southwest and JetBlue. Detroit auto companies have been doing this for three decades.

The RIAA started negotiating with companies such as Napster in 1999. Remember, their negotiating posture was one that required the Napster genie to get back into the bottle. In this case they used outsize force to bend the hand of the other party. In December 1999 the RIAA sued Napster for 20 billion dollars (it was seeking damages of $100,000 for each of the 200,000 songs in the system). "Napster CEO Eileen Richardson seemed caught off guard by the suit. "This came as a surprise; we've been spending so much time trying to figure out ways to work with the RIAA," said Richardson.[162] The music industry charged them with fostering copyright infringement by its millions of users, and that the services "cause serious and irreparable harm" to the music business. The established music industry did eventually destroy Napster – but the genie did not get back into the bottle. The Internet itself would not go away. They of course didn't see that in the new paradigm they had to look at their strategy and ponder whether it made sense in this world. This was a world where people wanted the choice to download a single song or a whole "CD equivalent." The old practice of wrapping several mediocre songs around a hit title and charge $15.99 for that CD could not work anymore. The new world included people who wanted a choice between an instant download of their favorite tune and a trip to the music store to buy it. The music industry would not provide the products and services that the new market demanded. As soon as Napster was slain other file-sharing services such as Kazaa fulfilled the demand.

4. Despair

In a last-ditch attempt to get control of the genie and put it back in the bottle, the five major record labels started two music downloading service companies: Pressplay and MusicNet. MusicNet was owned by AOL Time Warner, Bertelsmann, EMI and RealNetworks, and Pressplay was started by Sony and Vivendi Universal. The concept of the major industry players getting together to sue everyone (companies and individuals) to prohibit them from downloading music from the Internet while starting their own such service struck most as a lame monopolistic attempt.

The fourth stage of the loss grieving process is despair. Managers and their boards start believing that there's little they can do. They despair, lose hope, and become guilty and remorseful. Why didn't we see it coming? What were we thinking? Maybe we could do something to control this new beast?

Both American and European Union judges promptly struck back at the music industry's desperate attempts. "These record companies do not throw money into black holes and the commission fears that if they come together, it could make them into a cartel and make it virtually impossible for a rival model to compete," said European competition lawyer Peter Alexiadis. California judge Marilyn Hall Patel, who was in charge of the RIAA lawsuit against Napster, said that this anti-competitive attempt "looks bad, sounds bad and smells bad."[163] This latest attempt by the music industry tried and failed to control the new paradigm through old ways of doing business.

5. Acceptance

By the end of 2004, the record labels were ready to accept that music downloading was here to stay and would not necessarily be under their control. The market had no sympathy for the major record labels.

"Major record labels have spent years fighting tooth and nail through courts, legislatures and on the airwaves, to destroy music file-sharing networks on the Internet. But they now seem to have accepted that they cannot stop people using such networks and have decided instead they may as well find a way to profit from them," said *The Economist*.[164]

The last stage of the five stages of grieving is acceptance. Managers start thinking rationally. They accept that the world has changed. They seek new frameworks and deal with real information with open rational minds. They seek to adapt the company to the new environment. They accept the new world order and verbalize their grief about the loss of the old. They may even start pointing confidently to new ways in which they company can transition into the new world.

Apple had proved through its iPod and iTunes that the market was willing to pay for downloading music. The fact that Apple sold a million downloaded songs within a week of launching its iTunes store and a nearly a billion over the following two and a half years was proof of that. Apple was clearly listening to customers and offering them value. At the same time CD sales rose by 10% the fourth quarter of 2004. Both CD sales and online sales were going up.

Denial, however, creates opportunities for new players. For the strategic planner it is interesting to look at which companies in the value chain are going through these five same stages of the grieving process. If an incumbent (like Kodak) is denying the importance of a threat (like digital photography) you may have an easier time entering that market. If a whole industry is denying or fighting the new paradigm, there may be room for a company to enter and become a leader. While the music distribution industry was busy hiring lawyers to develop its strategy in the courtroom Apple entered the music distribution industry through its iTunes Store. It quickly became the leader in online music distribution and a force to be reckoned with in the whole music distribution world.

WHY NEW ZEALAND TELECOM SHOULD FEAR EBAY

Who knew that eBay would enter the telecommunications market? By acquiring voice-over-IP telecom company Skype, eBay started competing directly with companies such as Vonage, SBC Communications (now AT&T), and New Zealand Telecom. Should these companies be worried? If they haven't already changed their strategy, it may be too late!

If you're in a great tech business, someone is creating a product or service to kill your core business. Call it creative destruction or destructive creation. Ask not whether you're paranoid, ask whether you're paranoid enough! Here are some pointers to help the entrepreneur compete in the hyperdynamic world of high tech.

Look beyond your category

Nearly every company keeps careful track of their competition. The only problem is that they carefully define who their competitors are and follow mainly these companies. These competitors are likely to be in the same narrowly defined product category or industry. What many managers may not be careful in doing is anticipating competitors from outside this carefully screened set of companies.

Did the former AT&T see companies like Skype as competitors? Probably not. They probably focused on MCI and Sprint as competitors because these were in the classic "long distance phone company" category. And yet, the advent of the Internet and more specifically voice over IP (VOIP) technology may have done more to accelerate AT&T's demise than any of their competitors could have done.

Clearly denial is not going to make your competition go away. They exist whether you want it or not. Paranoia might be a better competitive strategy than denial. Expand the field of vision rather than narrowing it. What you learn may not be pretty, but the competitive realities seldom are.

In late 2005 Yahoo! and Google dominated the web search market. They beat or acquired their direct competitors like Excite, Lycos, and Overture (see Rule 2). Could they possibly rest on their laurels? Hardly. They knew they make pretty nice targets from adjacent companies. Google had a product called "Froogle" which found product bargains on the net. Should Amazon.com and eBay feel threatened? eBay owned Half.com where users could buy and sell books. Was Amazon worried? Conversely, how hard would it be for Amazon.com, eBay, or Microsoft to come up with search engines of their own that shadowed Google and Yahoo!? Amazon.com has the A9 search engine that competes with Google. At the same time, Google created GooglePrint–a service that lets users search book contents. This service may strike at the heart of Amazon's book selling business. Microsoft hasn't made it a secret that they are building the next generation search engine--or Google-killer. In fact, it released a free software program to perform Google-like search on personal computers. At the same time Google is releasing free products to compete with Microsoft's bread and butter Office Suite.

Watch for new business models

Threats don't always come directly from competitors, but can come instead from changes in business models. New organizations can offer products and services with similar benefits to your user. The difference is that they make their revenues in different ways from yours. In the 1990s Siebel Systems rose to stardom making and selling salesforce automation and customer relationship management software. A typical installation of a Siebel CRM would run into the millions of dollars (sometimes tens of millions) and take months or years to install. A new breed of companies such as Salesforce. com offered salesforce and CRM software with substantially similar benefits to users as Siebel's. The major difference is that Salesforce. com charged about $79 per user per month. The difference in business models meant that Siebel may have lost billions in revenue to an upstart that charged orders of magnitude less for similar value to the individual end user.

When performing a threat analysis take a look not just beyond your obvious competitors but also far beyond your industry. You need to combine and project price/performance growth in several technologies and imagine the environment that they enable and how they would affect your business.

In 2005 one of Microsoft's main threats didn't come from any specific company. Rather it came from a growing movement with a new business model–the open source movement. Linux has already grabbed nearly a third of the enterprise server market. Mozilla Firefox grabbed 5% or so of the web browser market just weeks after being released and maybe 10%-15% of the whole market soon after. An Information Week survey in late 2004 found that two out of five companies used open source databases.[165] It also found that two-thirds of companies used open source software. There are now open source applications for email, calendaring, word processing, and other functions that compete with Microsoft's core Office software.

Open Office, for example, combined a spreadsheet, word processor, multimedia presentation, graphics software, and database software. When OpenOffice.org 1.1 was released in October 2004, more than 16 million copies were downloaded.[166] Microsoft has proven adept at competing with companies that threaten them. From Lotus to Novell to Netscape, we have seen how Microsoft has focused on and beat company after company. The new threat to their business comes from and has been enabled by organizations with new business models (enabled in turn by the technology environment) rather than any specific company.

Today Microsoft competes with "free" software provided by these organizations. A new business model could enable a company to actually pay PC users to use their applications that compete with Microsoft. These applications would be supported by an advertising revenue model. Sure, the user would have to put up with watching commercials while she's using her word processing software, but millions of users already have made that choice while watching broadcast television, listening to the radio or surfing the web. Is there a market segment that would rather get paid $50 to use a word processor or spreadsheet with similar features as MS Word or Excel instead of paying $300 to use Microsoft's? My guess is that we will find out very soon.

Watch for convergence

We have seen the convergence of technologies that forever changed the music industry. Personal computing technologies, CD recording, MP3 encoding, the Internet, and peer-to-peer technologies made it possible for Napster and others to enter and disrupt the record companies' business. As soon as the RIAA sued Napster out of existence, someone else like Kazaa picked up their business because the technology environment that made Napster possible was not going to be sued out of existence. Lawyers and their lawsuit-happy clients haven't figured out a way to do that. Now, it is possible that strategists in the music industry did not see this convergence coming. If they even knew about the Internet, they probably saw it as a cool technology for geeks and Silicon-Valley types–not as a threat to their cozy business model.

To prevent these types of surprises strategic planning requires a broad view of changes in the tech world. For instance, if you are in any type of content business, your business might be under constant threat from technologies coming out of Silicon-Valley type businesses. Take storage technology. In 2005 a one-terabyte storage PC attachment could be purchased for under $1,000. According to Bob Reid, Chairman of Listen.com, "one terabyte stores the contents of over 25,000 CDs–far more than the combined active catalogs of all five major music labels plus all significant independent music labels."[167] Attaching a 1-terabyte music box to a PC then could constitute a major threat to the existing business models of several industries, including music publishers, conventional broadcast radio, digital radio and even satellite radio.

How hard is it to imagine an iPod with one terabyte of storage? The iPod I bought in the fall of 2005 had 20 gigabytes and cost around $249. My collection of over 300+ CD's fit easily–with almost half the iPod drive to spare! Computer storage has doubled its capacity while keeping the same cost every year for the last two decades. This means that today you can buy *two million times* the storage capacity you bought twenty years ago for exactly the same price. This growth in performance shows no signs of stopping in the foreseeable future. We thus can look forward to a one-terabyte iPod around 2010. Apple is advertising iPods that they say can carry 15,000 songs, 25,000 photos and 150 hours of video in a 60 Gig iPod. By 2010 (just around the corner) anyone will likely be able to carry 10 times that in their pocket (remember 10x changes?) That means we'll be able to carry 25,000 music CDs (or all the world's music production) or 1,500 to 3,000 hours of video (100-200 movies) in our pocket. It's going to happen! Denial or resistance is useless. Executives in the movie industry can't say they didn't see this one coming! Either they develop new product strategies to profit from this scenario or someone else will do it.

We may not need to wait. Podcasting is the distribution of content programming to the iPod and iTunes. Basically, anyone can be an iPod broadcaster. Anyone can send music, class audiotapes, interviews, or movie reviews to thousands or millions of users who subscribe to that podcast. Combine your iPod or similar device with podcasting content and you have an alternative to radio, both at home and on the road. Sign up for an automatic feed and add wireless connectivity to the iPod and you have a substitute for broadcast radio or even satellite radio.

The storage improvement curve also tells us that by the end of the decade Tivo-like set-top boxes should have storage for about 14,000 two-hour high-quality (MPEG-2) films.[168] Clearly several industries should feel the impact of this inevitable development. Broadcast television, cable television, movie rentals (off and on-line), and movie publishing are just some industries that come to mind. ABC TV, Comcast, Blockbusters, Netflix, and Universal are some of the companies that should see their business models altered because of this technology alone. Are they prepared for the onslaught? They had better be.

Given the success of podcasting, Apple decided to support it and make it part of its iPod and iTunes basic product. By September 2005 CEO Steve Jobs announced that iTunes had more than 15,000 podcasts in its directory, a figure that was growing by a thousand per week. There were more than seven million subscriptions to these podcasts. "This phenomenon is just exploding," said Jobs.[169] So much for a fad!

What about wireless technologies? WiMax, also known as 802.16, is a new wireless technology standard from Intel that promises broadband connectivity over distances as far as 30 miles. Imagine your PC, TV set-top box, mobile phone, iPod, or personal digital assistant (PDA) having the ability to transmit movie-size files over the air several miles away. Suddenly people don't need wires for a telephone call or even video call within the same city. Which businesses are in trouble now? Both cell phone companies like Verizon and wireline companies like SBC would see their businesses affected as users switch to voice-over-internet (VOIP) phone calling. Now imagine the Tivo-like box above with Wi-Max capability. Podcasting turns into Tivo-casting and it's easy to imagine that almost anyone could basically become a cable-like provider in their neighborhood. Suddenly cable companies like Comcast don't have a monopoly anymore.

These are of course just obvious and well known technologies. If you scan the technology universe and consider combinations or convergence of technologies you can imagine how your business can be affected. This is true whether you work in high tech or not.

Mind your value chain

The IBM PC burst unto the world in 1983–forever changing the information technology world. The most powerful technology company in the world did what very few thought possible: it designed and assembled a product with off-the-shelf components and stamped it with the top computer brand in the world. For a decade, IBM made billions of dollars and led a revolution from within that threatened to topple its own world of IBM mainframes. In 1999 IBM abandoned manufacturing PCs and in 2004 it sold off its PC division. The company that created the personal computer market and led it for many years abandoned it altogether. What happened?

IBM neglected to understand the evolving nature of the PC value chain. In 1983 IBM was the most important link in that value chain. It hired little-known companies such as Microsoft, Intel and many others to manufacture and supply parts of its upcoming PC. In 1986 Intel was so financially weak that IBM had to invest $400 million to keep it afloat (and buy a 20% stake in the company plus warrants for an extra 10%). Demand for PCs took off. Manufacturing them became such a simple exercise that many new manufacturers like Compaq, Gateway, Dell, and many others entered the market. As the PC market grew, the power evolved away from the PC manufacturers like IBM and into the operating systems (Microsoft) and CPU (Intel) makers. In 2004, Intel and Microsoft were each valued by the stock market at two to three times IBM's own market capitalization. IBM sold its equity stake in Intel as soon at the latter regained its financial stability. However, a 20% equity position in Intel was worth in 2000 about the same as the whole of IBM. That is how drastic the changes in the value chain had been!

Each value chain is different. The power resides in different links and evolves differently in each one of them. There is likely to be one company that is the key link in the value chain. This company provides the platform or infrastructure around which other companies build their products and services and deliver the final product to the market. The PC value chain today revolves around the operating system (Microsoft) and the CPU (Intel). There is plenty of room in this value chain for thousands of companies to build great businesses: storage, communications, monitors, application software, development tools, etc. No value chain is static and technology chains are especially dynamic. While Microsoft and Intel are at the key links in the PC value chain today, their place is by no means guaranteed. In fact, part of the competitive battle in a value chain involves grabbing more of the value for a given company and commoditizing other links in the chain. For instance, while Microsoft and Intel have been able to maintain or even raise their margins, much of the rest of the PC value chain is brutally competitive.

Understand how money flows in your company's value chain and who is keeping what portion of that value. These power relations will change according to many competitive factors. You should know how they're evolving and how it affects your product line. Margins are one area you want to keep track of. If your margins are consistently going down while your supplier's are going up, you may be looking at a shift in power. Look at your competition's value chain. Is the same thing happening to them? If so there may be an unmistakable trend. Otherwise the problem may be related to your own product or company, not the industry. Either way you need an early-detection mechanism before it's too late to act to solve the problem. Furthermore, in high tech today's partners are tomorrow's competitors. Today you may be winning together but that doesn't mean it's going to stay that way for a long time. Tech markets move much too fast for that to happen.

Last but not least, your whole value chain may be losing power to newer value chains that are competing for those same customers. Today the centrality of computing has moved from the PC to the Internet. Companies like Google are competing with Microsoft by creating a whole new net-centric platform. By shifting the battleground away from the PC Google is playing to its own advantage while Microsoft needs to learn about the new rules of the game to compete there. Other companies such as Nokia are betting on the centrality of the mobile phone value chain while Apple is creating its own new entertainment value chain. As usual the winners will take it all and the rest will hopefully pick up the pieces and live to fight another battle.

RULE 9 SUMMARY: YOU'RE DOING WELL. CONGRATULATIONS. NOW CHANGE OR DIE

High technology is all about change. Fast change. Everything changes in all kinds of direction: technologies, products, markets, value chains, competition, partnerships, user expectations, business models, and every thing in between. Winning leadership in a given market does not guarantee monopoly rents forever. Winners can take it all but they can also lose it all. Companies like MicroPro, Digital Equipment Corporation, Ashton-Tate were market leaders and the darlings of their time. Today they are only memories. Companies need to change their strategies or die.

Change is hard. Losing is hard. In dealing with loss to new competition brought about by massive changes in capabilities, technology, or the environment many companies go through a classic grieving process. The five stages of the process are: denial, bargain, anger, despair, and finally acceptance. Understanding this process, whether it takes place within your company or the environment, is important in crafting strategy.

New threats to your business come from many angles. Call it creative destruction or destructive construction. Threats come from new entrants into the market category. Google entered the Internet search market to unseat Yahoo! Threats come from new business models. Salesforce.com entered the CRM space as a service offering to unseat the traditional software distribution model provided by its leading proponent Siebel. Threats come from the convergence of several technologies that allow new "paradigms" to take hold. Personal computing technologies, MP3 encoding, the Internet, broadband connectivity, and peer-to-peer innovations made it possible for anyone to copy, store, and distribute massive amounts of music for negligible costs. Apple Computers put together an impressive product like iPod and iTunes and transformed itself and the music industry. Changing strategies to fit the new and upcoming environment is a must for technology companies that wish to remain leaders in the future. Ask not whether you're paranoid; ask whether you're paranoid enough!

ABOUT THE AUTHOR

Tony Seba teaches entrepreneurship courses including "Strategic Marketing of High Technology Products and Innovations", "Business and Revenue Models", "Finance for Entrepreneurs" at Stanford, and at international business schools such as the Auckland University Business School. He has an MBA from the Stanford University Graduate School of Business, and a BS in Computer Science and Engineering from Massachusetts Institute of Technology (MIT).

Tony Seba has two decades' experience of strategy, business development and operating performance in the high technology industry, designing, building, managing, and marketing more than two dozen products that range from sales force automation, to small business management, to integrated computer-aided software engineering, to Internet security software.

As PrintNation.com's founder, President and CEO, Seba raised more than $31 million in VC funding, and established the company as the undisputed leader in its market segment, listed as the *Upside* Hot 100 and the *Forbes*.com B2B "Best of the Web." As a Director of Strategic Planning at RSA Data Security he helped the company successfully enter new markets and in its $200-million merger with Security Dynamics.

Mr. Seba's leadership has been recognized in publications such as *Investors Business Daily, Business Week, Upside,* and *Success.* Mr Seba was cited as one of Bridgegate's 20 "difference makers".

Tony Seba has been on the board of directors of the San Francisco Jazz Organization and Stanford GSB Alumni Consulting Team. As a Mentor Capitalist he was also on the board of advisors of MediFirst Systems, a health care infrastructure software company and SalesEdge, a next-generation CRM software company. He has been a guest lecturer at major US business schools, and an international speaker on entrepreneurship and high technology subjects at numerous conferences around the world.

Endnotes

[1] Yahoo! Finance - http://finance.yahoo.com/

[2] http://www.bell-labs.com/about/awards.html

[3] Source: Craigslist company data, Alexa, Nielsen. Numbers are for consolidated companies rather than individual websites.

[4] David Gardner, "Craigslist Rips Up Classifieds," *Motley Fool*, June 25, 2005.

[5] Will Swarts, "Craigslist: Stopping The Presses?", *SmartMoney*, Sept 7, 2005.

[6] Lucas Conley, "Is it Still Craig's List?" *Fast Company*, Sept 2004.

[7] http://www.craigslist.org/about/mission.and.history.html

[8] Adam Lashinsky, "Where Dell is Going Next," *Fortune*, Oct 18, 2004.

[9] Timothy Archibald, "How Google Grow, and Grows, and Grows," *FastCompany*, April 2003

[10] Matt Hamblen, "Cisco's John Chambers at company's 20-year mark," *ComputerWorld*, Dec 9, 2004.

[11] Jim Duffey, "Internet pioneer says Net traffic growing faster than ever," *Network World Fusion*, August 16, 2001

[12] Andy Grove, "Only The Paranoid Survive," *Currency Doubleday*, April 1999

[13] *Symantec 2000 Annual Report*.

[14] *Symantec 2000 Annual Report*.

[15] Symantec press release, July 28, 2000.

[16] Anne Saita, "Profile: John Thompson," *Information Security Magazine* , Feb. 2003.

[17] Robert Mullins, "CyberVigilance," *Silicon Valley/San Jose Business Journal*, Sept 22, 2003.

[18] Alex Salkever, "Which Anti-Virus Stock is Safer?" *Business Week*, Sept 13, 2003.

[19] http://finance.yahoo.com/

[20] Keith Hammonds, "How Google Grows…and grows…and grows," *Fast Company*, April 2003.

[21] Rich Karlgaard, "Philippe Kahn interview," *Upside*, Sept 1991.

[22] Microsoft SEC form 10K, June 1995.

[23] Rick Karlgaard, "Philippe Kahn interview," *Upside*, Sept 1991.

[24] Catherine Ledner, "Borland Software: Back in the Black," *Fast Company*, July 2002

[25] Yahoo! press release, January 14, 1997,

http://docs.yahoo.com/docs/pr/release70.html

[26] Jim Hu and Melanie Austria Farmer, "Yahoo thinks entertainment with Launch buy," *CNET News.com*, June 28, 2001.

[27] Jim Hu, "Yahoo CEO Semel: Search is everywhere in 2004," *CNET News.com*, Jan 5, 2004.

[28] Saul Hansel, "Google Defies Its Warnings, Growning Briskly," *The New York Times*, Feb 2, 2005.

[29] Financial sources: Morningstar, Yahoo! Finance and SEC filings.

[30] Michael Liedtke, "Google Shares reach all time high," *San Francisco Chronicle*, Oct 21, 2005,

[31] Mary Eisenhart, "How Palm beat Microsoft," *Salon*, Sept 17, 1998.

[32] Richard McCaffery, "High Five for Palm," *Motley Fool*, Dec 14, 1999,

[33] *Detroit News*, Technology, Oct. 29, 2003.

[34] "PalmSource platform overtaken by Microsoft," *Silicon Valley Biz Ink*, Nov 19-25, 2004.

[35] Michael Singer, "Palmsource acquisition finalized," CNET News.com, Nov 14, 2005.

[36] *Detroit News*, Technology, Oct. 29, 2003.

[37] David Sims, "At-home's last mile," O'Reilly Network, Sept 29, 2001.

[38] John Borland, "Excite-at-Home Agrees to sell portal assets," *CNET*, Nov 9, 2001.

[39] Texas Instruments, "History of Innovations."

[40] David Lammers, "Agere passes Motorola in DSP rankings," *EE Times*, April 8, 2004.

[41] Associated Press "Intel Cancels TV Chip," In *Forbes*, Oct 22, 2004.

[42] John Markoff, "The Disco Ball of Failed Hopes and Other Tales From Inside Intel," *The New York Times*, Nov 29, 2004.

[43] Stock quote and financials source: *Morningstar*: http://www.morningstar.com/

[44] Tony Smith, "SGI Finally Sells off Cray," The Register, March 2, 2000.

[45] "Special Report: America's business recovery," *The Economist*, Nov 15, 2003.

[46] Michael Kanellos, "Intel's wireless ambitions lead to new acquisition," CNet News.com, June 26, 2000.

[47] StarMine company data.

[48] Source: Reuters / Yahoo! Finance : Full Company Description for TXN – Retrieved from http://yahoo.investor.reuters.com/FullDesc.aspx?ticker=TXN.N&target=companyprofile%2ffulldescription

[49] Katheryn Jones, "Don't Mess with Texas Instruments," *Business 2.0*, Sept 1. 2004.

[50] Michael Singer, "Microsoft Settles Netscape Lawsuit with Microsoft," Internet News, May 29, 2003.

[51] David Pogue, "From Apple A Tiger to Put in Your Mac," *The New York Times*, April 18, 2005.

[52] *Internet Systems Consortium*, http://www.isc.org/index.pl?/ops/ds/

[53] Real Vision, Facts and Figures, *TV Turnoff Network*, in http://www.tvturnoff.org/images/facts&figs/factsheets/FactsFigs.pdf

[54] United States Information Agency, "Portrait of the USA: The Media and its Messages," 1997, in, http://usinfo.state.gov/usa/infousa/facts/factover/ch12.htm

[55] Peter Lyman and Hal Varian, "How Much Information?" Retrieved from http://www.sims.berkeley.edu/research/projects/how-much-info-2003/index.htm on July 2004.

[56] Miller, George, "The Magical Number Seven, Plus or Minus Two," 1956, Retrieved from http://www.well.com/user/smalin/miller.html

[57] Denny C. LeCompte (2000), "3.14159, 42, and 7±2: Three Numbers That (Should) Have Nothing To Do With User Interface Design," Internetworking, April 30, 2000.

[58]Tom Ziegler (July 12, 2002), The Buzz Saw, Retrieved July 6, 2004 from

http://www.buzzkiller.net/innersaw.htm

[59] Jerome Bruner, *Making Stories*, New York: Farrar, Straus, and Giroux, 2002.

[60] Howard Gardner, *Leading Minds*, New York,Basic Books, 1995.

[61] Howard Gardner, *Leading Minds*, New York: Basic Books, 1995.

[62] "More Companies Say 'The DVD is in the Mail'," *The New York Times*, Dec. 26, 2004.

[63] Ibid.

[64] ScreenWriting Theories (2006, April 4). In Wikipedia, The Free Encyclopedia. Retrieved April 12, 2006 from http://en.wikipedia.org/wiki/Screenwriting_Theories.

[65] Syd Field (2006, February 11). In Wikipedia, The Free Encyclopedia, rRetrieved April 12, 2006, from http://en.wikipedia.org/wiki/Syd_Field

[66] Joia Shillingford, "Return of the Star Wars dollars," BBC News, May 19, 2005.

[67] Time Warner Businesses: New Line Cinema - Core Statistics in http://www.timewarner.com/corp/businesses/detail/new_line_cinema/index.html downloaded May 2006.

[68] Al Ries and Jack Trout, *Positioning, The Battle for Your Mind*, McGrawHill, New York, 1981.

[69] Hoover's Online www.hoovers.com

[70] Sybase Annual Report 2005.

[71] Evelyn Nussenbaum, "It's Take Two for Digital Hollywood", CNNMoney.com, Feb 21, 2005.

[72] "Super Bowl viewership slides," *CNN*, Feb 8, 2005.

[73] "Gmail," In Wikipedia, The Free Encyclopedia. Retrieved from http://en.wikipedia.org/wiki/Gmail

[74] Securities and Exchange Commission Sycamore 10K-K405 form October 24, 2000 and 10Q form 13 March 2001.

[75] Source: Morningstar, www.morningstar.com

[76] "Silicon Valley Office Vacancy Rate Stabilizes," *Silicon Valley Biz Journal*, May 6, 2003.

[77] Christopher Koch, "Nike rebounds," *CIO Magazine*, June 15 2004,

[78] "The Real ROI from SAP," *Nucleus Research, Research Note*, D23.

[79] Joshua Greenbaum, "Implementing Oracle? Fire your systems integrator,"*Managing Automation*, April 2001.

[80] IEEE, www.ieee.org

[81] Matt Hines,"RFID standards race may set early market leaders," *CNET News.com*, May 19, 2004.

[82] Matthew L. Wald, "Maintenance Lapse Blamed for Air Traffic Control Problem," *The New York Times*, Sept 16, 2004.

[83] "The ROI Challenge," *CFO Magazine*, Sept 1, 1999.

[84] David Stout and John H. Cushman Jr., "Defense System for U.S. Fails to Launch," *The New York Times*, Dec 16, 2004.

[85] Elisa Batista, "What your clothes say about you," *Wired News*, March 12, 2003.

[86] "Benetton explains privacy flap," *RFID Journal*, June 23, 2003.

[87] Alan Deutchman, "The Kingmaker,"*Wired*, May 2004.

[88] (Ibid).

[89] *Openwave Annual Report* 2004.

[90] The American Dictionary of The English Language, Fourth Edition, Houghton Mifflin Company 2000.

[91] Paul Leyland et al, "A discussion of RSA-129 Activity," in http://www.math.okstate.edu/~wrightd/numthry/rsa129.html

[92] Paul Leyland et al, "A discussion of RSA-129 Activity," in http://www.math.okstate.edu/~wrightd/numthry/rsa129.html

[93] Source:LinkedIncompanynumbersandTheSocialSoftwareWeblog, http://socialsoftware.weblogsinc.com/entry/9817137581524458/

[94] "The World's Wealthiest People," Forbes, Feb 26th, 2004.

[95] Nathan Myrhvold, 'The Next Fifty Years of Software," Presentation to ACM 97.

[96] "Study: Drug Reactions kill an estimated 100,000 each year," *CNN*, April 14, 1998.

[97] Keith Belows, "Pictures Then and Now," *National Geographic Traveler*, Jan-Feb, 2005.

[98] LinkedIn company data.

[99] "Browser Wars," In Wikipedia, The Free Encyclopedia. Retrieved from http://en.wikipedia.org/wiki/Browser_wars

[100] "The Empire Strikes Back," *Wall Street and Technology*, June 1, 2000.

[101] "The Rise of the Creative Consumer," *The Economist*, 11 March, 2005.

[102] "Paying Through the Nose," , *The Economist*, May 20, 2004.

[103] Alan Deutchman, "The Kingmaker," *Wired*, May 2004.

[104] Alan Deutchman, "The Kingmaker," *Wired*, May 2004.

[105] "The Gilder Effect," <u>*Gilder Technology Index*</u>, May 23, 2003.

[106] "Gillette to Buy 500 Million EPC Tags," RFID Journal, Nov 15, 2002.

[107] James Nicolai, "BEA lines up partners for midmarket push," *Infoworld*, Dec 23, 2003

[108] S. Dull, W. Mohn, and T. Noren, "Partners," *The McKinsey Quarterly*, 1995, no. 4.

[109] This is a slight variation of the graph in page 65 of the article by S. Dull, W. Mohn, and T. Noren, "Partners," *The McKinsey Quarterly*, 1995, no. 4.

[110] Zook, Chris, *Beyond the Core*, Boston: Bain & Company, 2004.

[111] Matthew Yi, "Intel, Micron Join Forces," *San Francisco Chronicle*, Nov 22, 2005.

[112] Financial data from Morningstar.com

[113] Dawn Kawamoto et al, "Apple Acquires Next, Jobs," *CNET News*, Dec 20, 1996.

[114] Google Inc. Securities and Exchange Commission SEC Form 10-Q Nov 14, 2005.

[115] Saul Hansell, "Time Warner Plans to Sell 5% of AOL to Google," *The New York Times*, Dec 16, 2005,

[116] Source: "CPU Museum" in: http://www.cpu-museum.com/4004_e.htm#Busicom%20141-PF Check it out. It's just a webpage!

[117] http://www.skype.com/company/news/2004/company_niklas_letter.html

[118] "eBay To Acquire Skype," Skype company press release in http://www.skype.com/company/news/2005/skype_ebay.html

[119] Teresa Mastrangelo, Broabbandtrends.com, *Trendsetter Reports*: Voice over Broadband: Vonage," May 2, 2005.

[120] Skype website data, www.skype.com

[121] John C. Hodulik and Aryeh B. Bourkoff, "UBS Investment Research, Telephony and HSD Update for 4Q04," March 10, 2005.

[122] Teresa Mastrangelo, Broabbandtrends.com *Trendsetter Reports*: Voice over Broadband: Vonage," May 2, 2005.

[123] Bill Dyszel, "Rio exits the MP3 business,"*PC Magazine*, 23 Aug. 2005.

[124] "Prices Down, Memory Up for iPods," *CBS News*, , Feb 23, 2005.

[125] Rick Moody "Against Cool," in *The Best American Essays (2004)*, Louis Menand, ed., Boston: Houghton Mifflin Company, 2004.

[126] Apple company data (SEC financials, press releases) and estimates for early numbers.

[127] Everett Rogers, *Diffusion of Innovations*, Fifth edition. New York: Free Press, 2003.

[128] Amy Leung, "Smartcards seem a sure bet," CNN.com, March 11, 1999.

[129] Ben Charmy, "Can Skype live up to the Net Phone hype?" *CNET News*,Sept 27, 2004.

[130] "Benioff Breakfast: Networks point the way to profit," *Ariadne Capital Journal*, Vol. 3, Ed.2.

[131] Paul Kallender, "Dual DVD HD-DVD disc developed," *PCWorld*, Dec 8, 2004.

[132] J. Sinur and J. Thompson, "Magic Quadrant for Pure-play BPMS, 2Q03,"*Gartner Research Note*, 2 June, 2003.

[133] Clint Boulton, "Vendors Eye slice of $1B BPM Pie," *Internetnews. com*, 14 Aug, 2004.

[134] Howard Smith and Peter Fingar, *Business Process Management: The Third Wave*. Tampa, Florida, Meghan-Kiffer Press, 2002.

[135] Howard Smith and Peter Fingar, "Workflow is just a Pi Process," *Business Process Trends*, BPTrends.com, Jan 2004.

[136] "Adobe/Macromedia Acquisition Close," Fact Sheet, December 5, 2004, in http://www.adobe.com/aboutadobe/acquisition.html

[137] Scott Woolley, "Broadcast Bullies," *Forbes*, Sept. 6, 2004.

[138] http://www.wordiq.com/definition/Segway_HT

[139] "Bush Fails the Segway Test," BBC News, June 14, 2003.

[140] "Defnition of Segway HT", WordIQ.

[141] Neil McCabe, "*Sommerville News*," Sept 6, 2004.

[142]Financial statements from Morningstar, www.morningstar.com

[143] Source: *Morningstar and Yahoo! Finance*, Nov. 2005

[144] Jonathan Silverstein,"iTunes: 1 Billion Served," ABC News, February 23, 2006.

[145] Peter Cohen, "Apple unveils Ipod Nano, ROKR phone, iTunes 5," *Macworld*, Sept 2005.

[146]Paul Barker, "Kahn talks tough in Wake of A-T Deal," *Computing Canada*, Aug 1991.

[147] Ken Polsson, "Chronology of Events in the History of Microcomputers," in http://www.microprocessor.sscc.ru/comphist/ comp1986.htm

[148] "WorldCom To Acquire CompuServe and AOL's Network Services Company, Ans Communications, in $1.2 Billion Internet Transaction," *MCI News*, Sept 8, 1997.

[149] America Online Annual Report, 1999.

[150] Dana Cimillucaand and Timothy Doyle "SBC CommunicaCations may keep rival's name after sale is finalized," Bloomberg News, in *Daily Record*, Sept 2, 2005,

[151] Thomas Kuhn, *The Structure of Scientific Revolutions*, second edition, enlarged. Chicago: ,The University of Chicago Press, 1970

[152] Jeffrey Tarter, Softletter (date?1984), in http://dba-oracle.com/oracle_news/2004_6_29_rittman.htm

[153] Clayton Christenses, The Innovator's Dilemma: When New Technologies Cause Great Companies to Fail," Cambridge: Harvard Business School Press, 1997.

[154] Matt Hamblen, "Cisco's John Chambers at Company's 20-year mark,"*ComputerWorld*, Dec 9, 2004.

[155] Andrew Grove, "Only the Paranoid Survive," *Currency*, 1996.

[156] Mike Musgrove, "Nikon Says It's Leaving Film-Camera Business," *The Washington Post*, Jan 12, 2006.

[157]Navitaire website, www.navitaire.com

[158] IBM Annual Report 1994.

[159] Joseph Nocera, "Kodak: the CEO vs. the Gadfly," *Fortune*,Jan 12, 2004.

[160] "Capitol: 'Electric Barbarella' release touches a nerve," *CNN.com*, Sept 10, 1997.

[161] Ashlee Vance, "The RIAA sees the face of evil, and it's a 12-year-old girl," *The Register*, Sept 9, 2003.

[162] Rich Menta, "RIAA sues music startup for $20 billion," *MP3Newswire.net*, Dec 9, 1999.

[163] BBC News, "EU threat over download sites," Oct 15, 2001.

[164] *The Economist*, "I want my P2P," Nov 18, 2004.

[165] Helen D'Antoni, "Open Source Software Use Joins the Mix," *InformationWeek*, Nov 1, 2004.

[166] http://www.openoffice.org/product/index.html

[167]Bob Reid with Mary Collins, "The Point of Lunacy," in *Gilder Technology Report*, Vol VII, No.2, Feb 2002.

[168] Grant Barry, "Glossary," *The New York Times*, WK, Dec 26, 2004.

[169]Peter Cohen, "Apple unveils Ipod Nano, ROKR phone, iTunes 5." *Macworld*, Sept 7, 2005.

Company and Name Index

5377440R0

Made in the USA
Lexington, KY
03 May 2010